The South African Tradition of Racial Capitalism

This book documents the emergence and development of the theory of racial capitalism in apartheid South Africa. It interrogates the specificity of this theory in the South African context and draws lessons for its global applicability.

Racism and capitalism have a long history of entanglement. Nowhere is this more evident than in South Africa, where colonial and apartheid regimes used explicit systems of racial hierarchy to shore up profit. It is therefore no surprise that South Africa has represented a key site for thinking about the role that racism plays in shaping state policy, labor markets, patterns of capital accumulation, and working-class struggle. Illuminating these dynamics, this volume develops a distinctive South African tradition of thought about the relationship between racism and capitalism.

The South African Tradition of Racial Capitalism contributes to a burgeoning literature on the concept of "racial capitalism," the origins of which many commentators trace back to apartheid South Africa. It pays particular attention to the crucial role of anti-apartheid activists as theorists, whose important insights remain relevant for scholars and activists around the globe. This book was originally published as a special issue of *Ethnic and Racial Studies*.

Zachary Levenson is Assistant Professor of Sociology at Florida International University, USA, and Senior Research Associate in Sociology at the University of Johannesburg, South Africa. He is the author of *Delivery as Dispossession: Land Occupation and Eviction in the Postapartheid City* (2022).

Marcel Paret is Associate Professor of Sociology at the University of Utah, USA, and Senior Research Associate in the Centre for Social Change at the University of Johannesburg, South Africa. He is the author of *Fractured Militancy: Precarious Resistance in South Africa after Racial Inclusion* (2022).

Ethnic and Racial Studies

Series editor: **John Solomos**, *University of Warwick, UK*

The journal *Ethnic and Racial Studies* was founded in 1978 by John Stone to provide an international forum for high quality research on race, ethnicity, nationalism and ethnic conflict. At the time the study of race and ethnicity was still a relatively marginal sub-field of sociology, anthropology and political science. In the intervening period the journal has provided a space for the discussion of core theoretical issues, key developments and trends, and for the dissemination of the latest empirical research.

It is now the leading journal in its field and has helped to shape the development of scholarly research agendas. *Ethnic and Racial Studies* attracts submissions from scholars in a diverse range of countries and fields of scholarship, and crosses disciplinary boundaries. It is now available in both printed and electronic form. Since 2015 it has published 15 issues per year, three of which are dedicated to *Ethnic and Racial Studies Review* offering expert guidance to the latest research through the publication of book reviews, symposia and discussion pieces, including reviews of work in languages other than English.

The *Ethnic and Racial Studies* book series contains a wide range of the journal's special issues. These special issues are an important contribution to the work of the journal, where leading social science academics bring together articles on specific themes and issues that are linked to the broad intellectual concerns of *Ethnic and Racial Studies*. The series editors work closely with the guest editors of the special issues to ensure that they meet the highest quality standards possible. Through publishing these special issues as a series of books, we hope to allow a wider audience of both scholars and students from across the social science disciplines to engage with the work of *Ethnic and Racial Studies*.

Fighting Discrimination in a Hostile Political Environment
The Case of "Colour-Blind" France
Edited by Angéline Escafré-Dublet, Virginie Guiraudon and Julien Talpin

Reexamining Racism, Sexism, and Identity Taxation in the Academy
Edited by Tiffany D. Joseph and Laura E. Hirshfield

Urbanization and Migration in Three Continents
Edited by Alejandro Portes and Margarita Rodríguez

The South African Tradition of Racial Capitalism
Edited by Zachary Levenson and Marcel Paret

For more information about this series, please visit:
www.routledge.com/Ethnic-and-Racial-Studies/book-series/ERS

"Viva FRELIMO" rally organized by the Black People's Convention (BPC) and South African Student Organization (SASO) outside of Curries Fountain Stadium, Durban, South Africa, September 25, 1974.
Credit: Vino Reddy

The South African Tradition of Racial Capitalism

Edited by
Zachary Levenson and Marcel Paret

LONDON AND NEW YORK

First published 2024
by Routledge
4 Park Square, Milton Park, Abingdon, Oxon OX14 4RN

and by Routledge
605 Third Avenue, New York, NY 10158

Routledge is an imprint of the Taylor & Francis Group, an informa business

© 2024 Taylor & Francis

All rights reserved. No part of this book may be reprinted or reproduced or utilised in any form or by any electronic, mechanical, or other means, now known or hereafter invented, including photocopying and recording, or in any information storage or retrieval system, without permission in writing from the publishers.

Trademark notice: Product or corporate names may be trademarks or registered trademarks, and are used only for identification and explanation without intent to infringe.

British Library Cataloguing in Publication Data
A catalogue record for this book is available from the British Library

ISBN13: 978-1-032-76616-4 (hbk)
ISBN13: 978-1-032-76620-1 (pbk)
ISBN13: 978-1-003-47929-1 (ebk)

DOI: 10.4324/9781003479291

Typeset in Myriad Pro
by Newgen Publishing UK

Publisher's Note
The publisher accepts responsibility for any inconsistencies that may have arisen during the conversion of this book from journal articles to book chapters, namely the inclusion of journal terminology.

Disclaimer
Every effort has been made to contact copyright holders for their permission to reprint material in this book. The publishers would be grateful to hear from any copyright holder who is not here acknowledged and will undertake to rectify any errors or omissions in future editions of this book.

Contents

	Citation Information	ix
	Notes on Contributors	xi
	Introduction: The South African tradition of racial capitalism	1
	Zachary Levenson and Marcel Paret	
1	The context of struggle: racial capitalism and political praxis in South Africa	23
	Andy Clarno and Salim Vally	
2	Merely liberals? Du Bois and Plaatje as radical critics of racial capitalism	46
	Mosa M. Phadi	
3	Articulating difference: reading Biko-with-Hall	60
	Ahmed Veriava and Prishani Naidoo	
4	Bernard Magubane on the political economy of race and class in South Africa	80
	Bongani Nyoka	
5	Whiteness and racial capitalism: to whom do the "wages of whiteness" accrue?	99
	Zine Magubane	
6	Reproducing "racial capitalism" through retailing in South Africa: gender, labour, and consumption, 1950s–1970s	118
	Bridget Kenny	
7	Geographies of racial capitalism: the July 2021 riots in South Africa	140
	Ashwin Desai	

| 8 | Racial capitalism: an unfinished history | 160 |

Robin D. G. Kelley

Index 167

Citation Information

The chapters in this book were originally published in the journal *Ethnic and Racial Studies*, volume 46, issue 16 (2023). When citing this material, please use the original page numbering for each article, as follows:

Introduction
The South African tradition of racial capitalism
Zachary Levenson and Marcel Paret
Ethnic and Racial Studies, volume 46, issue 16 (2023), pp. 3403–3424

Chapter 1
The context of struggle: racial capitalism and political praxis in South Africa
Andy Clarno and Salim Vally
Ethnic and Racial Studies, volume 46, issue 16 (2023), pp. 3425–3447

Chapter 2
Merely liberals? Du Bois and Plaatje as radical critics of racial capitalism
Mosa M. Phadi
Ethnic and Racial Studies, volume 46, issue 16 (2023), pp. 3448–3461

Chapter 3
Articulating difference: reading Biko-with-Hall
Ahmed Veriava and Prishani Naidoo
Ethnic and Racial Studies, volume 46, issue 16 (2023), pp. 3462–3481

Chapter 4
Bernard Magubane on the political economy of race and class in South Africa
Bongani Nyoka
Ethnic and Racial Studies, volume 46, issue 16 (2023), pp. 3482–3500

Chapter 5
Whiteness and racial capitalism: to whom do the "wages of whiteness" accrue?
Zine Magubane
Ethnic and Racial Studies, volume 46, issue 16 (2023), pp. 3501–3519

Chapter 6
Reproducing "racial capitalism" through retailing in South Africa: gender, labour and consumption, 1950s–1970s
Bridget Kenny
Ethnic and Racial Studies, volume 46, issue 16 (2023), pp. 3520–3541

Chapter 7
Geographies of racial capitalism: the 2021 July riots in South Africa
Ashwin Desai
Ethnic and Racial Studies, volume 46, issue 16 (2023), pp. 3542–3561

Chapter 8
Racial capitalism: an unfinished history
Robin D. G. Kelley
Ethnic and Racial Studies, volume 46, issue 16 (2023), pp. 3562–3568

For any permission-related enquiries please visit:
www.tandfonline.com/page/help/permissions

Notes on Contributors

Andy Clarno, Department of Sociology, University of Illinois at Chicago, Chicago, IL, USA.

Ashwin Desai, Department of Sociology, University of Johannesburg, Auckland Park, South Africa.

Robin D. G. Kelley, Faculty of History, University of California, Los Angeles, USA.

Bridget Kenny, Department of Sociology, University of the Witwatersrand, Johannesburg, South Africa.

Zachary Levenson, Department of Global and Sociocultural Studies, Florida International University, Miami, FL, USA; Department of Sociology, University of Johannesburg, Auckland Park, South Africa.

Zine Magubane, Department of Sociology, Boston College, Chestnut Hill, MA, USA.

Prishani Naidoo, Work and Politics Institute (SWOP), University of the Witwatersrand, Johannesburg, South Africa.

Bongani Nyoka, Department of Political & International Studies, Rhodes University, Makhanda, South Africa.

Marcel Paret, Department of Sociology, The University of Utah, Salt Lake City, UT, USA; Centre for Social Change, University of Johannesburg, Auckland Park, South Africa.

Mosa M. Phadi, Department of Sociology, University of the Free State, Bloemfontein, South Africa.

Salim Vally, Centre for Education Rights & Transformation, University of Johannesburg, Auckland Park, South Africa.

Ahmed Veriava, Department of Political Studies, University of the Witwatersrand, Johannesburg, South Africa.

Introduction: The South African tradition of racial capitalism

Zachary Levenson and Marcel Paret

Abstract
This introduction to the special issue on "The South African Tradition of Racial Capitalism" situates the South African tradition of racial capitalism (SAT) against the organizational backdrop of the anti-apartheid movement, outlines the key theses of the SAT, and presents the contributions of the special issue. We argue that the SAT rests upon four key theses: 1) class struggle from above – the pursuit of profit – generates racism; 2) the capitalist state is the primary agent of racialization; 3) racial ideology can divide, enabling capitalism, but it can also unify, facilitating resistance; and 4) racial capitalism is a strategic concept that emphasizes the inseparability of anti-racist and anti-capitalist struggle. The SAT underscores the centrality of struggle and the importance of conjunctural analysis in the study of racial capitalism.

The central argument of RC [racial capitalism] is that the class and national aspects cannot be separated ... [R]ace and class are intertwined and ... constitute one problem or contradiction. In other words, "apartheid" and "capitalism" do not represent two contradictions, but a single one i.e. racial capitalism ... At the level of strategy, RC means the rejection of the "two-stage theory" and the acceptance of the "one-stage theory" ... [For proponents of RC,] national liberation means the immediate destruction of racial capitalism and the construction of socialism ... RC does not facilitate a broad revolutionary movement at the level of various diverse components of struggle. The acceptance of CST [colonialism of a special type], on the other hand, facilitates the presence of socialists and non-socialists alike, in the struggle for national liberation.

––Cape Youth Congress (CAYCO), "Left-Wing Deviation: Discussion Article," 1987[1]

Racial capitalism: a South African tradition

What is the relative significance of race and class, respectively, in generating and reproducing inequality? Is one more fundamental than the other? And how do these distinctions translate into strategic terms? These questions were at the heart of debates within the anti-apartheid movement in South Africa in the 1970s and 80s. But what is often discussed as a singular movement turns out to be far more complex, containing multiple contending solutions to these questions. An outside observer might assume, for example, that a "class first" position maps neatly onto the South African Communist Party (SACP), and that a "race first" position corresponds to the Black Consciousness movement (BCM). But in practice, the truth was far closer to the opposite: the SACP defended an approach that prioritized the struggle for racial equality, and the BCM moved increasingly toward an emphasis on the struggle for socialism.

How can we make sense of this apparent paradox? A starting point is to recognize that many different anti-apartheid organizations shared the twin goals of opposing *both* racism *and* capitalism, but that they developed very different strategies for doing so. The SACP (1963 [1962], 43) came to understand South Africa as "colonialism of a special type" (CST), a "new type of colonialism ... in which the oppressing White nation occupied the same territory as the oppressed people themselves and lived side by side with them." In their view, CST implied that popular struggle must unfold in two distinct phases: first, activists should join forces with all organizations fighting apartheid, anti-capitalist or otherwise, to launch a "national democratic revolution" (NDR); and only once the fight against racism was complete could the second phase, the fight against capitalism, enter the discussion.[2] This prioritization of the struggle against racism led the SACP to align with the African National Congress (ANC), which became the hegemonic leader of the anti-apartheid movement and eventually the ruling party of South Africa.

The CAYCO pamphlet cited in the epigraph, however, underscores a very different tradition – racial capitalism – that strongly opposed the SACP's two-stage approach. As part of the United Democratic Front (UDF), the largest anti-apartheid coalition in this period, CAYCO worked firmly in the tradition of the ANC and the SACP. Following the CST thesis, CAYCO insisted that the struggle against apartheid needed to play out in a broad anti-racist popular front. Only once the NDR was achieved, they argued, could the fight against capitalism begin. In defending this position, however, CAYCO pointed to a range of organizations in the "racial capitalism" camp, including opponents of the SACP who refused to separate the struggles against racism and capitalism. Those in the racial capitalism camp understood racism and capitalism as necessarily linked: overthrowing apartheid required an anti-capitalist program.

Who were these proponents of "racial capitalism" so derided by the CAYCO pamphlet? There was Neville Alexander, often cited as the key South African theorist of the term (Burden-Stelly, Hudson, and Pierre 2020; Go 2021; Hudson 2017; Jenkins and Leroy 2021; Singh 2022), as well as his organization of the period, the Cape Action League (CAL). There was the Unity Movement, an early radical organization that attempted to unite all ethno-racial groups under the banner "Non-European," even prior to the beginning of apartheid in 1948. There was the Black Consciousness movement, which became increasingly anti-capitalist in the aftermath of the 1976 Soweto Uprising. And there were a variety of Trotskyist organizations, foremost among them the Marxist Workers Tendency (MWT). All of these tendencies came under fire by name in the CAYCO pamphlet. This was a remarkably diverse assortment of political organizations. And while we are far more sympathetic to the "one-stage" analysis than the "two-stage," we do find ourselves in agreement with CAYCO on one major point: *the theory of racial capitalism as developed in the anti-apartheid movement in South Africa held that race and class constituted a single site of struggle.*

The CST thesis, of course, also represents a theory of the relationship between racism and capitalism (SACP 1963 [1962] [1963 [1962]]). In using the term "racial capitalism," however, we mean something far more circumscribed. Our goal in this introductory essay is to identify a political milieu and approach to struggle that developed in opposition to both racial capitalism *and* the CST/NDR tradition – as suggested by the CAYCO pamphlet. We refer to this alternative tradition or milieu as the South African tradition of racial capitalism (SAT). On the side of domination, proponents of the SAT argued that capitalism generated racism, and that the capitalist state was simultaneously a racist state. This was not too far off from the SACP and ANC's analysis, though the SAT developed very distinct political responses. On the side of resistance, they argued that state-generated racial categories divided the population, but that oppositional forces could use new, broader racial categories to forge unity. Further, and perhaps most importantly, they emphasized that anti-racist and anti-capitalist struggle could not be successful alone; each required the other. We elaborate these points below in terms of four central theses we develop to characterize the SAT as a whole.

The SAT has become something of a specter haunting racial capitalism studies. Accounts of the concept's genesis have increasingly pointed to South African debates (e.g. Burden-Stelly 2020; Burden-Stelly, Hudson, and Pierre 2020; Go 2021; Hudson 2017; Jenkins and Leroy 2021; Koshy et al. 2022; Kundnani 2020; Taylor 2022). In his foreword to the latest edition of Cedric Robinson's (2021) *Black Marxism*, Robin Kelley argues (2021: xiv), "The phrase originated in South Africa around 1976," pointing to a pamphlet released by one of the Trotskyist groups identified above (Legassick and

Hemson 1976). Singh (2022, 28) dates the origins of racial capitalism to "the South African anti-apartheid struggle in the late 1970s."[3] Given the obvious centrality of these debates, we want to unpack their content. And we want to do so in context, thinking about the emergence of "racial capitalism" as a strategic political intervention in an unfolding conjuncture.

But contextualizing in this way does not necessarily render the SAT "specific to South Africa," as Koshy et al. (2022, 1) argue in a recent volume. It means, rather, as Hall (2021 [1986], 297) once put the point, that ideas "have to be delicately disinterred from their concrete and specific historical embeddedness and transplanted into new soil with considerable care and patience." This is what Taylor (2022, 17) seems to suggest in her call for a return to South Africa:

> I think we would be better served by going back to the development of the idea of racial capitalism, which was not in Cedric Robinson's *Black Marxism*, but in the Marxist tradition in South Africa. What is useful about that history? I think their development of the concept can be generalized beyond the South African context ... The question is how we use their thinking outside its original history and context to explain patterns of race and capitalism in the US ... [and] are there other contexts within which this works?

For Koshy et al. (2022, 1), the specificity of the SAT stands in contrast to Cedric Robinson (2021), whose "contribution was to generalize and theorize racial capitalism on a world scale. His thesis was that capitalism was racial capital-ism everywhere" (Koshy et al. 2022, 1). Conversely, Taylor (2022) suggests a generalizability with greater contingency: the SAT may apply elsewhere, but this is an open question. This point resonates with Stuart Hall's (2019 [1980], 213) intervention into South African debates, where he argues that "[r]acism is not present, in the same form or degree, in all capitalist for-mations; it is not necessary to the concrete functioning of all capitalisms." Within this Taylor/Hall frame, the key task for the researcher is to reveal the conditions under which capitalism *becomes* racial, or as Hall puts it, "how and why racism has been specifically overdetermined by and articulated with certain capitalisms." Our goal in this introductory essay, and with the special issue more generally, is to push the analysis of racial capitalism forward by distilling some of the key theses that emerged from the SAT. It will be up to future researchers to apply the theses to other contexts. After presenting the four key theses of the SAT, we present the contributions to the special issue.

Four theses on the South African tradition of racial capitalism

The SAT was forged in the "context of the struggle," as Clarno and Vally (2023) put it in this volume, against apartheid, colonialism, and racial capitalism. It emerged from a tremendously diverse ecosystem of movements that challenged – to varying degrees – the two-stage approach of the ANC/SACP. This ecosystem included, among others, the NEUM and its offshoot APDUSA; organizations linked to Neville Alexander such as CAL and the Workers' Organisation for Socialist Action (WOSA); Black Consciousness groups such as the South African Students' Organisation (SASO), Black People's Convention (BPC), and Azanian People's Organisation (AZAPO); the National Forum coalition; and the Marxist Workers' Tendency (MWT). Activists in these and kindred groups insisted that the national struggle and the class struggle were inseparable. And as varied as their positions were, we want to suggest that this broader ecosystem of struggle constituted a recognizable South African tradition of theorizing racial capitalism: the SAT.

In this section we outline four of the key theoretical claims that emerged from the SAT. We do not intend to posit these as eternal truths; they are better understood as hypotheses that one may test in other contexts. Following Hall (2021 [1986], 297), our goal here is to "delicately disinter" the key ideas of the SAT, enabling others to "transplant" them "into new soil with considerable care and patience."

I . Class struggle from above – the pursuit of profit – generates racism.

Capitalism generates racism: that was a fundamental point of departure for the SAT. But this argument was developed in a particular context, namely, the peculiar development of racial capitalism in South Africa. Theorists in the SAT never argued that all capitalism is racial, but rather, that capitalism assumes a racial guise under specific conditions. And South African conditions were quite specific, or at least extreme: throughout the late 19th and 20th centuries, capitalism developed in tandem with relentless white supremacy, including an especially draconian system of pass laws that enabled the hyper-exploitation of Black workers (Johnstone 1976; Hindson 1987; Crush, Jeeves, and Yudelman 1991). For proponents of the SAT, it was the pursuit of profit in this context that underpinned apartheid racism.

In positing the causal role of capitalism, the SAT departs from understandings of racial capitalism that emphasize the origins of racism independently of class struggle. This is the lesson, for example, of Cedric Robinson's (2021 [1983]) *Black Marxism*, which suggests that "racialism" preceded capitalism. In stark contrast, Black Consciousness leader Steve Biko is clear: "There is no doubt that the colour question in South African politics was originally introduced for economic reasons" (Biko 1996 [1978], 87–88). For him, racial divisions became a "moral justification" for exploitation, leading to a fusion of capitalism and racism: "Capitalistic exploitative tendencies, coupled with the overt arrogance of white racism, have conspired against us" (Biko 1996

[1978], 88, 96-97). For this reason, Biko suggests, Black movements will tend toward anti-capitalist challenge:

> "It will not be long before the blacks relate their poverty to their blackness in concrete terms. Because of the tradition forced onto the country, the poor people shall always be black people. It is not surprising, therefore, that the blacks should wish to rid themselves of a system that locks up the wealth of the country in the hands of a few" (Biko 1996 [1978], 63).

Tabata, of the NEUM and later APDUSA, made a similar argument just before the rise of apartheid. Like Biko, Tabata recognized both the class roots of racism and the ways in which the latter assumed an independent guise:

> While at first this racialism was fostered in the economic interests of the White employers, and while it was intended to facilitate the keeping of the Blacks in a subordinate position, so that they would be an every-ready source of cheap labor to feed the triple demands of the industrial machine, the gold-mines and the white farms, it gained so much momentum in the course of time, that now it exists on its own. (Tabata 1974 [1950], 3)

Biko (1996 [1978], 88) agreed that, even if racism was rooted in "the economic greed exhibited by white people, it has now become a serious problem on its own." In contrast to Biko, however, Tabata understood capitalism and class as far more central to the project of organizing resistance. He notes that,

> "The real cleavage is one of class, not one of color. But in the particular historical conditions attending colonial exploitation ... [whites found it] extremely convenient to utilize color differences to cover over and obscure the fundamental dividing line, that of class" (Tabata 1974 [1950], 4, see also 1, 3).

Racism had the effect of disorganizing the working class, but it appeared to facilitate capitalist unity. Tabata thus points to the way that British and Dutch colonists became "co-partners in the rape, in the conquest and in the plunder of South Africa ... both pursue ever more efficient methods for the exploitation of the Black man in the endeavor to maintain the source of limitless profits" (2). Once again, we see that class struggle from above, the search for profit, generates racism.

Foreign capital played an especially important role in generating racism. Legassick and Hemson (1976, 8) of the MWT, for example, underscore "the role that foreign capital has played not only economically in South Africa, but in the political endorsement and reproduction of South Africa's system of racial domination." They point especially to the collaboration between the "British state, acting on behalf of British capital," and the emergent South African state, itself forged by British interests in conjunction with Afrikaners. At the core of this collaboration, they suggest, was the policy of racial segregation, which "meant the division of the working class on a *racial* basis," and "on terms which perpetuated the profit rates of the mining industry"

(Legassick and Hemson 1976, 4, original emphasis). This policy of racial domination and division, cemented in the early years of the 20th century, "created the foundations of South Africa's racial capitalism and the modern apartheid regime" (Legassick and Hemson 1976, 4). Indeed, the apartheid regime merely represented "the emergence in new forms of the compromises and alliances between imperialist and local capitalist interests which had been continually renegotiated," with the key goal being to "sustain a cheap black labor force" (Legassick and Hemson 1976, 7).

Seen from the vantage point of white capital within South Africa, Alexander (1985 [1983], 43) notes that the "national bourgeoisie" relied on racial domination to secure cheap Black labor, cementing a compromise with British imperialism "to maintain their profitable system of super-exploitation of black labor." Like Legassick and Hemson (1976), Alexander (1985 [1983], 41) understood the apartheid regime as a reflection of a much deeper system – racial capitalism – that was the real target of resistance. Indeed, apartheid reflected a longstanding reliance of the capitalist class on ethnic and racial division to justify inequality – they "artificially created" such groups, "as a matter of state policy, because it was in the broad economic and political interests of the ruling class to keep them divided" (Alexander 1982b [1985], 9). This included, for example, the construction of a "split labor market" that divided white and Black labor (Alexander 1985 [1983], 43). In Alexander's (1985 [1984a], 117) view, then, South African capitalism rested firmly on racial segregation – including, especially, the migrant labor system – as a "fundamental organizing principle" (see also Alexander 1979: ch. 2, 4). Due to the capitalist underpinnings of racism, Alexander (1985 [1982a], 19–20) began to detect a shift from an "anti-white position" to "definitions [of the enemy] based on a class analysis."

Adherents of the SAT were not the only ones to recognize the key role of capitalism, and the imperatives of accumulation, in generating racism. Indeed, the SACP (1963 [1962] [1963 [1962]], 25) offered a parallel analysis in its foundational statement on the CST, noting that, "The South African and foreign monopoly capitalists and large-scale landowners, who, together, are the real rulers of this country, have cultivated racial differences and prejudices as their most effective instrument in their insatiable drive for cheap labour and high profits. The colonial status of the African people facilitates the maximum exploitation of their labour." Likewise, Magubane (1979:, 3), who was loosely aligned to the ANC, argues: "The seemingly 'autonomous' existence of racism today does not lessen the fact that it was initiated by the needs of capitalist development or that these needs remain the dominant factor in racist societies." He stresses the key role of foreign capital, racial segregation, and the use of racial domination to divide and dominate the working class in the service of profit. But despite the overlap with these analyses, as well as others coming out of the Congress tradition loosely defined (e.g. Davies, O'Meara, and Dlamini 1984; Saul and Gelb 1986 [1981]; Wolpe 1972), the *strategic* consequences members of the SAT drew from this analysis could not be further from that of the CST. SAT theorists were clear: because racism emerges from capitalism, it cannot be challenged independent of capitalism. By contrast, followers of the CST thesis insisted that racism should be challenged separately from capitalism – in a prior "stage." Only then could capitalism be confronted directly.

II . The capitalist state is the primary agent of racialization.

If capitalists promote racism, they do not do so on their own. The state is central to class struggle from above, waged (among other means) through racialization. This explains the centrality of Marxist state theory – above all, the work of Nicos Poulantzas – to South African debates in this period (Clarke 1978; Davies et al. 1976; Davies 1979; Innes and Plaut 1978; Morris 1976; cf. Nash 1999). Proponents of the SAT argued that the colonial/apartheid state developed and implemented racist policies – including segregation, influx control, political repression, and other forms of racial exclusion – *for the benefit* of capitalists. This key role of the state, in turn, underscored the historical specificity of racial capitalism. If South African capitalism rested upon racism and racial division throughout the late 19th and 20th centuries, the precise character of this racism – as implemented and secured by the state – shifted over time, typically in response to the contours of class struggle from above and below (Burawoy 1981). This was not a generalized and transhistorical racism, but rather a conjunctural one.

A key example here is Wolpe's (1972) classic "cheap labor" thesis, which differentiates between the periods of segregation (roughly 1870 to the 1930s) and apartheid (from 1948). The policies and practices of the apartheid state, Wolpe argues, reflected an attempt to shore up the migrant labor system established under segregation, and thus cheap labor itself, most notably through stricter regulation of movement, political repression, and the promotion of industry closer to the rural areas. In sum, the state protected capital by implementing racism in historically specific ways – the racism of apartheid differed from the racism of segregation. Wolpe (1988) would later extend and revise this conjunctural analysis, pointing to the greater contingency of racism and capitalism while continuing to insist that the racism of the capitalist state shifts alongside the economy and class struggle.

Wolpe's relation to the SAT, of course, is tenuous. As Burawoy (2004:, 666) notes, he "did not have the courage of his class convictions," and thus remained aligned with the ANC and the SACP (see also Friedman 2015; Lodge 2022). Yet, he was highly critical of both the CST thesis and its implication: the need for an NDR as part of a two-stage transition (Wolpe 1975, 1995). Much like the proponents of the SAT, Wolpe (1975) criticized the

SACP for imposing a singular version of "internal colonialism," which in reality may take varied forms across time and space. This critical view put him on shaky ground in the ANC/SACP (Friedman 2015), though he did not experience expulsion, as did his MWT counterparts. Further, Wolpe's analysis resonates closely with proponents of the SAT. Like Wolpe (1972), for example, Alexander (1979, 33–38) underscores the key role of the state in promoting the migrant labor system, including the preservation of rural areas as a basis for cheap Black labor. Interestingly, though, in doing so he draws only minimally from Wolpe and more so from the lesser-known Molteno (1977), who is quite critical of the CST and suggests that Wolpe's argument amounts to liberal pluralism. Mafeje (1981), who came out of the Unity Movement and aligned with APDUSA, also took Wolpe to task for his abstract Marxism, which, he argued, ignored everyday realities and culture on the ground in the rural areas, imputing monolithic identities from without.

Wolpe was part of a broader academic tradition, rooted in the UK, which pointed to the role of the state in using racism to protect and advance capitalist interests (Burawoy 1981; Davies et al. 1976; Legassick 1974; Marks and Trapido 1979; Morris 1976; Trapido 1971). Many of these academics remained somewhat distant from popular struggles on the ground in South Africa, and some, like Wolpe, aligned with the Congress tradition, though others, like Legassick, joined organizations that were part of the SAT. Nonetheless, periodization of the capitalist state – that is, conjunctural analysis of how state racism enabled capitalism in historically specific ways – was central to thinking within the SAT. In his address to AZAPO in 1982, for example, Alexander argued that racial capitalism and the apartheid state were confronting a crisis due to shifting conditions. Most crucial was the ascendance of manufacturing, the incorporation of Black workers into more skilled positions, and their growing confidence and demands enabled by their new structural power (Alexander 1985 [1982a], 23–27). The new conjuncture thus generated a crisis for "their system of racial capitalism": "The dilemma for the rulers in this connection is how to reconcile the iron laws of capitalist development with the bantustan/apartheid strategy designed for an earlier phase of that development" (Alexander 1985 [1982a], 25–6). In response, he argued, the capitalist state would have to shift yet again, with two possible options: greater repression, or compromise with the Black middle class (Alexander 1985 [1982a], 29–35). As Legassick (1974) suggested, a similar ruling class crisis and decision point in the 1940s led to the implementation of apartheid after 1948.

The central role of the capitalist state was a hallmark of left thinking under apartheid, including proponents of both the SAT and the CST, as well as academics with weaker ties to popular struggle. What is crucial, however, is that they came to different political conclusions. If the SAT and CST both recognized that capitalists and the capitalist state underpinned racism and apartheid, they disagreed about how to respond. In contrast to the two-stage transition implied in the analysis of CST, proponents of the SAT sought to link struggles against racism and capitalism: they viewed the two as inseparable. This was a consistent feature of the SAT, even if its proponents understood that the capitalist state and racist policies were conjunctural and historically specific. Not only did this lead to different strategy (thesis 4), but it also yielded very different conceptions of race (thesis 3).

III . Racial ideology can divide, enabling capitalism. But it can also unify, facilitating resistance.

Most tendencies in the SAT developed a theory of racial identity rooted in the strategic project of building a united front against racial capitalism. The idea was to reclaim broader conceptions of race that encompassed oppressed and exploited people in South Africa *against* divisive conceptions of race generated by the racial capitalist state. Activists began to recognize the artificiality of racial ideology even before the advent of apartheid in 1948. For example, the Non-European Unity Movement's (1997 [1943], 60) draft program describes "Segregation [a]s an artificial device of the rulers, and an instrument for the domination of the Non-European." As Alexander (1979, 64) puts the point, "Racism has been to the development of capitalism in South Africa what the doctrine of individual rights was to the development of capitalism in England and France." Racism, he argues, historically justified various forms of forced labor; but just as importantly, it had the effect of disorganizing the proletariat, "trapp[ing them] in a divisive and debilitating ethnic consciousness" (Alexander 1985 [1982b], 29). Afrikaner and British settler colonists collaborated to "retribalize" (Alexander 1979, 65; cf. Mafeje 1971; Magubane 1973, 2000) the African population beginning in the late 19th century, largely as a means of reproducing "non-capitalist" rural enclaves in which "tribes" had direct access to the land. This worked to subsidize the impossibly low wages of migrant workers in the mines, and later in heavy industry, maintaining a true semi-proletariat (Alexander 1979; Molteno 1977; Wolpe 1972). This is what Magubane (1979, 96) called, sardonically, "social security for the migrant workers."

The migrant labor system began to unravel once "tribal" subsistence producers were dispossessed, prompting a wave of mass urbanization. Apartheid represented both an attempt to stem this wave, as well as a new strategy of racial fragmentation in the face of growing resistance. As anticolonial struggles picked up pace across the continent, the apartheid regime fragmented race ("Natives," "Africans") into ethnicity (Xhosa, Tswana, Venda, Xhosa, and so forth), granting "independence" to each ethno-linguistic group and assigning them respective "homelands." This was both a strategy of cooptation, a transparent attempt to "decolonize" South Africa from above

THE SOUTH AFRICAN TRADITION OF RACIAL CAPITALISM 11

in response to burgeoning independence movements (Magubane 1979, 233), and an attempt to sow division within the category "African," as well as among "Coloreds," "Indians," and "Africans."

Proponents of the SAT criticized the Congress tradition for emulating this race-as-divisive formulation in their own organizing practices. Most famously, Alexander (1979) points out how the ANC's theory of "multi-racialism" – separate resistance organizations for each racial group as defined by the apartheid state – emulates, and even derives from, the apartheid schema.[4] He suggests that the SACP/ANC's multi-racialism shares the apartheid regime's class project of fostering indigenous bourgeoisies among each respective ethnic group. For the CPSA,

> "After 1924 ... the Party went over to a strategy of tacit and often open alliance with the liberal bourgeoisie. There was implicit (and often explicit) in its theory and practice the conception of a two-stage revolution: first for bourgeois democratic rights and later for socialism" (Alexander 1979, 50; Zumoff 2014, 345, 356).

And for the ANC and SACP of the 1960s and 70s, Alexander (1979, 99) suggests that by ignoring class in favor of the NDR, both parties were oblivious to "privileged classes" within each racial group being "pulled in the direction of the ruling classes in the South African state," i.e. collaborating with the apartheid state.

This is why Alexander had such disdain for the two-stage theory of the CST, as did most activists in the SAT. Going back to the NEUM's (1997 [1943], 61) draft program, "the Unity of all the Non-Europeans is a necessary precondition for this total fight against Segregation." A couple of decades later, proponents of Black Consciousness would agree with the spirit of this formulation but take issue with the Unity Movement's invocation of "Non-European" as a negative definition of race. BC activists demanded a positive definition, a reclaiming of "Black" as the basis for collective struggle (Biko 1996 [1978], 48; SASO 1970, 1–2). Unity was key here: Biko (1996 [1978], 49) argued that all Black people had "to operate as a group in order to rid themselves of the shackles that bind them to perpetual servitude." For Biko (1996 [1978], 48), blackness had two components: subjection to group-based oppression, including "those who are by law or tradition politically, economically and socially discriminated against as a group"; and self-identification with the category, because "by describing yourself as black you have started on a road towards emancipation, you have committed yourself to fight against all forces that seek to use your blackness as a stamp that marks you out as a subservient being." Sipho Buthelezi suggests that this politics derived from engagement with Cabral (1973; qtd. in Buthelezi 1991, 114), who argued that colonized people need to "rediscover an identity" as a basis for mobilization – a point which Buthelezi (1991:, 120) suggests was completely alien to the ANC's approach. Instead of letting the apartheid state define them, BC activists would reclaim "blackness" in "a deliberate attempt by all of us to counteract the 'divide and rule' attitude of the evil-doers" (SASO 1970, 2).

These reconstructions of race aim to simultaneously acknowledge the importance of racism while denying the existence of races. Alexander (1985 [1982a], 37) was at pains to illuminate "the scientific fact that 'race' is a non-entity," yet he also notes that, "though 'races' do not exist, racial prejudice, racialism and racism are as real as the food that you and I eat!" The ANC's multi-racialism, he argued, failed to grasp this complex reality, and as a result it was a false "nonracialism" that actually reinforced racial division. For this reason, Alexander and others associated with the National Forum often advocated for *anti*-racism, rather than *non*-racialism. In Alexander's (1985 [1983], 46) view, anti-racism encompasses both the rejection of race as a scientifically valid concept and opposition to capitalism: "the term not only involves the denial of 'race' but also opposition to the capitalist structures for the perpetuation of which the ideology and theory of 'race' exist." If capitalism generates racism, then anti-racism is about revealing this racism for the fabrication and justification of exploitation that it is.

A distinctive aspect of the SAT approach, then, was the pairing of a healthy skepticism of the divisive potential of certain racial categories with a recognition that these same categories could be rearticulated as a unifying force. The skeptical impulse identified a certain commonality between the thinking of the apartheid state and the multi-racialism of the ANC and the SACP. If the former insisted upon a hierarchy of essential differences rooted in biology and culture (MacDonald 2006, 6–16), the ANC's "four nations thesis" was similarly based in primordialism. This tendency is even evident in the SACP's theorizing (Slovo 1988), which drew heavily on Stalin's (1913) definition of the nation as "a historically constituted, stable community of people, formed on the basis of a common language, territory, economic life, and psychological make-up manifested in a common culture." For proponents of the SAT, apartheid formulations and the multi-racialism of the ANC and the SACP were two sides of the same coin: both took racial categories as relatively immutable. In response, SAT strategists sought to redefine race as a fundamentally political, and thus malleable, category that could either divide or unite.

IV . Racial capitalism is a strategic concept that emphasizes the inseparability of anti-racist and anti-capitalist struggle.

If the various groups discussed under the banner of the SAT all appear to converge on the Black working class by the early 1980s, this was not incidental. As a singular figure, this class fraction represents the strategic refusal to separate the national and social struggles into distinct "stages." Proponents of the CST aligned themselves with the ANC, arguing that the working-class was gaining influence within the organization (Everatt 1992, 34–8); supporters of the SAT, meanwhile, saw this as a dangerous mistake that would focus on the fight for legal equality at the expense of anti-capitalist struggle. But just as race alone was insufficient as the basis for revolutionary activity, so too was class, according to the SAT. It was the *Black* working class that had to play this role.

Why not the *entire* working class? At the first National Forum, AZAPO Chairperson Lybon Mabasa (Mabasa, Manthatha, and Sebidi 1983, 3) argued that "[r]acial capitalism is maintained and sustained by the white middle class ... and the 'white working class,' which is satisfied with the status quo and feel they have nothing in common with their counterparts, i.e. the black working class. The latter remains the only politically viable class who can wage a committed and successful struggle." From this perspective, the white working class was a potentially reactionary class fraction, materially invested as it was in the perpetuation of apartheid rule. But the Black working class was invested in the overthrow of this regime and, indeed, of capitalism itself. Mabasa's position is nearly indistinguishable from Alexander's (1985 [1983], 55–6), who, at the very same meeting, drew on the BC conception of blackness: "The black working class has to act as a magnet that draws all the other oppressed layers of our society, organizes them for the liberation struggle, and imbues them with the consistent democratic socialist ideas which alone spell death to the system of racial capitalism as we know it today." Alexander's subsequent group, WOSA, would maintain a similar position, as would the Marxist Workers Tendency. As Legassick (2019, 63) put it in his final published essay, the MWT view was that "in the course of the struggle white workers would move to reaction. The main class force was the black working class."

This position was nothing new in 1983. Even before the launch of the National Forum, at an AZAPO congress a year prior, Alexander (1985 [1982a], 28) argued, "The white working class became a junior partner in the class alliance that governed South Africa .... The white workers formally entrenched their vested interest in perpetuating the system of racial capitalism." This position had a long legacy in the Unity Movement as well. More than three decades earlier, Tabata (1974 [1950], 2) explained that "the White worker's bill of wages is subsidised from that of the Black worker ... That is why he is so willing to join the White bloc." This was not only because white workers were no longer trustworthy; racial capitalism had itself been transformed, and white workers no longer had a "virtual monopolisation of productive skills. Today, increasingly it is the black workers who are acquiring this strategic leverage. The white workers, on the other hand, are becoming more and more dispensable as a class." (Alexander 1985 [1982a], 25).

Racism was therefore crucial to the analysis, but it was not something separable that could be challenged prior to capitalism itself. Capitalism in South Africa was *racial* capitalism, or to cite Alexander's (1985 [1983], 53) speech at the first National Forum meeting, "The class struggle against capitalist exploitation and the national struggle against racial oppression become one struggle under the general command of the black working class and its organizations." This is a frontal assault on the notion that the national struggle can be waged independently of the fight against capitalism. So when the MWT's Legassick (2019:, 59), for example, argues that "national oppression could be overcome only through ending capitalism in South Africa," he is not advancing a reductive analysis that privileges class over race. As the MWT argued from the beginning (Legassick et al. 1980), "Just as national oppression is rooted in class exploitation, so the national liberation struggle is rooted in class struggle." The aim, in other words, is not to uncritically revert to a non-racial class politics, but rather to understand racial capitalism as a conflict "between capital and the black working class" (ibid.). This is rooted in a "logic of racial capitalism" in which "racial oppression and capitalist exploitation have come to feed on and reinforce one another" (Saul and Gelb 1986 [1981], 63–4). But the key is that anti-racism and anti-capitalism, while potentially analytically separable, are never empirically separable: "There can be no separation of stages" (Legassick et al. 1980). For Alexander, the goal of working-class struggle is to reconstitute the nation in a way that undermines ethnic and racial division: "the unmaking of ethnic identities through the nation-building process understood as a class struggle waged in the course of national liberation" (1985 [1984b], 151; see also 1985 [1983]).

In practice, this means that the SAT understands racial capitalism as a system co-constituted by twin forces – profitability and dehumanization – in which the latter initially served the former but has now become a force in its own right. Because these two forces are so substantially interlinked, it was the SAT's key intervention to redirect strategic forces to their point of articulation: a successful challenge to either racism or capitalism requires a unified and protracted struggle to challenge them both, simultaneously and together.

Overview of articles

Our special issue includes seven original articles and an afterword that develop a distinctively South African tradition of racial capitalism. A first set of contributions considers key thinkers in context, asking how their respective theories of racial capitalism square with theories from elsewhere. A second set of articles then puts the SAT to work across multiple time periods, from early 20th century segregation to high apartheid to the present. Finally, an afterword considers the SAT in relation to Cedric Robinson's theory of racial capitalism.

The first set of articles begins with Andy Clarno and Salim Vally's (2023) analysis of Neville Alexander, who developed a novel theory of racial capitalism in the "context of struggle," the key concept in Clarno and Vally's assessment. Alexander's theory can only be understood in relation to socialist strategy. Racial capitalism, they argue, was a radical critique of the SACP/ANC's two-stage theory of revolution, and was central to the project of building unity among BC activists and Marxists at the National Forum in 1983. They conclude with a global conjunctural analysis, identifying South African racial capitalism as a node in an imperialist system.

A second contribution from Mosa Phadi (2023) turns to a much earlier thinker, often unfairly omitted from debates over racial capitalism in South Africa: Sol Plaatje. Phadi rescues Plaatje from unfair characterizations of him as a liberal – which, she argues, parallel dismissals of the early writings of W.E.B. Du Bois. She maintains that both Plaatje and Du Bois, who actually met and corresponded with each other, developed incipient theories of racial capitalism in their work, long before Du Bois confronted racial capitalism in *Black Reconstruction*.

Third, Ahmed Veriava and Prishani Naidoo (2023) analyze Steve Biko's (1979) testimony at the 1976 BPC/SASO trial. Thinking Biko in relation to Stuart Hall, they develop a nuanced account of race-class articulation and present Biko as a radical critic of racial capitalism. Since the SAT is always about strategic thinking, they set their theory to work – Biko-with-Hall, as they put it – in making sense of debates that emerged from the recent wave of student struggles across South Africa.

The final contribution of the first section comes from Bongani Nyoka (2023), who analyzes the thought of Bernard Magubane. While he only infrequently invoked the term (e.g. Magubane 1977, 1983), Magubane consistently centers the relationship between racist policy and capital accumulation. Despite ties to the ANC and SACP, Magubane was a heterodox thinker, putting a theory of racial capitalism to work in analyzing the history of racist land dispossession in the pre-apartheid period. Nyoka concludes his analysis by contrasting the persistence of racial capitalism after apartheid with Magubane's vision of the socialism that a Black working-class insurgency might bring about.

After this initial set of articles, three authors analyze racial capitalism in various periods of South African history. First, Zine Magubane (2023) challenges the standard understanding of whiteness as a "psychological wage" paid to white proletarians. Through a bold new interpretation of the 1932 Carnegie Commission, a study of the "Poor White Problem in South Africa," she argues that the Afrikaner petty bourgeoisie that promoted the report never sought to forge an alliance with white workers by boosting their "public and psychological wage," as Du Bois famously put it. Rather, the

Carnegie Report boosted the actual wages of the Afrikaner petty bourgeoisie, and demonstrated the worth of Afrikaner smallholders to both mining capital and the segregationist state.

The second contribution in this section comes from Bridget Kenny (2023), who develops a relational analysis of white and Black women working in the service sector in Johannesburg in the 1950s through the 70s. Pairing Stuart Hall's theory of race-class articulation with Bridget O'Laughlin's emphasis on the struggles of "living labor," Kenny's analysis disturbs the standard functionalist analysis of the role of women under apartheid: as sources of reproductive labor. This piece – and Kenny's work more generally – demonstrates that women generated politics at the point of production: white women workers reinforced normative white femininity and legitimated apartheid rule, while Black women workers rejected such notions in favor of an oppositional race-class subjectivity. Kenny's work shows what the concept of "living labor" brings to analyses of racial capitalism.

The final piece in this section is by Ashwin Desai (2023), who brings racial capitalism to bear on the July 2021 riots in South Africa, which left over 350 dead. Desai explores the racial dynamics of the violence in an Indian township called Phoenix in Durban, the largest city in KwaZulu-Natal, where vigilantes set upon "Africans," who they immediately identified as "looters." He shows how racial capitalism continues to reinscribe apartheid historical geography by continuing to differentiate populations in the present. What will it take, he asks, to build a "non-racial inclusive democracy"?

The issue concludes with reflections from Robin D.G. Kelley (2023), whose work provides an ideal bridge between South African and American debates over racial capitalism. In the 1980s, he began research for a dissertation comparing the Black left in both countries (Camp and Kelley 2013; Kelley 2014). If today Kelley is celebrated for bringing Cedric Robinson's long-neglected work into the public eye, his graduate work demonstrates that Robinson's "Black radical tradition" was with him from the beginning. In one of his first academic publications, Kelley (1986) argues that the struggle for African self-determination was never imposed by the Comintern or even developed by the CPSA but was already latent in earlier African nationalist movements. His afterword, then, brings us full circle. While we have suggested in this introduction that the SAT is distinct from Robinson's approach to racial capitalism – a conjunctural, as opposed to a global, mode of generalization – following Kelley, we can see how Robinson might help us understand the emergence of the SAT in the first place.

Conclusion

We present this special issue on the SAT not as a definitive statement, but rather a point of departure. The anti-apartheid movement was vibrant and diverse. This collection of essays only scratches the surface in terms of uncovering the myriad viewpoints that emerged from the left amidst South Africa's particular combination of capitalism and racism. Nonetheless, we hope that readers will appreciate that South African theorizing is not only important because it coined a phrase – racial capitalism. It is useful, above all, because it offers novel insights that continue to hold relevance today, whether in South Africa or elsewhere. Indeed, exploration of the SAT helps us to recognize that racial capitalism has been a strategic, rather than a purely analytic, concept – a concept that was forged and developed in struggle. One of the most crucial lessons, then, of this foray into the SAT, is that we should appreciate the insights of radical organic intellectuals who are engaged in everyday battles, on the ground and beyond the academy.

Notes

1. "Left-Wing Deviation: Discussion Article" by Cape Youth Congress 1987, A2562, box 5, folder 1, Mark Heywood Papers, Historical Papers Research Archive, University of the Witwatersrand, Johannesburg, South Africa.
2. One may trace the SACP's stagist approach to at least the 1920s, when the Communist Party of South Africa (CPSA, predecessor to the SACP), embraced the idea of a Native Republic, as directed by the Sixth World Congress of the Communist International (Comintern). The CPSA's 1929 program called for building "[a]n Independent South African Native Republic as a *stage* towards the Workers' and Peasants' Republic" (CPSA 1929, emphasis added; see also Drew 1991, 2000).
3. Jenkins and Leroy (2021, 22) point out that Blauner's (1972) *Racial Oppression in America* used the term "racial capitalism" as early as 1972. Elsewhere we note that, to our knowledge, this is the first usage of the term in print (Levenson and Paret 2022). Since writing that piece, we have learned that South African sociologist Eddie Webster used the term in a December 1973 speech to the National Union of South African Students. This is the earliest usage of the term in South Africa that we have found (so far).
4. During the Third Period, the Executive Committee of the Communist International (ECCI) instructed the CPSA to build separate ethnic states even before the apartheid state made doing so official policy (Lodge 2022, 164), calling "[f]or the right of the Zulu, Basuto, etc. nations to form own Independent Republics" (ECCI 2003 [1931], 18), which, as party leader Lazar Bach argued, would "bring about a voluntary association of national republics – Sotho, Tswana, Swazi, Zulu, Xhosa – in a federation of independent native republics" (Simons and Simons 1983 [1956], 473; see also Legassick 1973, 52). But this position quickly faded into oblivion, with the CPSA's organizing work focused on industry rather than ethnicity.

Acknowledgments

For critical feedback on this introduction, we want to thank Allison Drew and Salim Vally, as well as participants in two workshops where we presented this paper: the

History Workshop at the University of the Witwatersrand in March 2023, and the International Workshop on Racial Capitalism at the University of Texas at Austin in April 2023. We are also deeply grateful to all contributors to this issue, whose thinking has greatly influenced our own.

Disclosure statement

No potential conflict of interest was reported by the author(s).

References

Alexander, Neville [No Sizwe]. 1979. *One Azania, One Nation: The National Question in South Africa.* London: Zed Press.

Alexander, Neville. 1985 [1982a]. "Let Us Unite in the Year of the United Front." In *Sow the Wind: Contemporary Speeches*, 1–17. Johannesburg: Skotaville.

Alexander, Neville. 1985 [1982b]. "The National Situation." In *Sow the Wind: Contemporary Speeches*, 23–40. Johannesburg: Skotaville.

Alexander, Neville. 1985 [1983]. "Nation and Ethnicity in South Africa." In *Sow the Wind: Contemporary Speeches*, 41–56. Johannesburg: Skotaville.

Alexander, Neville. 1985 [1984a]. "'Let Us Fight Against the Organ-Grinder': Background to the Nkomati Accords." In *Sow the Wind: Contemporary Speeches*, 98–125. Johannesburg: Skotaville.

Alexander, Neville. 1985 [1984b]. "Race, Ethnicity and Nationalism in Social Science in Southern Africa." In *Sow the Wind: Contemporary Speeches*, 126–153. Johannesburg: Skotaville.

Biko, Steve. 1979. *The Testimony of Steve Biko: Black Consciousness in South Africa.* London: Grafton.

Biko, Steve. 1996 [1978]. *I Write What I Like: Selected Writings.* Chicago, IL: University of Chicago Press.

Blauner, Robert. 1972. *Racial Oppression in America.* New York: Harper and Row.

Burawoy, Michael. 1981. "The Capitalist State in South Africa: Marxist and Sociological Perspectives on Race and Class." *Political Power and Social Theory* 2: 279–335.

Burawoy, Michael. 2004. "From Liberation to Reconstruction: Theory & Practice in the Life of Harold Wolpe." *Review of African Political Economy* 31: 657–675. doi:10.1080/0305624042000327813

Burden-Stelly, Charisse. 2020. "Modern U.S. Racial Capitalism." *Monthly Review* 72 (3): 8–20. doi:10.14452/MR-072-03-2020-07_2

Burden-Stelly, Charisse, Peter James Hudson, and Jemima Pierre. 2020. "Racial Capitalism, Black Liberation, and South Africa." *Black Agenda Review*, 16 December. Available online: https://www.blackagendareport.com/racial-capitalism-black-liberation-and-south-africa.

Buthelezi, Sipho. 1991. "The Emergence of Black Consciousness: An Historical Appraisal." In *Bounds of Possibility: The Legacy of Steve Biko and Black Consciousness*, edited by N. Barney Pityana, Mamphela Ramphele, Malusi Mpumlwana, and Lindy Wilson, 111–129. Cape Town: David Philip.

Cabral, Amilcar. 1973. *Return to the Source: Selected Speeches of Amilcar Cabral.* New York: Monthly Review Press.

Camp, Jordan T., and Robin D. G. Kelley. 2013. "Black Radicalism, Marxism, and Collective Memory: An Interview with Robin D. G. Kelley." *American Quarterly* 65 (1): 215–230. doi:10.1353/aq.2013.0007

Cape Youth Congress. 1987. "Left-Wing Deviation: Discussion Article," A2562, box 5, folder 1, Mark Heywood Papers, Historical Papers Research Archive, University of the Witwatersrand, Johannesburg, South Africa.

Clarke, Simon. 1978. "Capital, Fractions of Capital and the State: 'neo-Marxist' Analysis of the South African State." *Capital & Class* 2: 32–77. doi:10.1177/030981687800500103

Clarno, Andy, and Salim Vally. 2023. "The Context of Struggle: Racial Capitalism and Political Praxis in South Africa." *Ethnic and Racial Studies*. Advance online publication. doi:10.1080/01419870.2022.2143239.

Communist Party of South Africa (CPSA). 1929. "Programme of the Communist Party of South Africa Adopted at the Seventh Annual Conference of the Party, 1 January 1929." In *The Heart of Hope: South Africa's Transition from Apartheid to Democracy*, edited by Padraig O'Malley. Available online: https://omalley.nelsonmandela.org/index.php/site/q/03lv01538/04lv01600/05lv01606/06lv01608.htm.

Crush, Jonathan, Alan Jeeves, and David Yudelman. 1991. *South Africa's Labour Empire: A History of Black Migrancy to the Gold Mines*. Boulder, CO: Westview.

Davies, Robert H. 1979. *Capital, State and White Labour in South Africa, 1900–1960: An Historical Materialist Analysis of Class Formation and Class Relations*. Brighton: Harvester.

Davies, Robert, David Kaplan, Mike Morris, and Dan O'Meara. 1976. "Class Struggle and the Periodisation of the State in South Africa." *Review of African Political Economy* 3 (7): 4–30. doi:10.1080/03056247608703298

Davies, Robert H., Dan O'Meara, and Sipho Dlamini. 1984. "The Historical Development of Racial Capitalism, 1652–1948." In *The Struggle for South Africa: A Reference Guide to Movements, Organizations, and Institutions, Volume One*, 3–19. London: Zed.

Desai, Ashwin. 2023. "Geographies of Racial Capitalism: The 2021 July Riots in South Africa." *Ethnic and Racial Studies*. Advance online publication. doi:10.1080/01419870.2022.2131452.

Drew, Allison. 1991. "Social Mobilization and Racial Capitalism in South Africa, 1928–1960." (PhD dissertation). Department of Political Science, University of California, Los Angeles.

Drew, Allison. 2000. *Discordant Comrades: Identities and Loyalties on the South African Left*. Farnham, UK: Ashgate.

Everatt, David. 1992. "Alliance Politics of a Special Type: The Roots of the ANC/SACP Alliance, 1950–1954." *Journal of Southern African Studies* 18 (1): 19–39. doi:10.1080/03057079208708304

Executive Committee of the Communist International (ECCI). 2003 [1931]. "Resolution of Political Secretariat, ECCI, 18 October 1931 (Extracts)." In *South Africa and the Communist International: A Documentary History – Volume II: Bolshevik Footsoldiers to Victims of Bolshevisation 1931–1939*, edited by Apollon Davidson, Irina Filatova, Valentin Gorodnov, and Sheridan Johns, 18. London: Frank Cass.

Friedman, Steven. 2015. *Race, Class, and Power: Harold Wolpe and the Radical Critique of Apartheid*. Scotsville, South Africa: University of KwaZulu-Natal Press.

Go, Julian. 2021. "Three Tensions in the Theory of Racial Capitalism." *Sociological Theory* 39 (1): 38–47. doi:10.1177/0735275120979822

Hall, Stuart. 2019 [1980]. "Race, Articulation, and Societies Structured in Dominance." In *Essential Essays, Vol. 1*, edited by David Morley, 172–221. Durham, NC: Duke University Press.

Hall, Stuart. 2021 [1986]. "Gramsci's Relevance for the Study of Race and Ethnicity." In *Selected Writings on Race and Difference*, edited by Paul Gilroy, and Ruth Wilson Gilmore, 295–328. Durham, NC: Duke University Press.

Hindson, Doug. 1987. *Pass Controls and the Urban African Proletariat in South Africa.* Johannesburg: Ravan Press.

Hudson, Peter James. 2017. "Racial Capitalism and the Dark Proletariat." *Boston Review: Forum 1 – Race, Capitalism, Justice*, 59–65.

Innes, Duncan, and Martin Plaut. 1978. "Class Struggle and the State." *Review of African Political Economy* 5 (11): 51–61. doi:10.1080/03056247808703350

Jenkins, Destin, and Justin Leroy. 2021. "Introduction: The Old History of Capitalism." In *Histories of Racial Capitalism*, edited by Destin Jenkins, and Justin Leroy, 1–26. New York: Columbia University Press.

Johnstone, Frederick A. 1976. *Class, Race, and Gold: A Study of Class Relations and Racial Discrimination in South Africa.* London: Routledge and Kegan Paul.

Kelley, Robin D. G. 1986. "The Third International and the Struggle for National Liberation in South Africa." *Ufahamu* 15 (1/2): 99–120. doi:10.5070/F7151-2016995.

Kelley, Robin D. G. 2014. "Our South African Freedom Dreams." *Ufahamu* 38 (1): 239–244. doi:10.5070/F7381025030.

Kelley, Robin D. G. 2021. "Foreword: Why *Black Marxism*? Why Now?" In *Black Marxism: The Making of the Black Radical Tradition*, by Cedric J. Robinson, xi–xxxiii. Chapel Hill, NC: University of North Carolina Press.

Kelley, Robin D. G. 2023. "Afterword." *Ethnic and Racial Studies*. Advance online publication. doi:10.1080/01419870.2023.2219301.

Kenny, Bridget. 2023. "Reproducing "Racial Capitalism" Through Retailing in South Africa: Gender, Labour and Consumption, 1950s–1970s." *Ethnic and Racial Studies*. Advance online publication. doi:10.1080/01419870.2022.2146450.

Koshy, Susan, Lisa Marie Cacho, Jodi A. Byrd, and Brian Jordan Jefferson2022. *Colonial Racial Capitalism.* Durham, NC: Duke University Press.

Kundnani, Arun. 2020. "What Is Racial Capitalism?" Paper presented to the Havens Wright Centre for Social Justice, University of Wisconsin-Madison, 15 October. Available at: https://www.kundnani.org/ what-is-racial-capitalism/.

Legassick, Martin. 1973. *Class and Nationalism in South African Protest: The South African Communist Party and the "Native Republic," 1928-34.* Syracuse: The Program of Eastern African Studies.

Legassick, Martin. 1974. "South Africa: Capital Accumulation and Violence." *Economy and Society* 3 (3): 253–291. doi:10.1080/03085147400000014

Legassick, Martin. 2019. "Colonialism of a Special Type and the Approach of the Marxist Workers' Tendency of the African National Congress to the National Question." In *Race, Class, and the Post-Apartheid Democratic State*, edited by John Reynolds, Ben Fine, and Robert van Niekerk, 57–71. Scotsville: University of KwaZulu-Natal Press.

Legassick, Martin, Paula Ensor, David Hemson, and Rob Petersen. 1980. *South Africa: The Workers' Movement, SACTU, and the ANC: A Struggle for Marxist Policies.* London: Cambridgeheath Press.

Legassick, Martin, and David Hemson. 1976. *Foreign Investment and the Reproduction of Racial Capitalism in South Africa.* London: Anti-Apartheid Movement.

Levenson, Zachary, and Marcel Paret. 2022. "The Three Dialectics of Racial Capitalism: From South Africa to the U.S. and Back Again." *Du Bois Review: Social Science Research on Race*. Advance online publication. https://doi.org/10.1017/S1742058X22000212.

Lodge, Tom. 2022. *Red Road to Freedom: A History of the South African Communist Party 1921-2021.* Suffolk, UK: James Currey.

Mabasa, Lybon, Tom Manthatha, and Lebamang Sebidi. 1983. "In Search of National Unity: A Quest for Self-Determination," AK2117, file J2.2.B6, Gilbert Marcus Papers, Historical Papers Research Archive, University of the Witwatersrand, Johannesburg, South Africa.

MacDonald, Michael. 2006. *Why Race Matters in South Africa*. Cambridge, MA: Harvard University Press.

Mafeje, Archie. 1971. "The Ideology of 'Tribalism'." *The Journal of Modern African Studies* 9 (2): 253–261. doi:10.1017/S0022278X00024927

Mafeje, Archie. 1981. "On the Articulation of Modes of Production: Review Article." *Journal of Southern African Studies* 8 (1): 123–138. doi:10.1080/03057078108708037

Magubane, Bernard. 1973. "The "Xhosa" in Town, Revisited Urban Social Anthropology: A Failure of Method and Theory." *American Anthropologist* 75 (5): 1701–1715. doi:10.1525/aa.1973.75.5.02a00310

Magubane, Bernard. 1977. "The Poverty of Liberal Analysis: A Polemic on Southern Africa." *Review* 1 (2): 147–166. http://www.jstor.org/stable/40240766.

Magubane, Bernard. 1979. *The Political Economy of Race and Class in South Africa*. New York: Monthly Review.

Magubane, Bernard. 1983. "Imperialism and the Making of the South African Working Class." *Contemporary Marxism* 6: 19–56. https://www.jstor.org/stable/29765723.

Magubane, Bernard. 2000. "Race and Democratization in South Africa." *Macalester International* 9 (1): 33–82. https://digitalcommons.macalester.edu/cgi/viewcontent.cgi?article=1189&context=macintl.

Magubane, Zine. 2023. "Whiteness and Racial Capitalism: To Whom do the "Wages of Whiteness" Accrue?" *Ethnic and Racial Studies*. Advance online publication. doi:10.1080/01419870.2022.2143718.

Marks, Shula, and Stanley Trapido. 1979. "Lord Milner and the South African State." *History Workshop Journal* 8 (1): 50–81. doi:10.1093/hwj/8.1.50

Molteno, Frank. 1977. "The Historical Significance of the Bantustan Strategy." *Social Dynamics* 3 (2): 15–33. doi:10.1080/02533957708458200

Morris, M. L. 1976. "The Development of Capitalism in South African Agriculture: Clas Struggle in the Countryside." *Economy and Society* 5 (3): 292–343. doi:10.1080/03085147600000014

Nash, Andrew. 1999. "The Moment of Western Marxism in South Africa." *Comparative Studies of South Asia, Africa and the Middle East* 19 (1): 66–82. doi:10.1215/1089201X-19-1-66

Non-European Unity Movement (NEUM). 1997 [1943]. "Draft Declaration on Unity Provisionally Adopted at Unity Conference, Bloemfontein, 17 December 1943." In *South Africa's Radical Tradition: A Documentary History – Volume Two 1943-1964*, edited by Allison Drew, 60–61. Cape Town: University of Cape Town Press.

Nyoka, Bongani. 2023. "Bernard Magubane on the Political Economy of Race and Class in South Africa." *Ethnic and Racial Studies*. Advance online publication. doi:10.1080/01419870.2023.2195051.

Phadi, Mosa M. 2023. "Merely Liberals? Du Bois and Plaatje as Radical Critics of Racial Capitalism." *Ethnic and Racial Studies*. Advance online publication. doi:10.1080/01419870.2023.2186796.

Robinson, Cedric J. 2021. *Black Marxism: The Making of the Black Radical Tradition*. 3rd ed. Chapel Hill, NC: University of North Carolina Press.

Saul, John S., and Stephen Gelb. 1986 [1981]. *The Crisis in South Africa*. New York: Monthly Review Press.

Simons, Jack, and Ray Simons. 1983 [1956]. *Class and Colour in South Africa 1850–1950*. Johannesburg: International Defence and Aid Fund for Southern Africa.

Singh, Nikhil Pal. 2022. "Black Marxism and the Antinomies of Racial Capitalism." In *After Marx: Literature, Theory, and Value in the Twenty-First Century*, edited by Colleen Lye, and Christopher Nealon, 23–39. Cambridge, UK: Cambridge University Press.

Slovo, Joe. 1988. *The South African Working Class and the National Democratic Revolution*. Cape Town: South African Communist Party.

South African Communist Party (SACP). 1963 [1962]. "The Road to South African Freedom: Programme of the South African Communist Party." *African Communist* 2 (2): 24–70.

South African Students' Organisation (SASO). 1970. *SASO Newsletter*, September. Digital Innovation South Africa. Available online: https://disa.ukzn.ac.za/sasep70.

Stalin, Joseph. 1913. *Marxism and the National Question*. Available online: https://www.marxists.org/reference/archive/stalin/works/1913/03.htm.

Tabata, I. B. 1974 [1950]. *The Awakening of a People*. Nottingham, UK: Spokesman. Available online: https://www.apdusa.org.za/wp-content/books/awakening_of_a_people.pdf.

Taylor, Keeanga-Yamahtta. 2022. "It's Called Capitalism: Naming the System Behind Systemic Racism." *Spectre* 5: 12–26.

Trapido, Stanley. 1971. "South Africa in a Comparative Study of Industrialization." *The Journal of Development Studies* 7 (3): 309–320. doi:10.1080/00220387108421372

Veriava, Ahmed, and Prishani Naidoo. 2023. "Articulating Difference: Reading Biko-with-Hall." *Ethnic and Racial Studies*. Advance online publication. doi:10.1080/01419870.2023.2173977.

Wolpe, Harold. 1972. "Capitalism and Cheap Labour-Power in South Africa: From Segregation to Apartheid." *Economy and Society* 1 (4): 425–456. doi:10.1080/03085147200000023

Wolpe, Harold. 1975. "The Theory of Internal Colonialism: The South African Case." In *Beyond the Sociology of Development: Economy and Society in Latin America and Africa*, edited by Ivar Oxaal, Tony Barnett, and David Booth, 229–252. London: Routledge and Kegan Paul.

Wolpe, Harold. 1988. *Race, Class, and the Apartheid State*. Trenton, NJ: Africa World Press.

Wolpe, Harold. 1995. "The Uneven Transition from Apartheid in South Africa." *Transformation* 27: 88–101.

Zumoff, Jacob A. 2014. *The Communist International and US Communism, 1919-1929*. Chicago, IL: Haymarket.

The context of struggle: racial capitalism and political praxis in South Africa

Andy Clarno and Salim Vally

ABSTRACT

The South African critique of racial capitalism was developed during the struggle against apartheid, as Black South Africans engaged in urgent debates about how to understand the system they were fighting and how to win liberation for all. Rather than arguing that capitalism has always been racial, South African radicals developed a *conjunctural* analysis of racial capitalism with attention to time and space. In this article, we focus on the work of Neville Alexander to develop two arguments about the conjunctural critique of racial capitalism. First, we argue that the conjunctural analysis was closely tied to political praxis. The critique emerged as a theoretical framework that could inform political strategy in a context of struggle. Second, we demonstrate that the conjunctural analysis was always global, situating South Africa within a world historical moment and engaged in dialogue with radical intellectuals and anti-colonial, anti-capitalist, and anti-racist movements around the world.

"Our struggle for national liberation is directed against the system of racial capitalism, which holds the people of Azania in bondage for the benefit of the small minority of white capitalists and their allies, the white workers and the reactionary sections of the black middle class. The struggle against apartheid is no more than the point of departure for our liberation efforts. Apartheid will be eradicated with the system of racial capitalism."

– The Azanian Manifesto, 1983[1]

"It is simply a fallacy to claim that black workers are faced with two autonomous but intersecting systems of domination, viz a system of 'racial domination' and a system of 'class domination.' However valid it might be for specific analytical

purposes to distinguish between the 'racial' and the 'class' elements that constitute the system of racial capitalism, it is impossible to transfer such a dichot-
omy on to the social reality in political and ideological practice, except in terms
of, or for the purposes of, ruling class mystification of that reality."

– Neville Alexander[2]

In June 1983, radical South African political movements gathered north of
Pretoria under the banner of the National Forum to build what the late
Neville Alexander called a "fighting front for liberation from racist oppression
and class exploitation" (2008, 164). It was a time of militant struggle and contestation, as Black South Africans engaged in urgent debates about how to
understand the apartheid system they were fighting and how to achieve a
post-apartheid future that would bring liberation for all.

Building connections between the Black Consciousness Movement, anti-
racist working-class organizations, and independent Marxists, the 1983
National Forum convergence drafted the historic Azanian Manifesto quoted
in the epigraph. The Manifesto dissected the apartheid regime's reform proposals[3] and boldly envisioned a united front led by the Black working class
that would "mobilize the urban and the rural poor together with the
radical sections of the middle classes" to topple not just the apartheid state
but the racial capitalist system as a whole (Alexander 2008, 168).

Hudson (2017) and Kelley (2017) have noted a key difference between the
critiques of racial capitalism developed by South African radicals and by
Cedric Robinson. Robinson's argument is universal: there is no such thing
as non-racial capitalism. The analysis developed by Alexander and the
National Forum is *context-specific*: focused on a particular social formation.
As Kelley explains, Robinson developed his concept of racial capitalism
during a sabbatical year in England, where he "encountered intellectuals
who used the phrase 'racial capitalism' to refer to South Africa's economy
under apartheid. He developed it from a description of a specific system to
a way of understanding the general history of modern capitalism" (2017, 7).

The context specific analysis developed by South African radicals focused
not just on a particular location, but also on a particular moment in time. Considering this fact, we argue that it is more accurate to describe the South
African framework as *conjunctural*. Indeed, the analysis highlighted the shifting balance of racialized class forces within a particular conjuncture and the
role of structural racism "in enabling key moments of capitalist development"
in South Africa (Bhattacharyya 2018: ix).

To be clear, Kelley and Hudson do not present the distinction as a critique
of the South African tradition. Kelley points to the many commonalities
between Robinson and Alexander. Both were inspired by the radical writings
of W.E.B. Du Bois, C.L.R. James, Frantz Fanon, Walter Rodney, Amilcar Cabral

and others. And both engaged in a lively correspondence with members of the "Race and Class" collective in London during the late 70s, while writing *Black Marxism* (Robinson 1982/2000) and *One Azania, One Nation* (No Sizwe 1979)[4] both of which were published by Zed Press. Moreover, as Kelley (2021) explained at the 2021 Neville Alexander Commemorative Conference:

> Robinson and Alexander actually have much more in common than we might think, especially in the way we think about National Liberation as a class question, as historical context, or framework for class struggle. They both recognize national identities not as chimera but historical and they both reveal in their work exactly how racial capitalism deploys what Neville Alexander calls "racial fundamentalism" - that is racism, ethnocentrism and tribalism - to exploit the working class to extract surplus and to arrest national development.

As the framework of racial capitalism is increasingly deployed beyond South Africa, we believe it is important to add nuance, clarity, and an explanation for the conjunctural analysis developed by South African radicals. This is not a universal theory but a flexible framework for analyzing, envisioning, and strategizing from within a revolutionary conjuncture.

In this essay, we develop two arguments that help clarify and explain the conjunctural analysis deployed by South African radicals – best exemplified by Alexander - during the struggle against apartheid. First, we argue that a conjunctural analysis was important because the critique emerged in a *context of struggle* as a theoretical framework that could inform political strategy. Second, we demonstrate that the conjunctural analyses deployed by South African radicals was always situated within a broader analysis of global, imperial dynamics.

We begin this article with a brief biographical note on Alexander before describing the core features of his conjunctural analysis of racial capitalism. We then describe the context of struggle within which the analysis was developed and deployed, both locally and globally. In doing so, we demonstrate the importance of attention to shifting articulations of racial capitalism, racialized class alliances, and imperial strategies for efforts to envision and build pathways to liberation. We end the article by discussing the implications of this framework for understanding and combatting racial capitalism today in South Africa and beyond.

The praxis of Neville Alexander

South Africans belonging to different left political organizations – such as Martin Legassick, Bernard Magubane, and David Hemson – developed political-economic analyses that led to an understanding of South African racial capitalism. In this article, we focus on the praxis of Neville Alexander, who did more than anyone to use the framework of racial capitalism for political struggle in South Africa. Elevating the profile of Alexander's praxis is also a challenge to the dominant history of South Africa, which has largely reduced the anti-apartheid struggle to the African National Congress (ANC) and its alliance partners in what is known as the Congress tradition. Alexander was a key figure in political formations to the left of the Congress tradition. Recognizing his work is a way of remembering the revolutionary possibilities that existed during the 1970s and 1980s. The outcome of the South African transition and its present predicaments were not predetermined.

Alexander was born in the province of the Eastern Cape in 1936 to David James Alexander, a carpenter, and Dimbiti Bisho Alexander, a schoolteacher.[5] Alexander's maternal grandmother was among a group of enslaved Ethiopians freed and placed in the care of missionaries in Cradock.[6] He moved to Cape Town in 1953 to attend the University of Cape Town (UCT), where he spent six years obtaining a Bachelor of Arts in History and German, a Bachelor of Arts Honours and a Master of Arts by the age of 21. Politically, Alexander came under the tutelage of people who were members of the Teachers' League of South Africa and the Non-European Unity Movement. He joined these organizations and the Society of Young Africa with Archie Mafeje and others.[7] Alexander was also key to the establishment of the Cape Peninsula Students' Union.

He received a scholarship to attend the University of Tübingen, Germany, where he successfully completed his doctoral studies at the age of 26. Alexander joined the Socialist Democratic Students' Union and was close to Algerian and Cuban students involved in their liberation struggles. Deeply affected by the Sharpeville Massacre in March 1960, he returned to South Africa four months later. Alexander clandestinely formed the Yu Chi Chan Club to explore the feasibility of guerrilla warfare and subsequently, with Namibian and South African activists, established the National Liberation Front (NLF). Arrested in 1963 with ten other NLF members, Alexander was given a ten year prison sentence which he served on Robben Island Prison. Alexander was kept in the isolation section of the prison, along with Mandela and other ANC and Pan-Africanist Congress leaders. Despite their political differences, Alexander formed close relationships with all prisoners and helped organize political education classes that turned the prison into the "University of Robben Island" (Alexander 1994a).

After his release from Robben Island, Alexander was subject to a five year "house arrest" restriction order. After the restriction order was lifted, he began teaching part-time at UCT and re-engaged with community, worker and education struggles. He helped establishe various civic organizations, including the Cape Action League, and played an important role in the transformation of the South African Council for Higher Education Trust into one of the most important and vibrant organizations in the country and a home for radical and alternative educational practices. With other members of the National Forum Committee[8], Alexander convened the National Forum in June 1983, which was attended by 600 delegates from 200 organizations. The Forum adopted the socialist guiding document called the Azanian Manifesto and drew up plans to oppose the apartheid regime's latest reform proposals and to boycott the "Tri-Cameral Parliament." In April 1990, Alexander was elected head of a new political formation, the Workers Organization for Socialist Action (WOSA), committed to promoting working-class interests. With activists from key centres in South Africa, Alexander formed the Truth Movement in 2010, to discuss the realities of post-apartheid South Africa. He remained politically engaged and active until shortly before his passing.

Alexander passed away a mere eleven days after the tragic events in the mining area of Marikana in August 2012, where armed police opened fire on striking miners employed by the Lonmin Mining Company, killing 34 workers and wounding at least 78 others. The strike started when 3000 workers walked off the job in protest against the Lonmin bosses' lack of response to their demands for better wages and working conditions. Although in a weakened state, Alexander was aware of the massacre. His words two years earlier criticizing those who viewed the state as neutral or "developmental" were instructive, "The final disillusionment will come, of course, when the repressive apparatuses of the state ... turn their weapons on the masses to protect the interests of the capitalist class" (2010, 46).

An uncanny ability to predict South Africa's political trajectory made Alexander unpopular with members of the post-apartheid ruling establishment who were often unsettled by his critique of the dominant, largely celebratory discourse of national liberation and his condemnation of crony capitalism and the looting of public resources. But he was deeply respected because of his modest and humble lifestyle and because of the dignified, humanistic and principled positions he took on all issues and practices.

Alexander's polemical and scholarly writings, speeches and organizational activities were wide ranging and provocative because they often represented an alternative to the politically and socially dominant ideas both in the liberation movement and in the general intellectual climate of his times. Alexander's major scholarly contributions centred on the national question and on language, education and culture as well as organizational questions about how struggles against undemocratic systems should be carried out. As early as 1985, in his collection of speeches *Sow the Wind*, this is how he expressed his worldview and convictions:

> The abiding focus of my own contribution is on subjects such as the link between racism and capitalism; the need for and the inevitability of socialist solutions to our problems hence the crucial need to ensure working-class leadership of our struggle; the importance of nation-building in order to eliminate ethnic and racial prejudice; the link between women's liberation, national liberation and class emancipation; the vital need to initiate and to sustain educational and cultural practices today that will systematically and inexorably

undermine and counter the divisive and exploitative practices that derive from the pursuit of the interests of the dominating classes in an apartheid society (1985: p x).

Racial capitalism: a conjunctural analysis

For Alexander and the radical wing of the South African liberation movement, racism and capitalism were so deeply and historically interconnected that they would be nearly impossible to separate. Rather than theoretically necessary, however, they insisted that the link between racism and capitalism in the South African social formation was historically contingent. Alexander referred approvingly to both Legassick's (1985) and Wolpe's (1990) writing on the subject as clarifying the "contingent" relationship between racism and capitalism:

> At certain times racial ideology was and is functional for the accumulation of capital, whereas at other times it could be dysfunctional. So there is no necessary connection, it is a contingent one ... This is of course a different thesis from the liberal thesis[9], which is that racism is allegedly dysfunctional in regard to capital accumulation. (Callinicos 1992, 115–116).

In that sense, the South African critique of racial capitalism differs from Cedric Robinson's global critique in *Black Marxism* (1982/2000). It is more in line with Stuart Hall's insistence that, "Racism is not present, in the same form or degree, in all capitalist formations: it is not necessary to the concrete functioning of all capitalisms. It needs to be shown how and why racism has been specifically overdetermined by and articulated with certain capitalisms at different stages of their development" (1980, 338–339).

Hall's approach to conjunctural analysis was deeply informed by Gramsci's (1971) distinction between the "organic" and "conjunctural" aspects of a crisis. As Gramsci explains, the organic aspects of a crisis are determined by deep, structural contradictions that sometimes last for decades, whereas the conjunctural aspects define the "immediate terrain of struggle" on which "the forces of opposition organize" (1971, 178). A conjunctural analysis, therefore, examines political, economic, and ideological aspects of a social formation at a particular moment in time and space, recognizing that the status quo is a product of long-standing structural dynamics and constantly evolving struggles between social forces seeking to transform or defend existing structures. We see a conjunctural analyses at work in Hall's argument that "law and order" politics in the UK emerged in response to a crisis of capitalism and the state (Hall et al. 1978/2013). As Gramsci and Hall demonstrate, conjunctural analysis is an essential tool of political strategy and practice.[10]

Although the social category "race"[11] on its own is inadequate to explain capital accumulation or the exploitation of labour, it has "explanatory value in relation to class and the process of exploitation" (Motala and Vally 2010, 96). Bannerji (2020) convincingly argues that social class cannot be considered outside gender and "race" that, in the words of Saul, "so often significantly characterizes it in the concrete" (Saul 2006, 64–5). Capitalists make use of whatever mechanisms seem appropriate in specific imperially defined historical and geographical circumstances. Motala and Vally (2010, 96) elaborate:

> ... it is precisely because racist policies and strategies have been used in societies, both for capitalist accumulation and for engendering social conflict, and by dominant forces in imperialist states like the US to advance their global exploitative interests, that ideas about "race" (and other such discursive categories such as "civilization" and "culture") have such powerful meanings in the public consciousness, in global politics, and ultimately in the control over resources.

Kundnani (2021, 51) compellingly argues that "A racial idea of culture is the means by which neoliberalism manages and works through its own limitations. Above all, 'race' provides a means of coding and managing the material boundaries between different forms of labour under neoliberalism: citizen and migrant, waged and 'unexploitable,' bearers of entitlements and bare life."

The issue is therefore to identify the specific historical conditions under which a regime of accumulation takes shape. In South Africa, the conditions were imposed by the nature of the early mining/agricultural economies which required, from the point of view of accumulation, the kinds of racist control which evolved through and after the dispossession of indigenous people and the coercive extraction of labour from people enslaved in Dutch colonies and from Chinese and Indian indentured workers.

The peculiarities of racial capitalism in South Africa

Although racism has characterized capital accumulation from its earliest development, South African radicals developed their analysis of racial capitalism by examining the specific form it took in South Africa beginning in the late nineteenth – early twentieth century.[12] The distinct link between the development of capitalism in South Africa and racism is explained by Alexander in the following way:

> The peculiarities of capitalism in South Africa are determined by the pre-capitalist social relations that arose out of slavery and colonial conquest and, more specifically, by the ways in which the capitalist mode of production, once it became dominant following the late nineteenth-century mineral revolution, transformed those pre-capitalist social relations to appropriate surplus labour in particular ways. Racial capitalism is the appropriation of surplus labour in particular ways based on and defined by the colour of people's skin (Drew and Binns 1992, 257).

Alexander's analysis of racial capitalism in South Africa focused on three inter-related dynamics (Drew and Binns 1992, 257–8). First, *racialized dispossession*, which refers to the conquest of land by white settlers, the forced displace-ment of "Africans," and ongoing state laws that prevented "Africans' from owning or buying land in 87% of South Africa. Alexander insisted that accumulation by racialized dispossession was not limited to the pre-capitalist era but was an ongoing, structural feature of racial capitalism in South Africa due to laws that "sanctified the original conquest" and facilitated further dis-placement and dispossession (Drew and Binns 1992, 257).

Second, *racialized exploitation* or the processes through which mining, agricultural, and industrial capitalists maintained access to cheap Black labour. In twentieth century South Africa, this was grounded in the migrant labour system that was enforced by concentrating the "African" population in a series of rural "homelands" and later Bantustans and issuing "pass" laws that required Africans to obtain work permits to reside in so-called "white" cities. Through the migrant labour system, South African capital developed a particularly exploitative form of accumulation and social repro-duction. Throughout the world, capital's ability to extract surplus value from a working class that is presumed to be male depends on the unpaid, feminized labour of social reproduction, which is concealed by the form of the nuclear family (Federici 2004; James 2012; Bhattacharya 2017). In South Africa, mining, industrial, and agricultural capital paid "African" male migrant workers *less-than-subsistence* wages based on the assumption that "African" women remained in the "homelands" where they produced enough food to help support the family. This form of social reproduction depended on a legal system that limited the right to property ownership and upward mobi-lity for racially defined categories of people. In doing so, the migrant labour system gave rise to a legal form which demystified the supposed "free con-tract" between capital and labour.

Third, *racialized job reservations* known in South Africa as the "color bar" enabled the white working class to protect their access to high wages by excluding Black workers from skilled trades. While the strategies were similar to those used by craft unions in the US or the UK, in South Africa, Alex-ander explains, the process of exclusion was determined by "race." "The state defined the normal trajectory of skilled labour in racial terms and white workers reinforced that, quite apart from their own racial prejudices, because it was in their own economic interests to do so" (Drew and Binns 1992, 257). Alexander described racialized exploitation and racialized job reservations as two sides of the same process, demonstrating that white working class security was intimately connected to Black working class insecurity.

In apartheid-era South Africa, therefore, racial capitalism referred to the combination of accumulation by racialized dispossession, forcible exploitation of racially devalued populations, and exclusionary strategies to protect jobs for dominant groups. South African capital set out to shape the legal and state regime in ways that would facilitate super-exploitation through unpaid reproduction, while restricting mobilization by dividing and controlling workers along colour lines. But the contradictions of racial capitalism generated an organic crisis that deepened over time. The implication, for Alexander, was that addressing the crisis required confronting the "capitalist underpinnings" of racism in South Africa.

The context of struggle against racial capitalism in South Africa

Building on his analysis of the organic crisis, Alexander examined the ever-changing terrain of struggle in South Africa during the 1980s. In doing so, he was attentive not just to the geographical context but to shifting alliances and hegemonic strategies within a particular space-time conjuncture. This is what makes Alexander's conjunctural critique of racial capitalism so distinctive and so important for political praxis.

The political-economic analysis that grounds Alexander's conjunctural critique builds on frameworks deployed by Lenin and Gramsci to analyze relations between classes and class fractions. For Lenin, hegemony refers to the contingent process through which a particular class is able to establish its leadership by building alliances with other class fractions. Gramsci builds on this framework to analyze both the political strategies that a ruling class uses to manufacture consent as well as the possibilities for the industrial working class to build a hegemonic alliance with rural peasants and radical intellectuals.

More specifically, the South African conjunctural critique involved an analysis of the shifting relations between *racialized class fractions,* namely white capitalists, white workers, Black workers, and the Black petty bourgeoise. In that sense, Alexander's framework is closely related to Du Bois's (1935/1998) analysis of the shifting relations between Black workers, white workers, planters, and northern industrialists during and after the U.S. Civil War as well as James's (1963/1989) analysis of the dynamic relationship between enslaved Africans, "free Blacks and Mulattos," "small whites," and "big whites" that shaped the Haitian revolution. Like Du Bois and James, the conjunctural analysis carried out by South African radicals emphasized the shifting relationship between racialized class fractions.

Because of the deep, historical interconnections between racism and capitalism in South Africa, Alexander argued that they would be nearly impossible to disconnect. Yet Alexander and other South African radicals understood that, in the early 1980s, the white ruling class was embarking on a reform strategy that would reinforce the racial capitalist system through minor reforms that would appear to "deracialize" capitalism by coopting the Bantustan leadership and some members of the Black middle class. Moreover, they anticipated that "reactionary" sections of the Black middle class would embrace these reforms and call them "liberation." As a result, the reforms proposed by the apartheid state were a primary target of their critique. To better understand this point, it is crucial to understand the context of struggle within which they developed and deployed this analysis.

The South African critique of racial capitalism was forged in the crucible of the struggle against apartheid. The 1970s and early 1980s were marked by the emergence of the Black Consciousness movement, a resurgence of militant labour action by the Black working class after the Durban strikes of 1973, and waves of township uprisings that began in Soweto in 1976. Oppositional political organizations were banned and most of the leaders of the liberation movements were either in prison or in exile. As mass struggle and the contradictions of apartheid capitalism led the apartheid state to initiate a series of reforms, South Africans engaged in urgent debates about how to respond to various reform proposals and how to ultimately defeat the apartheid system. In this context, analytical frameworks were intimately tied to political strategies. Alexander's analysis of racial capitalism was thus inseparable from political praxis.

As Alexander explained in the introduction to his book *One Azania, One Nation*: "I wish to state it as bluntly as possible that this work is intended to meet both theoretical and practical political needs; it is not intended to be a mere juggling of words in the greyness of 'theory.' Only insofar as it is itself the result of, and capable of being a guide to, the action of the oppressed people is the writing of it to be understood at all" (1979, 4).[13]

The dominant bloc within the general liberation movement – the ANC and its allies in the South African Communist Party (SACP) – defined apartheid as "colonialism of a special type" and argued that liberation would come in stages (South African Communist Party 1981). First, a "National Democratic Revolution" (NDR) against the racist/apartheid state; and then in the second stage a struggle against capitalism.

In discussing the "National Democratic Revolution," Burawoy (2004) criticized the SACP's Harold Wolpe – and by extension the entire ANC/SACP alliance – because Wolpe:

> could not imagine separating the socialist project from the national bourgeois project. At most he saw this as a clash of the short term and long term interests so that the National Democratic Revolution would be the first stage and the socialist revolution the second stage. He didn't see what Frantz Fanon saw: two very different, opposed projects that existed side by side, that vied with each other within the decolonization struggle. If the national bourgeois road were taken then, according to Fanon, hopes for a socialist road would be ground to zero (2004, 22).

The radical wing of the movement rejected this "stagist" approach and embraced the socialist road to liberation. Black Consciousness theorists and independent Marxists engaged in long debates about the primacy of "race" vs. class in the freedom struggle, but ultimately found common ground in the framework of "racial capitalism."[14] It was understood by some at the time that the analysis was not only important for theoretical clarity but also had "great relevance to the question of political practice, the orientation of political organizations of the left to issues of class formation, class alliances and compromises, and the very strategies and tactics formulated in struggles for revolutionary social change" (Motala and Vally 2010, 100).[15]

The National Forum's analysis of the revolutionary conjuncture focused on shifting alliances between racialized class fractions. As John S. Saul and Stephen Gelb explained, the white ruling class responded to the deepening organic crisis of the early 1980s by envisioning a transition to "a more color-blind capitalism" (1986, 59). Through this so-called "deracialization" strategy, the white ruling class set out to shift its primary alliance from the white working class to the Black petty bourgeoisie and aspirant bourgeoisie, preparing to discard the most overt forms of state racism to protect the underlying system of racial capitalism. The National Forum anticipated that these reforms might enable increased mobility for some Black people but would not eradicate racial capitalism. As Alexander explained, "Even if you took away the legal and customary discrimination based on colour, as they have begun to do, the capitalist mode of production would continue to reproduce racial inequalities because of the peculiar historical development of capitalism in South Africa" (Drew and Binns 1992, 271).

The National Forum argued for a united front led by the Black working class that would mobilize the urban and rural workers as well as the radical sections of the Black middle classes in a struggle for "liberation from apartheid and capitalism" (Alexander 2008, 165) to counter the reform strategy of the apartheid state. As Alexander argued at the first National Forum convening,

> The black working class is the driving force of the liberation struggle in South Africa. It has to ensure that the leadership of this struggle remains with it if our efforts are not to be deflected into channels of disaster. The black working class has to act as a magnet that draws all the other oppressed layers of our society, organizes them for the liberation struggle, and imbues them with consistent democratic socialist ideas which alone spell death to the system of racial capitalism as we know it today (Alexander 1985, 55–56).

The South African critique of racial capitalism, therefore, is best understood as a theoretical tool that was developed in a context of struggle to facilitate an analysis of shifting racialized class alliances and to inform political strategy within a revolutionary conjuncture. It thus offers much more than a context-specific analysis of racial capitalism in one country.

To begin with, the critique is attentive to not just space, but space-time. It was developed to analyze the specific conditions in South Africa *during the 1980s*, including ruling class strategies and the shifting balance of racialized class forces. A conjunctural analysis should disabuse us of the assumption that the same dynamics will characterize other racial capitalist regimes. Indeed, as we describe below, neoliberal restructuring and the end of formal apartheid have reconfigured – but not abolished – racial capitalism in South Africa.

In addition, it was developed with attention to praxis. For Alexander, the analysis of racial capitalism in South Africa was always attentive to political/ strategic implications. Indeed, the analysis was intended to help guide political movements as they fought for liberation.

Moreover, the framework enables critical attention to multiple temporalities. This includes the enduring (organic) and the transitory (conjunctural) aspects of a social formation in crisis as well as alternative futurities. In this sense, the framework of racial capitalism provides a powerful lens for identifying the pitfalls of the national bourgeois road to liberation and for building a socialist alternative.

Finally, as we explain in the next section, the critique of racial capitalism was never narrowly focused on the South African context. Instead, it situated the South African conjuncture in relation to a world-historical moment shaped by global dynamics of uneven development and imperialism. In this sense, it was also attentive to processes playing out at multiple geographical scales.

Situating South Africa within the global context

While the framework emerged from an analysis of racial capitalism in South Africa, it was never narrowly focused on South Africa as an exceptional case. Instead, the South African conjunctural critique of racial capitalism situated South Africa within a world-historical moment. As Hudson (2017, 63) points out, it also drew on the knowledge generated by radical intellectuals and anti-colonial, anti-capitalist, and anti-racist movements around the world.

To be sure, unlike Robinson (1982/2000), South African radicals did not use the phrase "racial capitalism" to describe the capitalist world system as a whole. But theorists of racial capitalism in South Africa were in conversation with world systems theorists, dependency theorists, Althusserian Marxists, and others. As Hall (1980) points out, Southern Africa was a centrepiece – along with Latin America and the Caribbean – in global debates about the relationship between racism and capitalism during the 1970s. For instance, Wolpe's (1972) thesis that the migrant labour system in South Africa involved an "articulation of different modes of production" drew on the work of Althusser and Balibar (1970) to challenge explanations by dependency theorists and world systems analysts. Hall's own theory of articulation drew on Wolpe's work but departed from Althusserian structuralism by incorporating Gramsci's conjunctural analysis of struggles for hegemony. The radical intellectuals that developed the framework of racial capitalism were fully immersed in these debates and in the broader milieux.

Moreover, the analysis of racial capitalism built on knowledge generated through anti-colonial, anti-capitalist, and anti-racist movements throughout the world. Alexander and others learned from internationalist-oriented scholar-activists who came before them (Soudien 2019) and were in dialogue with radical movements and intellectuals throughout Africa, Latin America, Asia, and the Middle East as well those located in the heart of imperialist powers like the US and the UK.

In the National Forum meetings that generated the Azanian Manifesto, for instance, participants invoked the work of earlier theorists who analyzed the relationship between racism and capitalism. During debates about the formulation of "racial capitalism" in the Azanian Manifesto, many found inspiration in the words of C.L.R. James:[16]

> The race question is subsidiary to the class question in politics, and to think of imperialism in terms of race is disastrous. But to neglect the racial factor as merely incidental is an error only less grave than to make it fundamental (1963/1989: 283).

Perhaps the most important influences came from anti-colonial critiques developed by Fanon (1961), Cabral (1974), and Machel (1975), along with Brazilian educator Friere (1968/2018), members of the Black Panther Party in the US, and struggles against U.S. imperialism in Asia and Latin America.

Most immediately, Alexander's critique of the apartheid regime's reform strategy – and the bourgeois path to liberation more generally – was informed by radical critiques of national bourgeoisies across the African continent. Fanon (1961) famously warned that nationalist bourgeoisies would stifle anti-colonial revolutions and negotiate settlement with colonial regimes that created opportunities for Black elites without fundamentally transforming the capitalist/imperialist system. Building on that argument, and anticipating the negotiated settlement between the apartheid regime and the ANC, Alexander later argued that a struggle led by the Black working class "cannot be halted at the mere integration of the black people into the existing economic relationship on a basis of 'equality'" (1979, 178).

> A non-racial capitalism is impossible in South Africa. The class struggle against capitalist exploitation and the national struggle against racial oppression become one struggle under the general command of the black working class and its organizations (Alexander 1985, 53).

Alexander insisted that liberation in South Africa "means nothing else than the abolition of capitalism itself" (1979, 178). Similarly, Alexander's work on the "national question" was shaped by anti-colonial revolutions in Mozambique and Guinea Bissau. He often quoted Machel and Cabral, who argued that a "new nation" would emerge through a liberation struggle led by the working class. For instance, Machel insisted that the Mozambiquan nation was "historically new" because the struggle against colonialism "turned us progressively into Mozambicans, no longer Makonde and Shangane, Nyanja and Ronga ... " (Quoted in Alexander 1985, 51).

Alexander offered similar thoughts in his writings on the "national question." In *One Azania, One Nation,* he argued that the "The nation of South Africa is struggling to be born" (1979, 180) and that its birth would require "a determined and uncompromising struggle against all attempts to divide the population on the basis of language, religion, tribe, or caste" (1979, 178).

In addition to drawing lessons from radical intellectuals and revolutionary movements, Alexander's analysis of racial capitalism consistently situated South Africa in relation to historical processes of uneven development as well as shifting imperialist strategies, the reorganization of capital, and the changing balance of forces on the global scale during the late Cold War period. As Alexander explained, "Both the immediate and the ultimate enemy in South Africa is the capitalist class and its imperialist backers" (Drew and Binns 1992, 259). His analyses of racial capitalism in South Africa were ever attentive to shifting global dynamics, including competition between the United States and the Soviet Union, South African military and diplomatic relations in the southern African region, and the role of South African capital across the African continent.

In short, the South African critique of racial capitalism was built on a foundation of global anti-imperialist, anti-racist, anti-capitalist, and anti-colonial struggle. It provided tools for analyzing racialized class dynamics within a social formation while also situating that social formation within global patterns of capitalism and empire.

Racial capitalism in South Africa after apartheid

The last three decades have validated the Black radical tradition in South Africa. In 1994, legal apartheid was abolished and Black South Africans gained formal legal equality. This was a remarkable achievement, but it was not sufficient for liberation.

In 1992, Alexander (1994b, 88) argued that, "the present strategy of the ANC never was and does not have the potential to become the continuation of a revolutionary strategy for the seizure of power." Holding the ANC leadership accountable, he insisted that, "if the purpose is to place oneself in control of the levers of the state power within a capitalist framework, one has to realize and accept that the end effect will be to strengthen, not to weaken and much less destroy, that system" (Alexander 1994b, 87). Alexander foresaw a negotiated settlement between the apartheid regime and the ANC that would largely benefit the nationalist elites and not the Black working class and poor. The negotiated settlement was hastened by the collapse of the Soviet Union which provided significant support to the ANC/ SACP on the one hand and the pressure on the apartheid regime through the global sanctions campaign on the other.

Despite the democratization of the state, the South African transition did not address the structures of racial capitalism. During negotiations, the ANC made major concessions to win the support of white South Africans and global capitalist elites.

The post-apartheid government led by the ANC adopted neoliberal economic strategies from 1996. Neoliberal restructuring has reproduced racial capitalism while leading to important shifts in the racial composition of the elite, the dynamics of exploitation, and the constitution of a racialized surplus population. As Alexander predicted, South Africa has witnessed a partial "deracialization" of the capitalist class while the working class remains deeply racialized. Inequality is one of the most salient features of South Africa today and the country consistently ranks as the most unequal country in the world.

Formal legal equality coupled with neoliberal restructuring and affirmative action programmes has facilitated the emergence of a Black capitalist class and an expanding Black middle class (Van der Walt 2015; Southall 2016). Black elites now exercise control of 39% of companies listed on the Johannesburg Stock Exchange, although Black people comprise over 90% of the population (Department of Trade Industry and Competition, 2021). In 2021 the average income of the top 1% increased by 50% while that of the poorest half fell by more than 30% (The Economist 2021).

The lives of South Africa's Black working class are as precarious as ever. Deindustrialization, privatization and casualization have weakened the labour movement and intensified the racialized exploitation of the Black working class. Meanwhile, a growing racialized surplus population confronts permanent structural unemployment, landlessness, segregation, and repression. And the post-apartheid state's failed land redistribution policies have reinforced racialized dispossession by continuing to sanctify the original conquest.

For the first quarter of 2022, the unemployment rate was 63.9% for those aged 15–24. And while the official national rate stands at 34.5% (Stats SA 2022), the more accurate expanded definition of unemployment, including people who have stopped looking for work, stands at 44.1% (Ibid). Approximately 55% of South Africans live in poverty, with 25% of the population facing food poverty (World Bank 2020). And nearly half of all South Africans rely on meagre social grants to survive (SASSA 2021).

Poverty, inequality and unemployment correlates along colour, gender and spatial lines, with black women being the poorest. Importantly the most rapidly growing inequality over the past two decades has been within the "African" group rather than between groups (Statistics South Africa 2019).

Even while justifying the two-stage approach to liberation, the SACP's programmatic document, *The Road to Freedom* (1981), recognized the need for "profound economic changes" as part of the "National Democratic Revolution (NDR)," including:

> drastic agrarian reform to restore the land to the people; widespread nationalisation of key industries to break the grip of White monopoly capital on the main centres of the country's economy; radical improvements in the conditions and standards of living for the working people.

None of these benchmarks for the NDR has been achieved, despite nearly 30 years with the ANC as the ruling party and SACP leaders in key ministerial posts. Contrary to the *Road to Freedom*, there has been no "drastic agrarian reform" or "widespread nationalisation of key industries." In fact, key parastatals formed during the apartheid era have been hollowed out through corruption scandals and are well on their way to further neoliberal privatization.

The inevitable trajectory of the political compromise was precisely what Alexander foresaw (2002). Racial capitalism remains the foundation for social relations in South Africa today.

Using the sectors of housing and transport as examples, Ashman writes that the spatial geographies of apartheid-era racial capitalism remain despite the removal of apartheid laws.

> Housing and transport systems, combined with patterns of work (and the lack of work), have left these dynamics largely untransformed since 1994, with weak infrastructure provision in black areas, poor housing often long distances from centres of employment, an inefficient and expensive transport network, and a general weakness in the social wage. Racial spatial segregation remains except for the minority which has "escaped" to the suburbs (Ashman 2022, 35).

In a 2006 lecture in Pretoria, Alexander discussed the moral responsibility of intellectuals to combat the entrenchment of racial capitalism in South Africa after apartheid.

> Ardent as well as "reluctant" racists of yesteryear have all become convinced "non-racialists" bound to all South Africans under the "united colours of capitalism" in an egregious atmosphere of Rainbow nationalism. The same class of people, often the very same individuals, who funded Verwoerd, Vorster and Botha are funding the present regime. The latter has facilitated the expansion of South African capital into the African hinterland in ways the likes of Cecil John Rhodes or Ernest Oppenheimer could only dream ... In this connection, it is pertinent to point out that the strategy of Black Economic Empowerment

– broad-based or narrow is immaterial – is no more than smoke and mirrors, political theatre on the stage of the national economy. The only way that erstwhile Marxist revolutionaries in the liberation movement can justify their support and even enthusiastic promotion of these developments is by chanting the no longer convincing mantra: There is no alternative! (Alexander 2012, 34).

In a revealing interview in 2019, Gwede Mantashe – Minister of Mineral Resources and Energy, the national chairperson of the ANC and a South African Communist Party Politburo member – unwittingly confirmed Alexander's prescience:

One of the mistakes we make in talking about broad based black economic empowerment is making as if it is a social programme that will benefit everyone. Until we are categorical that [the] programme is about creating black capitalists, once we understand that, then we'll assess its success and failure on the correct basis (Seccombe 2019, 2).

Significance for today

This article sets out the importance of conjunctural analysis by situating the critique of racial capitalism by South African radicals in its historical and contextual milieu. In particular, it references the evolution of socio-political, economic, legal and other institutions which constituted the foundations on which the process of capitalist exploitation arose.

Such an analytical framework is critically important for several reasons. First, it informs our understanding of racial capitalist development in particular times/spaces and our analyses of the durability or otherwise of such systems. Second, it opens the possibility for examining the contradictions that racial capitalist systems produce and are likely to face. Third, such an analysis provides a firmer ground for understanding the globally interconnected nature of capitalist formation, with attention to the position of countries in the "periphery" relative to more powerful global imperial and corporate interests.

From the perspective of the radical wing of the liberation movement in South Africa, and explicitly for Alexander, the analysis of racial capitalism was also about political strategy and praxis. This directed their attention to the shifting relationships between racialized class fractions. Alexander developed his analysis while resisting petty-bourgeois nationalism and its capitulation to the interests of capital, fatally premised on the "stages" approach to revolution. For Alexander and his comrades, it was only through a generalized struggle against racial capitalism that the entrenched institutions of apartheid could be overcome.

The suggestion that the struggle for liberation in Southern Africa was best prosecuted through two stages – first against racism and thereafter against exploitative regimes – was at best capricious but, even more disconcertingly, shaped by the objective of solidifying the class interests of an emerging Black elite and an aspirant Black bourgeoisie with strong political ambitions. Alexander and others – especially in the worker's movement – warned against this real possibility, which is why he was so deeply committed to a struggle led by conscious elements of the Black working class and its political allies.

Given how events have unfolded in South Africa, it is easy to say that the approach to racial capitalism adopted by radicals in South Africa has been vindicated. Regrettably, this is not due to the realization of their strategic political approach. The struggle to overcome racial capitalism in South Africa has not succeeded, due in large part to commitments by the present ruling elite and the classes whose interests it represents to develop a "deracialised" social system. Wracked by irresolvable contradictions, as even a cursory examination of the present social system will evince, racial capitalism continues to fail, even while accumulation continues apace, resulting in some of the most egregious inequality imaginable. For us, the failure is deeply systemic, rooted in the marriage between racial domination and capital accumulation in South Africa.

The sociologically grounded framework developed by Alexander and other South African radicals provides a powerful tool for contemporary analyses of and struggles against racial capitalism. Attention to historical structures, hegemonic projects, and racialized class alliances can help identify the organic contradictions, conjunctural dynamics, and possibilities for liberation in a particular time and space.

An important direction for future work is to improve our conceptual frameworks for analyzing the multi-scalar dimensions of racial capitalism. At the global scale, Robinson is correct that capitalism has always been racial. But this does not invalidate Hall's insistence on a conjunctural analysis of the historically grounded relationship between racism and capital accumulation in particular contexts. How do we situate our analysis of racial capitalism in a particular social context in relation to these broader, global dynamics? For this, the work of Du Bois (1935/1998) and James (1963/1989) will be most instructive.

Another important direction for future work is to complicate the analysis of racialized class fractions. Alexander and other South African radicals recognized that subject position does not translate directly into political ideology. Indeed, their political vision distinguished between the reactionary segments of the Black middle class and those that allied with the working class struggle for socialism. Yet the most prominent radical intellectuals in these debates were men, and they did not centre gender and sexuality as axes of power and difference. There is a growing body of literatures analyzing the gendered dynamics of racial capitalism.[17] Moving forward, queer of colour critiques by scholar-activists such as Cohen (1997) and Ferguson (2004) can help guide our praxis by complicating assumptions about the stability of racialized class categories. As Cohen argues, "Only through recognizing the many manifestations of power, across and within categories, can we truly begin to build a movement based on one's politics and not exclusively on one's identity" (1997, 459).

Notes

1. Reprinted in Alexander 2008, 168–169.
2. Alexander 1986, 71.
3. The reforms centred around the "Koornhof Bills" and the "Tricameral Parliament" which promulgated new influx control laws and local government structures for what the regime called "urban Africans" and a limited franchise and separate "chambers" in parliament for those classified "coloured" and "Indian."
4. No Sizwe was the pseudonym used by Alexander.
5. For a more detailed biographical outline, see Vally (2014), from which this profile is partly derived.
6. www.sahistory.org.za/people/bisho-jarsa
7. Nyoka (2017) https://uir.unisa.ac.za/bitstream/handle/10500/23899/thesis_nyoka_b.pdf;sequence=1 see also Alexander (2013).
8. The National Forum Committee included then Bishop Desmond Tutu, General Secretary of the South African Council of Churches; Lybon Mabasa, then President of the Azanian People's Organization (AZAPO) and Saths Cooper, a close comrade of Steve Biko and former prominent member of the South African Students Organization (SASO) and the Black People's Convention (BPC).
9. Alexander was referring to the liberal view that racism was an aberration from capitalist accumulation and that free-market capitalism would eventually render racism obsolete. From the 1970s through the early 1990s, debates between liberals and radicals concerning the link between racism and capitalism characterized a vast array of South African writings in history, sociology, political science, education, economics, and other disciplines.
10. A growing number of radical scholar-activists have taken direction from Gramsci and Hall to develop conjunctural analyses of racial capitalism. Indeed, Robinson (2007) developed the concept of "racial regimes" to analyze the dynamics of racism within a particular conjuncture. See Al-Bulushi 2022; Camp 2016; Camp 2022; Hart 2002; Hart 2014; Heatherton 2022; Kundnani 2020.
11. An explanatory note on the terminology used in this article is important. The apartheid state marshalled a taxonomy of racial classifications to aid in the pursuit of its segregationist policies: "African", "white", "coloured" and "Indian." The Black Consciousness Movement in the 1970s rejected and actively opposed these classifications as well as the collective phrase "non-white" preferring instead the term "Black" as a political term for all who were oppressed. Despite these efforts, the apartheid terms took on a salience and an acceptance, both under apartheid and after, amongst many people classified in this way by the apartheid regime. While we reject the discredited and debunked notion of "race" as a biological entity (see Fields and Fields 2014), we use the apartheid categories for pragmatic explanatory purposes and use "race" as a social construct. We signal our discomfort with the apartheid categories through the use of quotes and embrace the term "Black" when referring to all oppressed groups.

12. Wolpe 1972; Legassick 1974; Magubane 1979.
13. Alexander also explains that the book was motivated "by the desire to facilitate the unification of the national liberation movement" (Alexander 1979, 1). In fact, Steve Biko's final tragic journey in 1977 was a failed attempt to meet clandestinely with Alexander to discuss arrangements for bringing together all liberation movements, including their armed formations. Both Alexander and Biko were under restrictive banning orders and, although in disguise, Biko was recognized by the security police at a roadblock on his way back from Alexander's house in Cape Town on August 18, 1977. He was jailed in Port Elizabeth (now Gqeberha), severely assaulted by the security police, then driven naked and shackled in a police van to Pretoria (a distance of 740 miles), where he died of a massive brain hemorrhage on September 12, 1977 (Villa-Vicencio 1996; Alexander 2008).
14. For more on this history, see Alexander 2008.
15. Marx (1992) speaks in detail to these debates in the National Forum and those who left the National Forum to form the United Democratic Front. See also Murray 1987 and Lodge and Bill 1991.
16. One of the co-authors of this article (Vally) was present at all National Forum conferences and was appointed by the National Forum Committee to assist the national coordinator Lusiba Ntloko. He observed that Walter Rodney's seminal work, *How Europe Underdeveloped Africa* was where James's analysis was first seen (1982, 89).
17. Ashman 2022; Bannerji 2020; Bhattacharya 2017; Davis et al. 2022; Magubane 2004; Gilmore 2022.

Acknowledgements

Thanks to Enver Motala for comments on our draft, Lybon Mabasa for discussions on the National Forum, and Rowayda Halim for literature on the National Forum. And thanks to everyone who provided feedback during the November 2021 workshop on "The South African Tradition of Racial Capitalism" organized by Marcel Paret and Zachary Levenson and the February 2022 "Portal Project" workshop organized by the Social Justice Initiative at the University of Illinois at Chicago.

Disclosure statement

No potential conflict of interest was reported by the author(s).

References

Al-Bulushi, Yousuf. 2022. "Thinking Racial Capitalism and Black Radicalism from Africa: An Intellectual Geography of Cedric Robinson's World-System." *Geoforum; Journal of Physical, Human, and Regional Geosciences* 132: 252–262.

Alexander, Neville (as No Sizwe). 1979. *One Azania, One Nation: The National Question in South Africa*. London: Zed Press.

Alexander, Neville. 1985. *Sow the Wind: Contemporary Speeches*. Johannesburg: Skotaville Publishers.

Alexander, Neville. 1986. "Approaches to the National Question in South Africa." *Transformations* 1: 63–95.

Alexander, Neville. 1994a. *Robben Island Dossier: 1964–1974.*

Alexander, Neville. 1994b. *South Africa: Which Road to Freedom?* San Francisco: Walnut Publishing Company.

Alexander, Neville. 2002. *An Ordinary Country: Issues in the Transition from Apartheid to Democracy in South Africa.* Scottsville: University of Natal Press.

Alexander, Neville. 2008. "An Illuminating Moment: Background to the Azanian Manifesto." In *Biko Lives! Contesting the Legacies of Steve Biko*, edited by A. Mngxitama, A. Alexander, and N. Gibson, 157–170. New York: Palgrave MacMilllan.

Alexander, Neville. 2010. "South Africa: An Unfinished Revolution?" The 4th Strini Moodley Annual Lecture, University of KwaZulu-Natal, 13 May 2010 In Enough is as Good as a Feast – A Tribute to Neville Alexander. Braamfontein: Foundation for Human Rights.

Alexander, Neville. 2012. "South Africa Today." In *Enough is as Good as a Feast – A Tribute to Neville Alexander*, edited by Hanif Vally and Maureen Isaacson. Braamfontein: Foundation for Human Rights.

Alexander, Neville. 2013. *Thoughts on the New South Africa.* Auckland Park: Jacana Media.

Althusser, Louis, and Etienne Balibar. 1970. *Reading Capital.* London: New Left Books.

Ashman, Samantha. 2022. "Racial Capitalism and SA's Changing Race-Class Articulations." *New Agenda: South African Journal of Social and Economic Policy* 2022 (84): 29–35.

Bannerji, Himani. 2020. *The Ideological Condition: Selected Essays on History, Race and Gender.* Leiden: Brill.

Bhattacharya, Tithi. ed. 2017. *Social Reproduction Theory: Remapping Class, Recentering Oppression.* London: Pluto Press.

Bhattacharyya, Gargi. 2018. *Rethinking Racial Capitalism: Questions of Reproduction and Survival.* London: Rowman & Littlefield.

Burawoy, Michael. 2004. "From Liberation to Reconstruction: Theory and Practice in the Life of Harold Wolpe." Paper presented at the harold wolpe memorial lecture, harold wolpe trust, Cape Town.

Cabral, Amilcar. 1974. *Return to the Source: Selected Speeches.* New York: Monthly Review Press.

Callinicos, Alex. 1992. *Between Apartheid and Capitalism: Conversations with South African Socialists.* London: Bookmarks.

Camp, Jordan. 2016. *Incarcerating the Crisis: Freedom Struggles and the Rise of the Neoliberal State.* Oakland: University of California Press.

Camp, Jordan. 2022. "Gramsci and Geography." *Oxford Bibliographies.*

Cohen, Cathy. 1997. "Punks, Bulldaggers, and Welfare Queens: The Radical Potential of Queer Politics?" *GLQ: A Journal of Lesbian and Gay Studies* 3 (4): 437–465.

Davis, Angela Y, Gina Dent, Erica R Meiners, and Beth E Richie. 2022. *Abolition. Feminism. Now.* Chicago: Haymarket Books.

Drew, Allison, and David Binns. 1992. "Prospects for Socialism in South Africa: An Interview with Neville Alexander." *The Journal of Communist Studies and Transitional Politics* 8 (4): 251–274.

Du Bois, W. E. B. 1935/1998. *Black Reconstruction in America, 1860-1880.* New York: Free Press.

The Economist. 2021. "Unpicking Inequality in South Africa." 23rd September. https://www.economist.com/middle-east-and-africa/2021/09/23/unpicking-inequality-in-south-africa.

Fanon, Frantz. 1961. *The Wretched of the Earth.* New York: Grove Press.

Federici, Silvia. 2004. *Caliban and the Witch: Women, the Body, and Primitive Accumulation*. Brooklyn, NY: Autonomedia.

Ferguson, Roderick A. 2004. *Aberrations in Black: Toward a Queer of Color Critique*. Minneapolis: University of Minnesota Press. Introduction.

Fields, Karen E., and Barbara J. Fields. 2014. *Racecraft: The Soul of Inequality in American Life*. London: Verso Press.

Friere, Paolo. 1968/2018. *Pedagogy of the Oppressed*. New York: Bloomsbury.

Gilmore, Ruth Wilson. 2022. *Abolition Geography: Essays Toward Liberation*. London: Verso.

Gramsci, Antonio. 1971. *Selections from the Prison Notebooks*. New York: International Publishers.

Hall, Stuart. 1980. "Race, Articulation, and Societies Structured in Dominance." In *Sociological Theories: Race and Colonialism*, edited by UNESCO, 305–345. Paris: UNESCO.

Hall, Stuart, Chas Critcher, Tony Jefferson, John Clarke, and Brian Roberts. 1978/2013. *Policing the Crisis: Mugging, the State, and Law and Order*. New York: Palgrave MacMillan.

Hart, Gillian. 2002. *Disabling Globalization: Places of Power in Post-Apartheid South Africa*. Berkeley: University of California Press.

Hart, Gillian. 2014. *Rethinking the South African Crisis: Nationalism, Populism, Hegemony*. Athens, GA: University of Georgia Press.

Heatherton, Christina. 2022. *Arise! Global Radicalism in the Age of the Mexican Revolution*. Berkeley: University of California Press.

Hudson, Peter James. 2017. "Racial Capitalism and the Dark Proletariat." *Boston Review: Forum 1 – Race, Capitalism, Justice*: 59–65.

James, C. L. R. 1963/1989. *The Black Jacobins: Toussaint L'Ouverture and the San Domingo Revolution*. New York: Vintage Books.

James, Selma. 2012. *Sex, Race, and Class: The Perspective of Winning – A Selection of Writings 1952-2011*. Oakland: PM Press.

Kelley, Robin D.G. 2017. "Introduction." Boston Review: Forum 1 – Race, Capitalism, Justice, pp. 5-8.

Kelley, Robin D.G. 2021. "Presentation at the Neville Alexander Commemorative Conference (online) 'The Struggle Against Racial Capitalism in the USA, SA and Palestine,'" hosted jointly by the Centre for Education Rights and Transformation and the Centre for Sociological Research and Practice at the University of Johannesburg, 30 March 2021.

Kundnani, Arun. 2020. "What is Racial Capitalism?" Unpublished lecture at the Havens Wright Center for Social Justice, University of Madison-Wisconsin. https://www.kundnani.org/what-is-racial-capitalism/ (accessed September 9, 2022).

Kundnani, Arun. 2021. "The Racial Constitution of Neoliberalism." *Race & Class* 63 (1): 51–69.

Legassick, Martin. 1974. "South Africa: Capital Accumulation and Violence." *Economy and Society* 3 (3): 253–91.

Legassick, Martin. 1985. "South Africa in Crisis: What Route to Democracy?" *African Affairs* 84 (337): 587–603.

Lodge, Tom, and Nasson Bill. 1991. *All Here and Now: Black Politics in South Africa in the 1980s*. New York: Ford Foundation.

Machel, Samora. 1975. *Mozambique: Revolution or Reaction?* Richmond, BC: LSM Press.

Magubane, Bernard. 1979. *The Political Economy of Race and Class in South Africa*. New York: Monthly Review.

Magubane, Zine. 2004. *Bringing the Empire Home: Race, Class, and Gender in Britain and Colonial South Africa*. Chicago: University of Chicago Press.

Marx, Anthony W. 1992. *Lessons of Struggle: South African Internal Opposition, 1960-1990*. Oxford: Oxford University Press.

Motala, Enver, and Salim Vally. 2010. "Class, 'Race' and State in Post-Apartheid Education." In *Class in Education: Knowledge, Pedagogy, Subjectivity*, edited by Deborah Kelsh, Dave Hill, and Sheila Macrine, 87–107. New York: Routledge.

Murray, Martin. 1987. *South Africa: Time of Agony, Time of Destiny*. London: Verso.

Nyoka, Bongani. 2017. *Archie Mafeje: An Intellectual Biography*. Doctoral thesis. University of South Africa.

Robinson, Cedric. 1982/2000. *Black Marxism: The Making of the Black Radical Tradition*. Chapel Hill: University of North Carolina Press.

Robinson, Cedric. 2007. *Forgeries of Memory and Meaning: Blacks and the Regimes of Race in American Theater and Film Before World War II*. Chapel Hill: University of North Carolina Press.

Rodney, Walter. 1982. *How Europe Underdeveloped Africa*. Washington, DC: Howard University Press.

Saul, John S. 2006. *Development After Globalization*. Scottsville: UKZN Press.

Saul, John S., and Stephen Gelb. 1986. *The Crisis in South Africa*. New York: Monthly Review Press.

Seccombe, Allan. 2019. "Ready to do Battle." *Business Day*, 4 Oct 2019.

Soudien, Crain. 2019. *Cape Radicals: Intellectual and Political Thought of the New Era Fellowship, 1930s-1960s*. Braamfontein: Wits University Press.

South African Communist Party. 1981. "The Road to South African Freedom." In *South African Communists Speak: Documents from the History of the South African Communist Party, 1915-1980*, edited by Brian Bunting. London: Inkululeko Publications.

South African Social Security Agency (SASSA). 2021. *Report on Social*. Grants: Fifth Statistical Report.

Southall, Roger. 2016. *The New Black Middle Class in South Africa*. Sunnyside: Jacana Media.

Statistics South Africa. 2019. *Inequality Trends in South Africa: A Multidimensional Diagnostic of Inequality*. Pretoria: Statistics South Africa. https://www.statssa.gov.za/publications/Report-03-10-19/Report-03-10-192017.pdf.

Vally, Salim. 2014. "The Battle for the Truth–youth Resistance, Neoliberalism and an Appreciation of Neville Alexander." *Critical Arts* 28 (1): 69–75.

Van der Walt, Lucien. 2015. "Beyond 'White Monopoly Capital': Who Owns South Africa?" *South African Labour Bulletin* 39 (3): 39–42.

Villa-Vicencio, Charles. 1996. "Neville Alexander: No Need for a God Hypothesis." In *The Spirit of Freedom: South African Leaders on Religion and Politics*. Berkeley: University of California Press.

Wolpe, Harold. 1972. "Capitalism and Cheap Labor Power in South Africa: From Segregation to Apartheid." *Economy and Society* 1 (4): 425–456.

Wolpe, Harold. 1990. *Race, Class, and the Apartheid State*. Trenton, NJ: Africa World Press. Inc.

World Bank. 2020. "Poverty and Equity Brief – South Africa." https://povertydata.worldbank.org.

Merely liberals? Du Bois and Plaatje as radical critics of racial capitalism

Mosa M. Phadi

ABSTRACT
A wide range of scholars ratified Du Bois' *Black Reconstruction* as his radical turn. Prior to its publication, "liberal" was an epithet used in reference to his work. Across the Atlantic, Plaatje's *Native Life* invoked his appellation as a "Black Victorian". As a counter, this article argues that both intellectuals, who were in communication and whose work resonated with each other, understood the historical development of modern capitalism as an "extension" of an old racialised system. Common threads are found through their analysis; firstly, capitalism required and depended on the exploitation of Black labour. Secondly, the Land dispossession of Black people was a congruent rationale for the accumulation and expansion of capitalism. Lastly, the making of Black people as inferior is entangled with salvaging the white working class. Thus, Plaatje and Du Bois articulated this historical development within the problematic *of racial capitalism.*

In the now massive and growing literature on W.E.B. Du Bois, there appears to be a consensus that it was only with the publication of his 1935 book *Black Reconstruction* that he turned into a proper radical. Jeff Goodwin, for example, notes that "Du Bois argues in *Black Reconstruction* that two characteristic features of capitalism— capitalists' competition for labour and workers' competition for jobs— are the root cause of conflicts that seem to be driven by racism" (Goodwin 2022, 55). In contrast to earlier work, he further asserts that in *Black Reconstruction* "not only is Du Bois not a Marxist but his ideas clearly transcend Marx's. Marx gave theoretical primacy to class, they say, whereas Du Bois grasped the "intersectionality" of class and race … " (Goodwin 2022, 56). Likewise, Adolph Reed (1997) insists that Du Bois' early work was reformist and concerned with "moral laxity" within the Black community. Moreover, he promoted the "social agenda" of the Black elite (Reed 1997, 36). Other scholars (Allen 2002; Mullen 2016) argue likewise, as does Cedric Robinson, who maintains that the *Black Reconstruction* was a moment in which Du Bois assertively argued that "beneath its appearance as a "feudal agrarianism" lay the real relation of slavery to the emergence of modern capitalism". Before 1935, however, Du Bois tends to be characterized as a liberal, reduced to the elitist politics of his concept of the "Talented Tenth", which "occupied a more significant place in his early work"(Reed 1997, 35–6).

A similar phenomenon is observable in treatments of Sol Plaatje (see Limb 2003; Odendaal 2016; Saunders 2016), the first General Secretary of the South African Native National Congress, which later became the African National Congress. His classic 1916 book *Native Life in South Africa*, for example, has been dismissed as an appeal to the British empire (Mkhize 2016), with Plaatje himself labelled a "Black Victorian" (Mkhize 2016). Likewise, Limb notes (2003, 33) claims that Plaatje was a "British Empire enthusiast". Indeed, a growing chorus of critics has dismissed this key South African intellectual as merely an appellant to the "moral conscious'.

The present article seeks to challenge these twin charges. It is useful to show that scholars in both South Africa and the United States were developing roughly parallel analytic frameworks, suggesting that their critiques of racial capitalism were part of a broader set of global political debates. Both Du Bois' early work and Plaatje's *Native Life*, roughly contemporaneous, were grounded in a *radical* analysis of racial capitalism. While neither writer used that term, both developed sophisticated theoretical understandings of race and class as integral to the expansion of capitalism. Despite the absence of the word *capitalism* in their writings from this period, concepts such as "world market", "economic revolution", "economic foundation" and "superstructure" were a crucial part of their lexicon. Their work highlights the importance of economic relations, which have indelibly shaped Black people's reality in the world. As Du Bois notes, "the Negro problem" has a "long historical development" which has changed "with the growth and evolution of the nation" (1898, 3). The long development, he explains, includes "incalculable world movements ... a movement so vast that we call it the economic revolution" (Du Bois 1898, 5). This "economic monstrosity" changed all spheres of production and reproduction – the "industrial conditions' and "the demands of the world market" (Du Bois 1898, 5). Similarly, Plaatje insists that the South African "economic foundation" is linked to the exploitation of Black people (2007, 138). He asserts that "for example, if the 200,000 Natives on the mines were ... to "down" tools ... if the farm labourers at harvesting time refused to work ... the beautiful white superstructure which had been built on it would come down with a crash" (2007, 138). Clearly, then, both thinkers developed a radical critique of racial capitalism even in this earlier period. This paper will provide evidence demonstrating that this is indeed the case.

Chandler (2022, 5) reminds us that, "if nothing else", there is a need for a "new reading or rereading" of Du Bois' work. The same argument could well be made for Plaatje. By opening Plaatje and Du Bois' thoughts to a "radical historiography", we begin to see aspects of how their "theory [was] based on a foundation of economic analysis and class struggle" (Robinson 2000, 195) - a framework of *racial capitalism* that exposes and explores "the dialectic of colonialism, plantocratic slavery, and resistance from the sixteenth century forward, and the formations of industrial labour and labour reserves' (Robinson 2000, 67).

Taking cues from Chandler (2022), this article will evoke Du Bois' "epistemological formulation", which remained "on many registers across his entire career" (Chandler 2022, 14).

Chandler (2022, 15) notes that, Du Bois, "half dozen years before the publication of his most famous book [*Souls*], the American context and its historical process were seen as part of the "global horizon" and "global modernity". Thus, Du Bois' thought from his earlier work was epistemologically rooted in the understanding that the historical developments of the Renaissance, European imperialism, modern colonialism and the emergence of capitalism depended on slavery, which embodied a racialised, cheap and exploited form of labour. This observation was already present in Du Bois' *Study of the Negro* (1898). Moreover, this article will argue that an in-depth reading of Plaatje's work shows how the author laments and vividly demonstrates how, in the making of South Africa, the removal of Black people from their land was institutionally orchestrated and integral to the country's capitalist expansion. Plaatje (2007) argues that the racial nature of this expansion was not accidental, but signalled an embedded dependency on cheap Black labour.

Underpinning Plaatje and Du Bois' work is the premise that modern capitalism is an "extension" of the old racialised system, which Robinson (2000, 10) refers to as "the social, cultural, political, and ideological complexes of European feudalisms'. While neither author explicitly used the term, this article will show that their thoughts operated within the *problematic of racial capitalism,* breaking with Western Marxist articulations of historical development. Plaatje and Du Bois arrive at similar conclusions about the *problematic* of *racial capitalism.* In both contexts, by design, an expansion of accumulation further racialised the state and its bureaucratic apparatus. Moreover, all aspects of life - political, cultural and social conditions, including class structures, were shaped by this dependency on making Black people inferior.

Du Bois and Plaatje highlight three common threads of the *problematic of racial capitalism.* Firstly, both authors demonstrate how primitive accumulation in the historical development of capitalism required the exploitation of Black labour – thus, Black inferiority is part of capitalism's *modus operandi.* Secondly, as Robinson (2000, 203) correctly observed, "Du Bois understood that the relationship between slavery and democracy was not a question of the clash of ideas'. Therefore, legal frameworks and institutions implemented coincide with the racialised nature of capitalism. Plaatje eloquently shows that the Land Act, which forcibly removed Black people from their land, was not an incongruent ideology but entangled within the rationale of capitalism and the making of Black people as inferior. Lastly, although recognizing that "territorial states and empires acquired lands in plenty" (see Robinson 2000, 20). Plaatje and Du Bois argue that to expand this wealth accumulation through "uncharted" landscapes, the salvaging of the white working class was used as a mechanism.

In their articulation of *racial capitalism,* Du Bois and Plaatje force us to "inquire somewhat more carefully into the form under which the Negro problems present themselves today.." (Du Bois 1898, 7). Both noted that the changing nature of *racial capitalism*, its fundamental structure depended on its racialised character - the oppression and exploitation of Black people. Yet, at the same time, Black people's experiences do not remain changeless. In the making of Blackness, "one cannot study the Negro in freedom and come to a general conclusion about his destiny without knowing his history of slavery" (Du Bois 1898, 12). Du Bois and Plaatje have shown the relevance of narrating the Black experience critically. Revisiting their work beyond the banal labels of "liberals' allows thinking more "carefully" about the mutation of capitalism and its racist character.

Misreading Du Bois and Plaatje as liberals

Mullen (2016, 4) describes Du Bois' *Black Reconstruction* as a "majestic study of the Civil War and the end of slavery". The book, he further notes, meticulously details how American capitalism was fundamentally built on slavery (Mullen 2016, 4). He adds that it remains a "classic in the history of Marxist scholarship" (Mullen 2016, 4). In his recent publication, Goodwin (2022, 54) describes the book as a "towering work of history" and an embodiment of the "Marxist tradition". The conclusion drawn from these scholars, however, is that the work Du Bois produced before *Black Reconstruction* was not radical. Mullen (2016, 5) asserts that Du Bois was a "race liberal" in his earlier life and proposed "parliamentary and democratic" reforms as solutions to racism. Goodwin (2022, 55) declares that it took "three decades' for Du Bois to craft a radical position.

Reed (1997, 36) adds to the onslaught by noting that Du Bois was part of the elite and thus advocated for his class interests. Reed (1997, 28) positions Du Bois' early work as a patient liberal. While he did not ignore historical economic development, Reed argues that Du Bois did not have a "critique of capitalism" (Reed 1997, 31). Du Bois, he asserts, had too much "faith" in the "Talented Tenth" as the catalyst of change. The cardinal sin of the

"Talented Tenth" is often repeated as the fundamental indicator of Du Bois' "liberal" tendencies (see Robinson 2000, Allen 2002). Here we should return to Chandler's point about the need for a "new reading" and "rereading" of Du Bois' texts. In this process, Chandler (2022, 134) shows that Du Bois used the word "duty" in his definition of the Talented Tenth. On a close reading of the word "duty", Chandler contends that "the supposed "talented tenth" is quite something other than a practice of elitism" (2022, 134). Du Bois sought freedom, and "duty" emphasized an individual and a collective responsibility to deal with the past, present and future – to think beyond immediate realities and fight for the possibility of something that is "yet to come" (Chandler 2022, 134). Chandler's analysis points to the negation of Du Bois' radical thought by those who interpret his earlier work as "elite" and "liberal" – pinpointing the limitations of existing scholarship to "think" with Du Bois and with the complexities of his thought.

The narrow analysis of Du Bois is also reproduced in scholarly reflection on Sol Plaatje's work. Saunders (2016, 152) notes that Marxist scholars have paid little attention to Plaatje's work, often referring to his work as part of a capitalist class project. Saunders (2016, 154) agrees that Plaatje's work "deserves to be appreciated as a great liberal text". Mkhize (2016, 96) argues that Plaatje's liberal tendencies stem from his schooling, educated by missionaries of the Berlin Mission Society. As a result, he became part of the "Black Victorian" intellectuals - a class, Mkhize (2016, 97) notes, "formed through the sensibilities of British imperial liberalism" at the turn of the twentieth century which aimed "for the end of racial and colonial oppression through empire" (2016, 97). Odendaal (2016, 126) argues that Plaatje played out his "Britishness' to pursue a political agenda. He appealed to the British moral conscience, hoping they would "protect their loyal and black subjects in South Africa" (Odendaal 2016, 125). Yet the British evocation, Odendaal adds, was laced with a "deep sense of African identity", another side of the "black Victorian" (2016, 126).

Keith Breckenridge (2016, 176) goes a step further in his attempt to understand the liberal tendencies of Plaatje's work by comparing him to Mohandas Gandhi. He argues that as white "progressives' were moving towards a separatist, racist model, "figures like Gandhi and Plaatje became increasingly fervent in their appeals to the liberal justifications of imperial government" (2016, 178). In this comparison, Breckenridge does not fully explain Plaatje's critical position vis-à-vis the Indian community.[1] Plaatje made it clear that the plight of Indian people was different from that of Black people because international actors, in particular interventions by the Indian government, derailed the "abominations' the South government wanted to impose on them.

Although Plaatje's work can be read through his pro-liberal and pro-capitalist interests, this analysis can be blunt and tend towards caricature (see Saunders 2016). It limits explorations of how Black intellectuals also shared experiences. It further annihilates their articulation of capitalism and how it shaped culture, social, economic and political spaces. In a context in which it was tactically prudent to agitate for reform, the exact dynamics of this process can be "difficult to pin down" and contradictory. It can manifest in a "complex mixture of opposites' (Barker 1987, 221). Hence a host of ideologies can exist simultaneously and at different points within their intellectual thoughts and changing conditions. Scholarship which paints both Plaatje and Du Bois as mere "liberals' disavows the radicalism and resistance which was present in their work and which ruptured Western Marxism and its historiography.

Du Bois and racial capitalism

In *The Study of the Negro* (1898, 3), Du Bois describes the United States in the latter part of the seventeenth century as a "young country" going through rapid expansion. This growth radically changed the global economic and political landscape, driving global historical development (Du Bois 1898). Demand for crops, especially in America's South, changed labour and "industrial conditions' generally through implementing a "large plantation slave system" (Du Bois 1898, 5). This "economic monstrosity", which also grew to become a "political menace", made the distinction between slaves and servants, applying different laws and giving Black people non-human status during slavery. When "emancipation" occurred, they were relegated to "serfdom" - making the "condition[s] of the free Negro unbearable" (Du Bois 1898, 5). In the course of these developments, the world came to be confronted with the "negro problem" (Du Bois 1898). Du Bois argues that the indelible logic of wealth accumulation operated within the vicissitudes of the "negro problem"- "English-speaking Negroes' born in the United States "mixed blood" through "illicit intercourse and inter-marriage", and a "new class of free Negroes' emerged after "emancipation" (Du Bois 1898, 4). This produced "a plexus of social problems, some new, some old, some simple, some complex" (Du Bois 1898, 3). The Black body further complicates this peculiarity – "physical unlikeness to the people with whom he has been brought into contact" (Du Bois 1898, 19). Modern capitalism, through its historical and material development, the vital component depended on making Black people inferior.

By the time *The Souls of Black Folk* (1903) was published, the "problem of the colour line" was understood as a "global problem" (see Chandler 2022). Du Bois showed that economic revolutions do not break with the old. Still, they created new dimensions: "the world old phenomenon of the contact of diverse races of men is to have new exemplification during the new century" (Du Bois 2003, 117). These historical and economic developments continuously bring "war, murder, slavery, extermination, and debauchery"

(Du Bois 2003, 117) and depend heavily on oppressed and "proscribed" Black people for its growth. The "modern world" rationale operates within the "fated triumph of strength over weakness, of righteousness over evil, of superiors over inferiors' (Du Bois 2003, 117). These economic structural relations permeated into social and political relations. Moreover, this order manifests itself at the ideological level:

> [T]here are the economic relations — the methods by which individuals cooperate for earning a living, for the mutual satisfaction of wants, for the production of wealth ... [T]here are the political relations, the cooperation in social control, in group government, in laying and paying the burden of taxation ... [T]here are the less tangible but highly important forms of intellectual contact and commerce, the interchange of ideas (Du Bois 2003, 118).

This economic structure, entangled with racism, shaped all aspects of "everyday life, in travel, in theatres, in house gatherings, in marrying and giving in marriage" (Du Bois 2003, 119). Urban planning also came to be underpinned by this *problematic*: "It is usually possible to draw in nearly every Southern community a physical colour line on the map, on the one side of which whites dwell and on the other Negro" (Du Bois 2003, 119). Du Bois described these processes as forming part of the "economic relations of the races' (2003, 120).

This central component of capitalism's historical development and the evolution of efforts to render Black people inferior was juxtaposed with land dispossession. Du Bois notes that an average person might think the "rich lands' in America's South might be "awaiting development and filled with black labourers' (2003, 120). However, he laments, it is "by no means as simple as this, from the obvious fact that these workingmen have been trained for centuries as slaves' (Du Bois 2003, 120). Black workers in the new dispensation were "left alone and unguided, without capital, without land, without skill, without economic organization, without even the bald protection of law, order, and decency" (Du Bois 2003, 120–1). These Black workers had to compete in an economic system with people who did not endure this reality (Du Bois 2003, 121). In this period, capitalism was reconfiguring and rebuilding, while the new and old capitalists acquired a "new thirst for wealth and power" (Du Bois 2003, 121). These "new captains of industry" exploited all workers. But Black workers had to deal with "race prejudice". They were saddled with the "wretched economic heritage of the freedmen from slavery" with limited access to opportunities compared to white workers (Du Bois 2003, 121).

Black elites who acquired some land and property were too small of a class to dent the economic system with any significant impact (Du Bois 2003). The new structure created an elite "who were without land" and regarded their freedom between "the devil and the deep sea" (Du Bois 2003, 28). The land was promised to the small elites, but only a few with "tools and capital" could accumulate it. Thus, the "vision of ""forty acres and a mule" ... was destined in most cases to bitter disappointment" (Du Bois 2003, 28). Most lands remained in the hands of the former slaveowners and landowners. The success of this class was "left to chance and accident, and not to any intelligent culling or reasonable methods of selection" (Du Bois 2003, 122). Du Bois argues that "the exploitation and debauchment of the worst" kind were exacerbated in denying Black people the right to vote (Du Bois 2003, 126). The "American civilization" was founded on "proscription and prejudice", with Black people "classed" as the "lowest" human (Du Bois 2003, 132). Therefore, the "colour line" in capitalism is not only a social and economic condition. Du Bois argues it is laced in continuously making Black inferior by dispossessing them from land.

In *Black Reconstruction*, Du Bois elaborates on how race and class are inherently integral to expanding American capitalism. The book should not only be read as a "radical" turning point for Du Bois. But, as an ambitious theoretical work with roots stemming from his earlier work. Du Bois illustrated how the economy shifted from the plantation of sugar, rice and tobacco towards growing cotton which "clothed the masses of a ragged world". The rapid speed of cotton production brought various changes – an "economic revolution in a dozen different lines' (Du Bois 1935, 55). Trade became globalized, and new cities were built. These developments depended on the Black labourers who built cities and worked in factories and farms (Du Bois 1935, 55). "It was thus the black worker", Du Bois proclaimed, who stood "as the founding stone of a new economic system in the nineteenth century and for the modern world" (Du Bois 1935, 78). However, the racialised character of capitalism advanced the white working class in the new dispensation by humanizing them: 'They wanted a chance to become capitalists' (Du Bois 1935, 85). Some quickly became "property holders and an aristocracy of birth and learning" (Du Bois 1935, 71). The ideology of racism excluded Black people economically:

> They said: Slavery was wrong but not all wrong; slavery must perish and not simply move; God made black men; God made slavery; the will of God be done; slavery to the glory of God and black men as his servants and ours; slavery as a way to freedom—the freedom of blacks, the freedom of whites; white freedom as the goal of the world and black slavery as the path thereto. Up with the white world, down with the black! (Du Bois 1935, 95).

Du Bois argued that during slavery, poor whites served as police, harshly enforcing and guiding segregationist laws (1935, 71). Humanizing the poor white working, even in the lowest class, served as a crucial mechanism in the racialised nature of capitalism. This conception was present in Du Bois' earlier work. In the *Darkwater: Voices Within the Veil* (1920), he emphasized how, for capitalism to flourish, it ought to preserve white people:

> This is not Europe gone mad; this is not aberration nor insanity; this is Europe; this seeming Terrible is the real soul of white culture—back of all culture—stripped and visible today ... it has always been in the interest of "white Europe" to structure capitalism that divides and is based on racial nature and exploitation (Du Bois 2016, 22).

Thus, the white working class needed to be given some minimal power in the form of policing, yet this was a vital device for the "re-enslavement" of Black people (Du Bois 2003).

In his articulation of the *problematic* of *racial capitalism*, Du Bois demonstrates that modern capitalism and its expansion used the slave trade to fill the required labour demands. These historical and economic developments based on proscription made Black people inferior. Even after the abolition of slavery, all parts of the social, political and cultural milieu were shaped and contaminated by this rationale. Land dispossession was integral in making Black people inferior. The white working class, given nominal power, were superficially humanized while positioned as instrumental in "re-enslaving" Black people.

Du Bois' conceptualization of racialised capitalism appears to cross-pollinate with Plaatje's thoughts. Du Bois and Plaatje had a close relationship, marked by "intellectual, financial, and professional dynamics' (Chrisman 2003, 95). Their connection, Chrisman argues, illustrated the enduring, complex and long history of transatlantic exchange and politics (2003, 95). Plaatje, eight years Du Bois' junior, was highly influenced by his work (Chrisman 2003, 95). He corresponded with Du Bois on several matters, including his plans to translate some of Shakespeare's plays into Setswana and the difficulties of finding a publisher for *Native Life*. Du Bois delivered Plaatje's speech at the Second Pan African Congress in 1921 when the latter could not attend the conference due to financial constraints (Willan 2018; Massachusetts archives). Across the Atlantic, reflections on the dialectic of racism and capitalism resonated, although their context differed.

Plaatje and racial capitalism

In his most quoted phrase, Plaatje articulates how the expansion of modern capitalism played out in South Africa: "Awaking on Friday morning, June 20, 1913, the South African Native found himself, not actually a slave, but a pariah in the land of his birth" (Plaatje 2007, 21). Land dispossession was at the heart of this historical and economic development. This form of accumulation was embedded in the rationale of making the Black majority of "servants'. The strategy, simply put, was: "a Kafir who refused to become a servant should at once be consigned to the road" (Plaatje 2007, 76). Plaatje angrily accused the British government of using a "free hand" to ally themselves with the crude racist sentiments of the Dutch. Plaatje suggested that the Dutch had a staunch racist ideology even before the implementation of legislated segregation. Although he was aware that the British were racist, they held out the possibility of negotiation. Yet the British, he argued, "unreservedly handed over the Natives to the colonists' (Plaatje 2007, 25). What followed was the proclamation of the Land Act in 1913, which stripped Black people of their land and possessions and divided them:

> The 4,500,000 black South Africans are domiciled as follows: One and three-quarter millions in Locations and Reserves, over half a million within municipalities or in urban areas, and nearly a million as squatters on farms owned by Europeans (Plaatje 2007, 21).

These circumstances came to be felt by Black people a year after the Act's passing when it became impossible for Black tenants to renew their contracts with their white landowners (Plaatje 2007, 22). A sanction of "100 Pounds, or six months' imprisonment" was passed if any white landowner sought to provide accommodation to landless Black people (Plaatje 2007, 22). Some farm owners who once profited from renting out their farms were upset about the imposed law, whose purpose was to "eliminate" Black tenancy. Leasing farms to Black people thereafter was seen as an immoral act, labelled as "Kafir-farming" and "baby-farming" (Plaatje 2007, 30). These land removals created squatters which the government were unable to manage effectively: "A squatter in South Africa is a native who owns some livestock and, having no land of his own … " (Plaatje 2007, 21). The annexation of the land left the Black majority with "one-eighteenth part of the Union [which is present South Africa], leaving the remaining seventeen parts for the one million whites' (Plaatje 2007, 24). Thus, the law deemed it illegal for Black people to "buy or lease land, except in scheduled native areas' (Plaatje 2007, 30).

Land dispossession was integral in making Black people inferior. However, this form of accumulation depended on Black people to work the land. Plaatje, for instance, demonstrates that even before the Act was passed, white parliamentarians who debated its merits were fully aware of the importance of Black labour: "Who had built our railways, who had dug our mines, and developed this country as far as it was developed? Who had been the actual manual worker who had done that?" (Plaatje 2007, 35). The white parliamentarian answered precisely: "The Native: the coloured races of this country" (Plaatje 2007, 35). But the "docility of the Natives' was crucial in executing the Act (Plaatje 2007).

These white parliamentarians wanted to compete internationally, and the land was a key marker in worldwide capitalism: "the land held by Europeans per head was fifty times the amount held per head by the Natives' (Plaatje 2007, 40). The imagination of the British Empire was present among these parliamentarians – trade figures were evoked in debates contesting the Act:

> Let them take our trade figures and compare them with the trade figures of the other large British Dominions. Our figures were surprising when measured by

the white population, but if they took the richest Dominion that there was under the British Crown outside South Africa, and took the trade value of those figures per head of the white population (Plaatje 2007, 35).

Modern capitalism and its racialised nature at a local and international level fundamentally changed the social, cultural, and political fabric. Dependency on Black cheap labour jolted even the daily experiences of white people. Plaatje narrated a scene in which a white woman is nervous that her domestic worker might leave the job because she is in love:

> And if a town Kafir is going to marry Anna, where on earth am I going to get a reliable servant to whom I could securely entrust my home when I have occasion to go to town or to the seaside on a shorter or longer vacation? Who could cook and attend to my husband's and children's peculiar wants, if Anna is going to leave us? (Plaatje 2007, 84).

This dependency on Black labour also manifests itself intimately in capital expansion. Plaatje (2007, 57) notes that the Act aimed "to prevent the Natives from ever rising above the position of servants' (Plaatje 2007, 57). To remain in this status of servitude, Black people are pacified with intimate evocations: "We are told to forgive our enemies and not to let the sun go down upon our wrath, so we breathe the prayer that peace may be to the white races' (Plaatje 2007, 68).

In these attempts to pacify Black people, the "poor whites' were preserved, protected and salvaged. Plaatje (2007, 28) notes that the "Dutch" removed Black people from their farms and "replac[ed] them with poor whites'. For these poor whites, whose status was elevated, the Land Act permitted them to employ Black labour, even though many did not have money to pay them a wage (Plaatje 2007, 65). He provided an account of a poor white farmer willing to employ a landless Black family: the man worked in the field, the woman inside the house and their children assisted with various chores (Plaatje 2007, 64). To supplement the Black family's wage, the Black man was told "to leave his family at work on the farm and go out with his wagon and his oxen to earn money whenever and wherever he was told to go" (Plaatje 2007, 64). Moreover, "they were swept out of the Railway and Postal Service with a strong racial broom, in order to make room for poor whites, mainly of Dutch descent" (Plaatje 2007, 28).

For the Act to succeed fully, Plaatje (2007) highlights the ideological rationale which suffused the structural implementation. The white poor, in the majority of cases, were once again made into police, thus using their nominal power to evict Black people from their land and drag those who resisted to prison. Ideologically and in law, the rationale was clear: "Kafirs were inferior beings', therefore white people needed to have "undisturbed possession of their property" (Plaatje 2007). Black people and their livestock were not even spared. Plaatje laments:

THE SOUTH AFRICAN TRADITION OF RACIAL CAPITALISM 57

> The section of the law debarring Natives from hiring land is particularly harsh. It has been explained that its major portion is intended to reduce the Natives to serfs; but it should also be noted that the portion of the Act that is against Natives acquiring any interest whatsoever in land aims directly at dispossessing the Natives of their live stock (2007, 148).

Plaatje narrates how racialised forms of accumulation evolved and expanded in its daily practice:

> [O]ne of their cruelest acts of omission was that of giving us no hint that in very much less than a quarter of a century all those hundreds of heads of cattle, and sheep and horses belonging to the family would vanish like a morning mist, and that we ourselves would live to pay 30s. per month for a daily supply of this same precious fluid [milk], and in very limited quantities. (Plaatje 2007, 67).

The Land Act further emboldened the eradication of the Black elite, resulting in "overcrowded locations, with the logical result that sundry acute domestic problems' emerged (Plaatje 2007, 149). Plaatje, like Du Bois, understood that for the expansion of modern capitalism to occur, racism is integral to the process. Land dispossession is fundamental in making Black people perpetually inferior. A "required serfdom!" (Plaatje 2007, 353) of Black people is also embedded in the process of humanizing the white working class. Although their focus was on the unfolding of modern capitalism, both Plaatje and Du Bois worked within the framework of *racial capitalism*. Both understood the dialectic of capitalism and racism and its entangled relationship to "formations of labour and labour reserves' (see Robinson 2000).

Conclusion

This article has shown that Du Bois and Plaatje understood that racism is integral to capitalism even in their earlier writings. For Du Bois, this articulation did not start with *Black Reconstruction,* as scholars have claimed, but can be traced to his much earlier work. This article followed Chandler's (2022) provocation to read Du Bois' texts anew, but included Plaatje's work in this process of rereading. In this process, Chandler (2022, 17) asserts, *"a new sense of the whole* of Du Bois", and, this article proposes, a new sense of the whole of Plaatje, can be discovered. It is a "daunting" task, yet this "recalibration" is a "necessary task for critical thought in our time". Chandler (2022, 7) further notes this process is crucial, as "context is thus also always plural, configured in the movement of thought and not simply and purely given, beforehand".

Plaatje notes that the Native Land Act was institutionally implemented to expand capital in South Africa. Furthermore, the article has shown that the claim that Plaatje's *Native Life* and Du Bois' early work were merely "liberal" and did not evoke the role of capitalism is erroneous and misplaced. Du Bois and Plaatje's work challenge every scholar who studies and cares about humanity to think "carefully" about these "plexus of social problems'.

Their work, partly, traces the historical development of *racial capitalism,* forcing us to understand the whole world. "Perhaps it could also mean that in order to understand the world, it might be essential to understand" capitalism and its racial nature (Chandler 2022, 43).

This article has also assertively illustrated that both authors were working within the *problematic of racial capitalism.* Three common threads emerged from their descriptions of how race and class are inherently integral to capitalism expansion: Land, Black inferiority, and the salvaging of the white working class. Plaatje demonstrated how the implementation of the 1913 Natives Land Act aimed to ensure Black people remained "servants'. Du Bois noted that slavery was essential to the making of American capitalism. In both cases, Du Bois and Plaatje demonstrate how land dispossession was crucial in perpetuating Black people as inferior. The white working class were given minimal power, either as police or through land ownership, which both authors argue were tools designed to salvage the white working class while keeping Black people re-enslaved. Du Bois and Plaatje's work shows the dialectic of capitalism and racism and its entangled relationship to the formation of labour.

Note

1. Plaatje Sol. T. (Solomon Tshekisho) 1876-1932. Speech to the Pan African Congress 1921. W. E. B. Du Bois Papers (MS 312). Special Collections and University Archives University of Massachusetts Amherst Libraries.

Acknowledgements

Thank you, Joel Pearson. Sarita Pillay, I appreciate you. To my mother, I miss you.

Disclosure statement

No potential conflict of interest was reported by the author(s).

References

Allen Jr., E. 2002. "Du Boisian Double Consciousness: The Unsustainable Argument." *The Massachusetts Review* 43 (2): 217–253. http://www.jstor.org/stable/25091848
Barker, C. 1987. "Poland 1980-81: Perspectives." In *Revolutionary Rehearsals,* edited by I. Birchall, C. Barker, M. Gonzalez, M. Poya, and P. Robinson. London: Bookmarks.
Breckenridge, K. 2016. "African Progressivism, Land, and Law: Rereading *Native Life in South Africa.*" In *Sol Plaatje's Native Life in South Africa: Past and Present,* edited by J. Remmington, B. Willan, B. Peterson, and N. S. Ndebele, 175–195. Johannesburg: Wits University Press.
Chandler, N. D. 2022. *"Beyond This Narrow Now." Or, Delimitations, of W. E. B. Du Bois.* Durham & London: Duke University Press.

Chrisman, L. 2003. *Postcolonial Contraventions*. Manchester: Manchester University Press.

Du Bois, W. E. B. 1898. "The Study of the Negro Problems." *Annals of the American Academy of Political and Social Science* 11: 1–23. http://www.jstor.org/stable/1009474

Du Bois, W. E. B. 1935. *Black Reconstruction*. Harcourt: Brace and Company.

Du Bois, W. E. B. 2003. *The Souls of Black Folk*. New York: Barnes & Noble.

Du Bois, W. E. B. 2016. *Darkwater: Voices from Within the Veil*. London: Verso.

Goodwin, J. 2022. "Black Reconstruction as Class War." *Catalyst Magazine* 6 (1): 53–98.

Limb, P. 2003. "Sol Plaatje Reconsidered: Rethinking Plaatje's Attitudes to Class, Nation, Gender, and Empire 1." *African Studies* 62 (1): 33–52. doi:10.1080/00020180300989.

Mkhize, K. 2016. "African Intellectual History, Black Cosmopolitanism and *Native Life in South Africa*." In *Sol Plaatje's Native Life in South Africa: Past and Present*, edited by J. Remmington, B. Willan, B. Peterson, and N. S. Ndebele, 95–114. Johannesburg: Wits University Press.

Mullen, B. V. 2016. *W.E.B. Du Bois Revolutionary Across the Color Line*. London: Pluto Press.

Odendaal, A. 2016. "Native Lives Behind *Native Life*: Intellectual and Political Influences on the Early ANC and Democracy in South Africa." In *Sol Plaatje's Native Life in South Africa: Past and Present*, edited by J. Remmington, B. Willan, B. Peterson, and N. S. Ndebele, 115–146. Johannesburg: Wits University Press.

Plaatje, S. T. 2007. *Native Life in South Africa*. Northlands: Picador Africa.

Reed, A. L. 1997. *W.E.B. Du Bois and American Political Thought: Fabanism and the Color Line*. New York: Oxford University Press.

Robinson, C. J. 2000. *Black Marxism: The Making of the Black Radical Tradition*. Chapel Hill, N.C: University of North Carolina Press.

Saunders, C. 2016. "Whose Past? *Native Life in South Africa* and Historical Writing." In *Sol Plaatje's Native Life in South Africa: Past and Present*, edited by J. Remmington, B. Willan, B. Peterson, and N. S. Ndebele, 147–157. Johannesburg: Wits University Press.

Willan, B. 2018. *Sol Plaatje: A Life of Solomon Tshekisho Plaatje, 1876-1932*. Auckland Park: Jacana.

Archival Collections:

University of Massachusetts Archives, *Amherst Libraries Special Collections*, MS 312.

Articulating difference: reading Biko-with-Hall

Ahmed Veriava and Prishani Naidoo

ABSTRACT
This article centres a selected set of "race-class debates" from the 1970s that were characterized by a powerful reformulation of political critiques of the South African racial order, both from within Marxist thought and with the dramatic entry of Black Consciousness onto the political stage. Our discussion focuses on two exemplary interventions: Biko's testimony at the SASO/BPC trial and his presentation of the theoretical basis of BC's political strategy, and Stuart Hall's 1980 essay "Race, Articulation and Societies Structured in Dominance", and its reformulation of a Marxist perspective for thinking through race-class relations. With Hall we (re)discover theoretical terms for thinking through the problem of how relatively autonomous practices of domination come to be articulated. With Biko, we discover a strategic modality for approaching the political problem of collective subjectivity that holds lessons for how struggles against frameworks of domination might be politically articulated in their multiplicity.

*

To articulate the past historically does not mean to recognize it 'the way it really was' (Ranke). It means to seize hold of a memory as it flashes up at a moment of danger. (Walter Benjamin 1968)

Introduction

On the 6th of October in 2015 there was a protest at the University of the Witwatersrand (Wits). One of the banners prepared for the event marked *a new articulation*: "Decolonise Wits. End Outsourcing".

In 2015, the demand to end outsourcing at Wits was not new. It had emerged a decade and a half earlier with resistance to a restructuring plan that saw most of the blue-collar work required to keep the institution going contracted to outside private service providers. But, in that earlier moment, the demand to end outsourcing was *articulated* with an (ambivalently) expressed critique of neoliberalism that highlighted the ways in which the deepening orientation of public institutions towards market-centred practices was distorting processes of national democratic transformation (see Naidoo and Veriava 2005). When the #Fees Must Fall /#End Outsourcing (FMF/EO) movement emerged, just a week after the 2015 #October 6 protest, demands for "transformation" and critiques of neoliberalism had significantly receded. Forcefully taking its place was a new discourse of decolonization that brought together onto-epistemological critique and an anti-racist politics with economic demands to end outsourcing and deliver free higher education.

FMF/EO was expressive of a heterogeneous constitution. As a political form it was something like "a movement of movements", bringing together a range of formal student political organizations with more diverse and informal affinities.[1] At the level of its discursive representations as well, movement activists *articulated* a multiplicity of ideological elements, drawing together demands that belonged to an older discourse of transformation or the political sensibilities of the formations that comprised it, with more newly acquired concepts like "intersectionality", "coloniality" and/or "social death". And within this multiplicity, what was most acutely reflected in the lines of solidarity established between workers and students, and what came to underpin the discursive linking of economic demands and an anti-racist, decolonial politics, was a reconfigured Black Consciousness (BC) perspective. In 2015, the struggle for insourcing, just like the struggle for free education, was framed principally as a Black struggle. The Black workers who cleaned the university and maintained its grounds came out in support of students (effectively joining their occupation of the university), speaking in endearing terms of them as their children whose struggle was therefore also theirs. Student leaders, for their part, presented their common cause with workers in terms of a struggle to restore the dignity of their parents through insourcing – just as their struggle for free education was part of a struggle to make space for "the black child" in the otherwise alienating environment of the colonial university.[2]

In the 1970s and 1980s, the BC movement emerged as an important component of the broader liberation movement. While it maintained affinities with both the Pan Africanist Congress (PAC) and the African National Congress (ANC), it expressed and energetically defended an independent political and ideological identity alongside its own organizational structures and framework.[3] But as South Africa entered into a process of negotiated transition to democracy, the BC movement's decision to oppose this process left them outside of newly minted political frameworks. And by the 1990s the formations of BC were in decline, coming close to disappearing completely.

BC, as an theoretical perspective, however, started to find residence in the political imagination of a new generation – one which grew up on the other side of the transition.

Part of the ideological work FMF did, then, was in reasserting a BC politics, and in a way that allowed it to push from the older economic demands for free education and insourcing towards a far reaching critique of the post-apartheid political order and the institutions that belonged to it. Extending from the problematization of the colonial university to the national context, the BC perspective that developed in FMF/EO helped put into question the worn-out narratives of rainbow nationalism and, more broadly, the terms of the political settlement that in 1994 installed liberal democracy. And over the course of its contentiously fought campaigns (which literally brought the sector to a standstill), the movement not only forced the insourcing of workers at many institutions and an overhaul of the framework for funding higher education, but also (re)installed imperatives towards decolonizing the curriculum, extending student and worker representation in institutional processes, and for transforming the relations governing the everyday life of the university community and beyond.

Ironically, at Wits BC operated in this re-radicalizing milieu as an ambient current. Where in the 1980s and 1990s, the respective symbols of the different factions of the liberation movement still travelled with difficulty, by 2015 things had changed. The absence of BC formations on campus meant that, as an theoretical perspective, BC could circulate outside of its traditional sites of association.[4] In this context, the idea of a common blackness now appeared as a potent symbol to temporarily unite competing agendas and organizations.

The resurgence of a BC politics within the FMF/EO movement was, however, also met with suspicion, especially from quarters of an "older left". At the height of the 2015/2016 mobilizations, representations of political subjectivity and solidarity centreing blackness, were critiqued for lacking an adequate class perspective or as a regression from the non-racial politics of the Congress movement. Although these kinds of critiques were themselves often made on the basis of a narrow class perspective, or reflected a contentious, if not misplaced assessment of the "non-racialism of Congress", their appearance re-introduced the terms of an older set of debates that unfolded between and within factions of the liberation movement, as well as in what got counted in academic publics as "the race-class debate".

This article was provoked by the movement that emerged at Wits in 2015/2016, and our attempt to orientate to the questions and debates that it surfaced. For us, an important dimension of the theoretical challenge presented by FMF/EO's practical critique of the present is how to conceptualize the relations between forms of racial and economic domination within concrete

social processes, as well as in their relationship with the political representations of antagonistic subjects. These questions, with their deep strategic
implications, are not easy to answer, especially if you assume the historical
specificity of such relations or contingency in the processes through which
political subjects are articulated with particular discourses.

In marking out one path in this direction, in this article we undertake a
detour through a selected set of theoretical debates that emerged in the
1970s. This turn to the 1970s is strategic since it is a period marked by a
powerful reformulation of political critiques of the South African racial
order, both from within Marxist thought and with the dramatic entry of BC
onto the political stage. In bringing these frameworks into relation, we
focus on two exemplary interventions: Biko's (1976) testimony at the SASO/
BPC trial in which he presents the theoretical basis of BC's political strategy,
and Stuart Hall's entry into South African race-class debates in his 1980 essay
"Race, Articulation and Societies Structured in Dominance", which opens onto
a reformulated Marxist perspective for thinking race-class articulations.

Part of what made FMF/EO so inspiring was exactly the way it brought
together economic demands for free education and an end to outsourcing
with a struggle against white supremacy and for decolonization. At the
same time, on campuses like Wits sectarian politics often wrecked
moments of unity in action, and in the end, the competing political organizations and agendas that characterized this movement failed to cohere into a
constitutive political project. In this context, the reading of Biko-with-Hall that
follows is an attempt at drawing out of the debates of the past tactical poin-
ters for today's struggles.

For us, Biko-with-Hall works towards the clarification of the terms of a
"double theory of articulation" that would allow us to grasp how systems
of domination come to be bound together, and even more importantly,
how different struggles might be brought together.[5] In this sense, it is an
attempt at expressing a framework to generalize what the best moments
of FMF pointed towards. Reading Biko-with-Hall doesn't, however, deliver a
ready-made-politics that once and for all says "what is to be done?" Instead
it marks out one potential starting point for developing the theoretical
terms of a constitutive politics in the present, and in a way that articulates
economic, sociological and ontological critique, with a framework focussed
on the political problem of collective subjectivity.

Rescripting BC into race/class debates

The relationship between the BCM and the development of a Marxist critique
of "racial capitalism" in the 1970s is a complex one. Read off bibliographies of
interventions in academic race-class debates or, for that matter, off the forms
of claim making present in the BCM of the late 1960s and early 1970s, this

movement was not actively engaged in the problematic that informed the academic terms of "the race-class debate". The organic intellectuals of the BC movement in the 1970s were, however, engaged in race-class debates of a different sort, linked to the terrains of political action their formative struggles were unfolding on, and often given expression in their critique of existing practices of political solidarity on the left.

It is therefore possible, as Ally and Ally (2008) have shown, to place BC within a rescripted intellectual history of "the race/class debate". And in this re-telling of the story, the emergence of BC provided the impetus and urgency to white theorists who were developing a critique of racial capitalism, which is to say, to their efforts to clarify the relationship between racial domination and class exploitation. For Ally and Ally the BC movement of the 1970s helped provoke socialists to deepen their critique of the link between capitalism and racism, just as the resurgence of BC today is provoking a return to the debates of this important period. It is, however, a mistake to reduce the BC of the 1970s to a race-based ideology unable to mount an organic critique of class exploitation and the historical link between apartheid and capitalism. What is more important to emphasize in this respect, especially in accounting for BC's impact on the "class analysis" of the 1970s and 1980s, is its insistence on theorizing from the lived experience of oppressed subjects. For this reason, it seems more appropriate to rescript BC's intervention in "the race/class debate" in relation to the impetus and form it gave to a critique of class reductionism.

In the 1970s the BC movement was a young movement, and so were its leaders. Emerging in the late 1960s following a breakaway of a prominent group of Black students from the National Union of South African Students (NUSAS), this movement was from the very beginning marked by its ambition to develop a new philosophy of liberation. It did so, like FMF/EO decades later, by articulating ideological elements present in the milieu of Black student activists, enmeshing the aesthetics and politics of the Black power movement in the United States (US) with theoretical forms transposed from readings of theology, the likes of Freire, Cesaire, Senghor and (especially) Fanon, and placing them alongside elements drawn from local traditions of struggle against colonialism and racial domination. BC was made from ideological elements that were "close at hand", and in relation to an intellectual attitude that was both expansive and insistent on making a politics grounded in Black experiences under apartheid.

By the 1980s the philosophical perspective self-consciously being constructed by the representatives of the movement now included a visibly Marxist perspective on class exploitation, but in a way that remade it within a BC politics vocally opposed to Eurocentrism and class reductionism. For the proponents of BC (even after it explicitly became a BC-with-Marxism), the central antagonism in South Africa remained the racially coded one, even as it drew into its discursive repertoires forms of analysis foregrounded by concepts of class and racial capitalism. BC's clunky, and admittedly reductionist, theoretical formulation that race was "a class determinant" (popularized in the 1980s), can therefore be linked to a more complex sensibility towards the ways in which race and class were articulated. And while the new language of critique that became part of the BC of the 1980s marked a significant moment in the development of this political philosophy, it can also be seen as an attempt to recode aspects of BC's already existing critique of the South African racial order into what had recently become the terms of a neo-Marxist critique of racial capitalism.

Returning to the BC of the 1970s, and specifically to the thought of Steve Biko, you already find there a concrete illustration of Hall's thesis that race comes to work as "the modality through which class is 'lived', the medium through which class relations are experienced, the form in which it is appropriated and 'fought through'" (Hall 2019, 216). What Biko represents, however, is not simply the case study that confirms the theory, but a political perspective that is beginning to place the political implications of such a view within a strategic framework aimed at the "destruction of the existing state of things". Listening for Biko's voice we encounter the movement's most important theoretical innovation – the articulation of a political framework for opposing the racist interpellations of the apartheid order with a complex and simultaneously constitutive project of self and for society.

To draw out this argument, in the next section we briefly mark out some of the theoretical points of inspiration of Hall's approach to articulations between race and class before showing how this perspective can be productively read with Biko's (1976) testimony at the SASO/BPC trial.

Race, class and the concept of articulation

In a 1986 interview, Stuart Hall clarified that his deployment of a metaphor of articulation (which extends far beyond his analysis of structures of racial domination) draws in its double valence. In one sense, articulation denotes the contingent linking of relatively autonomous elements. Elaborating on this sense of the term, Hall gives the example of an "articulated lorry" – a vehicle in which a "front (cab) and back (trailer) can, but need not necessarily be connected to one another" (Hall 2019, 234). With emphasis on this sense of the term, articulation came to play an important role in the theoretical framework spawned from the research conducted by Althusser and his students, figuring there as a component of their explicit attempt at shifting beyond the economic reductionism of orthodox Marxism. So, when in 1972 the South African theorist, Harold Wolpe, put out his soon to become canonical formulation of the relationship between the reproduction of cheap labour power and the racist governmental framework of apartheid, he did so precisely by way of a deployment of this sense of the Althusserian inspired concept (see Wolpe 1972).

The argument presented in Wolpe's "Capitalism and Cheap Labour Power in South Africa: From Segregation to Apartheid", was part of a broader challenge presented by Marxist scholars to a "dual economy" perspective associated with "liberal" historiography. In its rudimentary form the dual economy thesis emphasized the division between white and Black forms of life in relation to a structurally independent modern (capitalist) sector, set apart from a "traditional" sector. This view, however, also sat alongside a form of economism in which (irrational) Afrikaner racist ideology was seen standing in conflict with (rational) market relations and economic growth, impelling movement in the long run towards its transcendence. Critically developing his work in conversation with other radical theorists of the period (Legassick, Frank, Meillassoux, Laclau, to name a few) Wolpe simultaneously put both of these assumptions into question by drawing attention to the historically contingent processes through which capitalist economic development in South Africa came to be linked to a migrant labour system with its "foundation" in the non-capitalist economy.

Briefly, Wolpe's argument might be summarized as follows. Under segregation (as the governmental framework preceding apartheid), and in a context where the demand for African labour tended to be for low skill migrant workers, production in the reserves had become crucial to meeting the material needs necessary for reproducing African labour, however precariously. In this context, capital could secure a higher rate of profit based on the availability of a ready supply of cheap, short term, migrant labour (paid below the cost of their reproduction). The development of capitalism in South Africa, therefore, depended on the existence of the non-capitalist mode of production, but it also worked to undermine it. Part of what Wolpe emphasized, then, was the ways in which, under segregation, the migrant labour system, and "its boost" to "the rate of profit", implied a specific set of historical relations between the "capitalist and the African pre-capitalist modes of production" (Wolpe 1972, 425) – that is to say, an articulation of these modes of production (but in a domination-subordination relation).

In shifting away from the reductionist explanation of apartheid as merely a reflection of a racist ideology at odds with the rationality of capitalist market relations, the Althusserian framework adopted by Wolpe sought to delineate "the historical conjuncture" between ideological, political and economic practices, apprehended now in relation to the contradictory relationship between the capitalist and non-capitalist modes of production:

> This relationship between the two modes of production ... increasingly produces the conditions which make impossible the continuation of the pre-

capitalist relations of production in the Reserves. The consequence of this is the accelerating dissolution of these relations and the development, within South Africa, towards a single capitalist mode of production in which more and more of the African wage-labour force ... is freed from productive resources in the Reserves. This results in important changes in the nature of exploitation and transfers the major contradiction from the relationship *between* different modes of production to the relations of production *within* capitalism ... .Here we arrive at the critical point of articulation between ideology, racial political practice and the economic system. Whereas Segregation provided the political structure appropriate to the earlier period, Apartheid represents the attempt to maintain the rate of surplus value. (1972, 432)

The thrust of Wolpe's argument ends up being a functionalism in which apartheid, as a response to this crisis and an attempt to maintain the rate of profit, worked at the suppression of African consumption by violently consigning African life to the *barest* conditions of life (sanctioned and reproduced in relation to forms of juridical-governmental management).

Hall's debts to the Althusserian concept of articulation, and to Wolpe's deployment of it, are apparent in "Race, Class and Societies Structured in Dominance". However, as we noted above, Hall's usage of this concept also works in the direction of the second sense of the term, which is to say, the more widely used sense denoting "languaging" and modes of expression. With this inflection, the seminal set of essays published by Laclau in 1977 is a nearer genealogical relation than *Reading Capital*, especially for the ways the concept is renewed there in the analysis of ideological practices. At this level, articulation is framed as a way of theoretically working through problems of the unity of discourses by focussing attention on the practices through which different and distinct ideological elements come to be bound together and to specific political subjects. The Laclauian inspiration for this formulation, however, sits in the emphasis on the contingency of the relations between ideological elements, and more especially, in the "non-belongingness" that characterizes the relation between a discourse and a political subject:

> The theory of articulation, as I use it, has been developed by Ernesto Laclau, in his book *Politics and Ideology in Marxist Theory*. His argument is that the political connotation of ideological elements has no necessary belongingness, and thus, we need to think the contingent, the non-necessary, connection between different practices – between ideology and social forces, and between different elements within ideology, and between different social groups composing a social movement. He uses the notion of articulation to break with the necessitarian and reductionist logic which has dogged the classical Marxist theory of ideology. (Hall 2019, 235)

In Hall's hands the concept of articulation is part of a framework of analysis centred on the exercise and contestation of power (grasped in Gramscian terms) that works to mark out the historical development and contingent linking of both the discursive and non-discursive elements that characterize social forms, and the relations of effectivity that underlie these articulations. But, it is arguably in the specific ways in which he genealogically develops and deploys this concept as part of his analysis of "the work racism does", that an idea of articulation distinctly his own is most apparent.

Drawing off the South African case, Hall showed that something like race had to be understood in its specific historical context, which is to say in relation to the practices that organize, transform and reproduce racial identifications as structuring dimensions of social life, and which can potentially be articulated with class or gendered relations and practices. The takeaway from this discussion is therefore an analytic practice centred on the historical formation and transformation of the "economic, political, and ideological practices" that underlie particular racialized relations and categories, and the ways these practices have been articulated with other practices within a social formation. In a context like South Africa under apartheid, race becomes a modality through which class is lived, then, because of how it comes to be linked to the process of "fracturing" and "fractioning" of economic classes, but now linked and shaped by complex processes through which hegemonic projects are constituted and challenged.

This view complicates the strategic question as much as it enriches it. As we noted, from Hall's perspective there is no necessary link between a political subject and the discourses that become linked to it. But this also implies that the character of social antagonism cannot be read off the contradictions deductively apprehended between and within the modes of production, or in the sums of the theory of exploitation. Attention to economic relations is necessary in understanding the historical constitution of forms of racism, but it is not sufficient. Social conflicts and antagonisms must, then, be analysed also in their subjective expression and as dimensions of historically contingent experiences underpinned by a multiplicity of social forms, their shifting determinations, and the struggles that arise over them.

When, in the last section of "Race, Articulation and Societies Structured in Dominance", Hall begins to draw out the political implications of this approach to the analysis of racially structured social formations, the problem that comes to be foregrounded is that of subjectivity. If the ideology of racism works through a de-historicizing gesture, producing, "as the natural and given 'authors'" of a spontaneous form of racial perception, the naturalized "racist subject", this he says has implications as well for those who must "live their relation to their real conditions of existence, and the domination of the dominant class in and through the imaginary representations of racist interpellation, and who come to experience themselves as 'the inferiors', 'les autres'" (2019, 218). And the processes through which subjects are interpellated as white or Black, superior and inferior, and so on, are themselves caught within and are reflective of "ideological class struggles".

In this context, Hall cautions against any summary dismissal of political redeployments of "racist interpellations" by dominated subjects:

> The racist interpellations can become themselves the sites and stakes of the ideological struggle, occupied and redefined to become the elementary forms of an oppositional formation – as where "white racism" is vigorously contested through the symbolic inversions of "black power". The ideologies of racism remain contradictory structures, which can function both as vehicles for the imposition of dominant ideologies and as the elementary forms for the cultures of resistance. Any attempt to delineate the politics and ideologies of racism which omit these continuing features of struggle and contradiction win an apparent adequacy of explanation only by operating a disabling reductionism. (2019)

The structuralism that seems to still inspire this perspective bends in the direction of a functionalism that retains the analytic primacy of class and an abstract model of capitalism without race.[6] Nonetheless, Hall's is an analysis that motivates for a mode of theoretical and strategic analysis attuned to the lived experience of domination and the struggle against it, and thereby potentially builds into this statement the methodological terms for unsettling such theoretical investments. Given his immersion in the literature on South Africa, it is also likely that the BC movement of the 1970s was partly what Hall had in mind when he pushes our assessments of Black anti-racist politics in this direction. But in the case of BC, as we shift from the abstract to the concrete, and from the example to the actual movement, something more than "elementary forms for a culture of resistance" are visible.

In turning to Biko's thought, as one of the key ideologues of the BCM of the 1970s, what you find is a complex analysis of the structure of social antagonisms under apartheid and a well-developed perspective on the contingency of racial interpellations, expressed through an organic political discourse. But you also find something else. In Biko, the critique of the apartheid order, and antagonistic political action, is immediately linked to a constitutive project grounded in a new non-essentialized political identity.

Biko in court

At the beginning of May in 1976 Steve Biko appeared as a witness for the defense in the South African Student Organisation/Black People's Convention (SASO/BPC) trial. The nine defendants on trial were charged under the 1967 Terrorism Act and if found guilty potentially faced the death penalty. Under this act, as proponents and popularizers of BC, they were accused of participating in a conspiracy to "transform the state by unconstitutional, revolutionary and violent means"; "to create and foster feelings of racial hostility and antipathy by the Blacks towards the white population group of the Republic" and "to discourage, hamper, deter or prevent foreign investment in the economy of the Republic" (RSA in Biko 2017, 8). Biko – as a founder member of SASO and the BPC and a key individual in synthesizing the emerging ideas of his peers – was called by the defense as something like an expert witness (that is, someone able to give the court a representation of the movement and its philosophy). His testimony over six days covered an impressively wide range of subjects, but in this essay what we want to pick out is Biko's response to the specific charge that BC promoted racial hostility as a way of getting at Biko's perspective on the constitution of antagonistic racialized subjects.

The accusation that BC and the formations that subscribed to it were in some way involved in creating and fostering "feelings of racial hostility and antipathy" towards whites was not an easy one to refute. For one, much of what SASO and BPC had to say about whites and the apartheid order was in a critical register and, in fact, was set apart for the ways it pushed beyond the norms of "acceptable" political discourse for Blacks. The state could also point to an extended list of political statements, theatre productions and poems, and even decisions in which antagonism toward whites and the political order was not only expressed, but expressed in increasingly strident terms. At the same time, neither the movement nor the individual accused were inclined to disown or attempt to mitigate their public critiques in any way. Biko's response to the charge, which he returns to more than once in his six days of testimony, is important because rather than accept the terms of the state's argument and try to disprove it, he shows that antagonism is the truth of apartheid relations.

Biko's response to the state's accusation is straightforward. "To cause racial feeling, racial hostility", he says, is what "the system does to us. You know, they constantly knock against your head so that you can respond" (Biko 2017). Antagonism towards white society is not created by BC, but it is the starting point of a discussion amongst those who call themselves Black.

Biko keeps circling back to this fact (which he expresses in many ways), but the complexity of his response to the state's case is in the extended exposition he gives of it in relation to Black experience:

> I think basically Black consciousness refers itself to the Black man and his situation, and I think the Black man is subjected to two forces in this country. He is first of all oppressed by an external world through the institutionalized machinery, through laws that restrict him from doing certain things, through heavy work conditions, through poor pay, through very difficult living conditions, through poor education – these are all external to him – and secondly, and this we regard as the most important, the Black Man in himself has developed a certain state of alienation. (2017)

The first thing to notice here is the binding of a critique of the governmental-institutional machinery (the laws and practices of exclusion; Black living conditions and the system of education) to a critique of the economic

THE SOUTH AFRICAN TRADITION OF RACIAL CAPITALISM

circumstances (work conditions, poor pay, living conditions). These are articulated as external elements of oppressions. BC is, however, also, and perhaps more acutely, centred on an "internal" manifestation of oppression as the basis of Black inaction in the face of these external forces. The alienation Biko comes to describe in this respect is not the alienation of Marx's worker, but is instead about the Black self's relation to itself mediated by the racist conception of the human.

Biko's concept of alienation thus centres a form of a rejection of the self – narrated for the court as self-negation:

> [The Black man] rejects himself, precisely because he attaches the meaning White to all that is good; in other words he associates good – and he equates good – with White. This arises out of living and it arises out of his development from childhood. When you go to school, for instance, your school is not the same as the white School, and ipso facto the conclusion you reach is that the education you get there cannot be the same as what the white kids get at school ... Now, this is part of the roots of self-negation which our kids get even as they grow up. The homes are different, the streets are different, the lighting is different, so you tend to feel that there is something incomplete in your humanity, and that completeness goes with whiteness. This carried through adulthood when the black man has got to live and work. (2017)

Although he begins in general terms, he also offers to the court more specific anecdotes – which stand out precisely as illustrative of the binding of economic and racial oppression. In fact, the first story, that of a "so-called Indian" driver, is about the character of work for Black people under apartheid, illustrating through a description of his day how this worker no longer works "in order to live", but lives "in order to work" (2017). This situation, which Biko says is (with "some variance") typical for Black workers, is articulated with the very socio-spatial character of apartheid and compounded by a work environment in which the bosses are constantly sitting on the worker "to eke out of him even the last effort in order to boost up production". But as we see in the next story, the violence meted out on Black workers is not simply about boosting production, and it takes on a gratuitous character.

We would like to quote Biko at length again here because in this anecdote he resurfaces and distills many of the themes introduced above:

> I had a man working in one of our projects in the Eastern Cape on electricity – he was installing electricity, a white man with a black assistant. He had to be above the ceiling, and the black man was under the ceiling and they were working together pushing up wires and sending the rods in which the wires are and so on, and all the time there was insult, insult, insult from the white man: push this, you – that sort of talk, and of course this touched me. I know the white man very well, he speaks very well to me, so at teatime we invite them to tea, I ask him: Why do you speak like this to this man? And he says to me in front of the guy: this is the only language he understands, he is a lazy bugger. And the black man smiled. I asked him if it was true and he

says: No, I am used to him. Then I was sick. I thought for a moment I do not understand Black society. After some two hours I come back to this guy, I said to him: Do you really mean it? The man changed, he became very bitter, he was telling me how he wants to leave any moment, but what can he do? He does not have any skills. He has got no assurance of another job – his job is to him some form of security. He has got no reserves; if he does not work today he cannot live tomorrow. He has got to work, he has got to take it. And if he has got to take it, he dare not show any form of what is called cheek to his boss. (2017)

Readers of Biko are likely to spot a recurring theme of his earlier writing, centreing a division in Black discourse. But in his 1976 testimony, what Biko emphasizes is not so much this divided discourse of the worker or even the gratuitous violence of the white boss (even if collectively these and other anecdotes show this as well-established aspects of apartheid relations). Instead Biko shows the court what sits behind the Black electrician's ambivalence and muted response. As we saw, he calls this force alienation/self-negation, which comes to be expressed in a "two faced attitude of the Black man to this whole question of existence in this country".

Black as the name of a political subject

In his presentation of a critique of apartheid South Africa – and its articulated systems for distributing racial privilege and constituting particular subjects – Biko shows the court how BC operates to establish something like a politics of "de-subjectification" in relation to apartheid racial governmental categories, but which at the same time expresses a politics of self-valorization working to articulate the term "Black" with a new order of political meaning.

During his first day of testimony, two interwoven threads are apparent. The first thread tightens with Biko narrating a series of experiences, first in NUSAS and then within SASO, in which a growing group of students begins to develop a collective identity – a sense of being a "we" – positioned in opposition to the political order, but also distinctly different in their political orientation from existing anti-apartheid formations. Alongside this account – going from his experience and critique of NUSAS's non racialism, through his detailed descriptions of the first consultative meetings of Black students, to the formal establishment of SASO and its approach to movement building – Biko describes how there developed within the emerging collective the sense that their "attitude, which constitutes BC, was a unique approach" (2017). And crucially, the testimony shifts to a more theoretical register and begins to give an account of this attitude when it turns to explain SASO's decision to reject the term "non-white" and to self-describe as a Black formation.

The political passage from the rejection of "non-white" to the affirmation of "Black" as a political identity is a foundational moment in the development of the Black consciousness movement. Reflecting on the position taken by SASO with respect to the latter term, Biko tells the court:

> [S]tudents in fact took a decision to the effect that they would no longer use the term Non-Whites, nor allow it to be used as a description of them, because they saw it as negation of their being. They were being stated as 'non something', which implied that the standard was something and they were not that particular standard. They felt that a positive view of life, which is commensurate with the build up of one's dignity and confidence, should be contained in a description which you accept, and they sought to replace the term Non-White with the term Black. (Biko 2017)

It is easy to lose sight of the nuance of Biko's deployment of the terms "white", "non-white" and "Black" as distinct *political* identities. In a 1971 essay, written as a speech for a SASO leadership school (held close to the time of the decision Biko is describing above) with the title "The Definition of Black Consciousness", he insists that "being black" was not a matter of pigmentation. This does not, however, mean that it had nothing to do with race. "We have in our policy manifesto", he says, "defined blacks as those who are by law or tradition politically, economically and socially discriminated against as a group in South African society and identifying themselves as a unit in the struggle towards the realization of their aspirations" (2015, 52). And he goes on to mark, as a matter of "paramount importance", "the interrelationship between the consciousness of the self and the emancipatory programme" (2015, 53).

There is a famous moment in the trial when the court asks Biko about the decision to self-describe as Black, motivating his question by adding "Why not brown people? I mean, you people are more brown than black". Biko's response is important for two reasons. The first is that it is an example of an attitude that rejects any essentialist racial interpellation. "In the same way" Biko shot back, "I think white people are more pink and yellow than white". The point, however, that Biko goes on to underline after the magistrate manages to quiet the laughter provoked by his response, is the crucial one:

> I think really, historically, we have been defined as Black people, and when we reject the term Non-White and take upon ourselves the right to call ourselves what we think we are, we have got available in front of us a whole number of alternatives – starting from natives to Africans to Kaffirs to Bantu to Non-Whites and so on – and we choose this one precisely because we feel it is most accommodating. (2017)

What is striking about this exchange is the way it draws attention to the historical contingency of racial interpellations, as well as of BC's mode of self-identification. This political turn is essential: Black becomes the name of a political subject, and the name that the political subject gives to itself when it rejects the structure of racial interpellations.

During the first day of cross examination, Biko was also asked about the SASO leadership school text quoted above and, specifically, the definition of non-whites found there: "If one's aspiration is Whiteness but his pigmentation makes attainment of this impossible then that person is non-white. Any man who calls a white man "baas", any man who serves in the police force or security branch is ipso facto a Non-White". Biko affirms this as SASO's position and his own:

> I must state categorically that there is no such thing as a black policeman. Any Black man who props up the system actively has lost the right to be considered part of the Black world … They are extensions of the enemy in our ranks. (2017)

In the 1970s, association with a statement like this was a scandal and when he got pressed on his response, Biko again emphasizes the political character of his usage of the term Black in BC:

> I think what you must see here as being juxtaposed in that paragraph is the political concept Black with the descriptive concept Black. Now, in our definition of a Black man … you will find that we not only refer to people who are psychologically, socially and so on oppressed, but also identify as a unit in the struggle towards realization of their aspirations. Now that is a political definition. (Biko 2017)

Notably, the strict political meaning of Black is not sustained throughout Biko's discourse, and he uses the term simply as a signifier for belonging to a group oppressed based on the colour of their skin. But in the more politically qualified sense, it was something like a class already *a class for itself*. In Biko's explanation those who call themselves Black take on this identity when they undertake to fight as part of a wider movement to oppose the forces of their oppression.

The negation of non-white (as a designation of negated being) is absolute, and BC moves to establish itself as a "positive" ontology by creating the conditions for the appropriation of Black as an affirmed identity; a *political* identity that owes nothing to the negated term. But it is not just the term "non-white" that is rejected. BC extends the work of de-subjectification to all the categories of racial interpellation that characterize the white supremacist ideology of apartheid. "So called" Indians and "coloureds" also take on the political identity, Black, when they reject the names given to them within the racial hierarchy and become part of a movement imagined as re-building the conditions of possibility for both an individual and collective expression. An important aspect of Biko's collective subject, one often overlooked in commentary on his work, is therefore its multiplicitous form. By insisting that Black was not a matter of pigmentation, not a racial designation as such, Biko avoids BC becoming "just another racial nationalism" or nativist discourse. And even where Biko acknowledges a common, so to speak, across racially oppressed groups, BC's collective subject is a one that remains a many, a one characterized by internally differentiated experiences and expressions of self, affirmed in this diversity.

Finally, and along the same lines, we should also note that in Biko's discourse the term "white" functions also as a general designation and one that is more political. In court, for instance, when Biko is pressed on SASO resolutions that characterize "whites in general" as oppressors, his response is not to try to pick out any innate characteristics on the part of white people to justify these kinds of statements. What makes whites whites, which is to say, part of an oppressor class, is not in the first place their skin but their social position: the position of privilege they have been given in the white power structure based on the colour of their skin, as well as their interpellation and participation within that structure. Biko takes seriously both the formal structure of white citizenship in apartheid's nation state and its principle of popular sovereignty:

> Generally speaking, it is White society who vote at election time, it is they who return a government into power – be it Nationalists … the United Party, the Progressive Party. And it is that government which maintains legal provisions that creates problems for Black people – problems of oppression, problems of poverty, problems of deprivation, and problems of self-alienation … It is White society as a whole. Some may vote one way, some may vote another, but all of them belong to the electoral college, if one may speak in those terms, of the whole society, which is jointly responsible for the government that does all these things, or that makes all these provisions applying to black people. And in this sense therefore they lose the natural right to speak as co-planners with us in our way of determining the future … they define themselves in other words as the enemy. (2017)

What makes whites white, then, is their participation in the benefits of the system of racial privilege and, more crucially, their participation in the sovereignty of the apartheid state.

It is important to hold on to this point, because much of the strategic framing of BC in terms of a dialectical struggle between a white and Black bloc (which is of real concern to the court) should be read in relation to Biko's perspective on white popular sovereignty under apartheid. BC establishes itself as a philosophy of liberation by telling the truth about Black experiences under apartheid, and a hard truth about the Black self, about its alienation and its division in constituting a way of life. And it tells this truth in order to provoke Black people to undertake work on the self, and in fact in order to establish a new relation of the self to itself. This begins by taking on the identity Black as a political identity. On the one hand, this leads to the development of a whole set of practices that are about infusing in the name Black, and around it, a new sense of positivity and pride. Black people and the products of the Black world are affirmed and made as sites of ongoing development as a matter of political importance (in a wide range of fields). But taking on the name, Black, will for Biko also mean taking on a combative and militant attitude towards the white power structure.

BC establishes itself by telling a truth – publicly (with all the risks entailed) – about the political order in its relationship with racial-capitalism and the systems of racial subjectification established with it. But at this level, BC is now also working at constituting an organized collective subject now explicitly positioned in antagonistic relation to this order and the political subject, whites. In the 1971 essay (quoted above) for the SASO leadership school, after giving the political definition of Black (see above), this is set down in dialectical terms:

> The overall analysis ... based on the Hegelian theory of dialectic materialism, is as follows. That since the thesis is white racism there can only be a valid antithesis i.e. a solid black unity to counterbalance the scale. If South Africa is to be a land where black and white live together in harmony without fear of group exploitation, it is only when these two opposites have interplayed and produced a viable synthesis of ideas and a modus vivendi. We can never wage a struggle without offering a strong counterpoint to white races that permeate our society so effectively. (2015)

Arguably, the dialectical frame Biko takes up in this passage is too rigid to capture the dynamic becoming of Black as a political subject. By 1976 this perspective had significantly deepened, and during the state's cross examination Biko reworks it into an account of the struggles of racially oppressed subjects as the dynamic point in the historical movement of South African society.

The idea of a Black collective subject, engaged in an antagonistic struggle with a white power bloc, was a prominent part of BC discourse all the way into the transition from apartheid (and remains a recurring point of entry into Biko's thought). For the state's case, however, it was yet another example of how BC fostered animosity towards whites and the state. In his testimony, Biko makes the surprising decision to characterize the clash between a white and Black bloc as one of bargaining. It soon becomes clear, however, that what he means by bargaining is, in fact, a set of dialectical exchanges apprehended at a high level of abstraction. Seen in more concrete terms, Biko's process of bargaining – which is always in a sense an ongoing one – will take the form of different responses of white society to acts of resistance on the part of oppressed classes to white rule and exploitation (from simple acts of refusal, through participation in formal negotiations, to explosive expressions of anger and violent revolution). In these terms Biko's process of bargaining is a theory of a social in motion – a social propelled by antagonisms and political struggles, but now grasped in relation to a theoretical imagination focussed on the dynamic development of collective subjectivity.

Conclusion

Theory is important. As Stuart Hall says, theory potentially "has direct or indirect practical consequences". No less importantly, "political circumstances" are "one of the conditions of existence of theory" (Hall 2019, 175).

Theory is important, amongst other things, because it has strategic implications. If one argues that racial antagonisms and conflicts represent expressions of a deeper economic contradiction, or that they are "superstructural phenomena" whose forms of determination must be sought in relation to the base level of production, this has implications for how one goes about organizing and struggling against racial domination, or how one makes the case for an alternative to capitalism. Equally, if one insists on the irreducible specificity and absolute autonomy of systems of racial domination, or that the latter ought to be grasped in relation to its own "principle of structuration" disconnected from any kind of economic determination, then anti-racist struggles when properly understood belong to an independent domain of political action. And then, finally, if race (and racism) is seen as the determining feature of a social formation, or if one links such to a hard-pressed and immovable ontological framework delimiting forms of political subjectivity and agency, any struggle against capitalist exploitation will appear not only as secondary (at best) but also destined to play out the contradictions of the anti-Black world.

These three positions (which schematically, and borrowing something from Hall, we are calling the economic, sociological and ontological) represent polar extremes and in our hyperbolic representation of them, are, just as obviously, open to a charge of reductionism or even theoretical banality. However, precisely in their crudeness, they open up a rudimentary way of mapping a spectrum of tensions in the ways in which theoretical perspectives on racial domination have been surfaced in contemporary mobilizations. In FMF for instance, alongside a range of competing ideological elements, expressions of the economism of the first position sat in the shadow of the ontological fatalism of the third. To be clearer, while an imprint of Marxism (expressed with varying degrees of nuance) was present in the political milieu that developed around FMF at Wits, it showed up, arguably, only at the back end of the politics of competing nationalisms, a more open politics of decolonization, and a reconfigured Black consciousness shifting in the direction of what has been self-described as an afro-pessimist perspective.

The articulation of Biko-with-Hall is productive, especially in taking us beyond such competing reductionisms. But, it is not enough. With Hall we (re)discover theoretical terms for thinking the problem of how relatively autonomous practices of domination come to be articulated in particular conjunctural contexts. With Biko, we discover a strategic modality for approaching the political problem of collective subjectivity that holds lessons for how struggles against frameworks of domination might be politically articulated in their multiplicity. Hall makes us confront the multiplicity of domination. Biko points to a way of making ourselves a multiplicity in action.

This article is just a start. Biko articulated with Hall is productive, but it is still not enough, and as we step beyond the problem space of the 1970s to our that of our present, an open series of terms will still need to articulated. Theory is important, but it will have to be remade in relation to practical demands of people in struggle. Our modest contribution for this work has been to mark out two points for a relay already getting going.

Notes

1. The term 'movement of movements' emerged in the 2000s to describe the Alter-Globalisation Movement (AGM). It captured the heterogeneous character of a movement composed of struggles and political formations that were diverse in their composition while sharing a common enemy in the form of neoliberalism.
2. For a discussion of the modalities of solidarity that emerged between workers and students at Wits during the 2015 protests, see Motimele 2019; Veriava 2019; see also Pontarelli 2019.
3. For instance, where the ANC's vision of a liberated South Africa was framed through the statement of the Freedom Charter, the BC movement organised around the alternative, and arguably more radical, Azanian People's Manifesto.
4. For example, the South African Students' Congress (SASCO), aligned to the ANC, produced T-shirts that proudly displayed the image of Biko, laying claim to his legacy alongside those icons and leaders more traditionally associated with the Congress movement, like Chris Hani.
5. Notably, in a far more ambitious return to the "subversive" movements of the 1970's, Michael Hardt has also brought together Hall's theory of articulation, with the intellectual productivity of feminist and anti-racist political movements, in developing such a double theory of articulation (forthcoming 2023). The position developed in this article emerges in conversation with this project.
6. By our reading, when Hall answers the question of the "work" that racism does, his answer appears to refer back to an abstract conception of capitalism formed in the canon of structuralist Marxism and in relation to which the particular dynamics of a specifically racialized social formation are explained.

Acknowledgements

This article was written in conversation with the contributors and editors of this special issues as well as the spaza writers collective. We are also grateful for our conversations with Asher Gamedze, Kelly Gillespie, Leigh-Ann Naidoo, Efthimios Karayian-nides, Zen Marie, Tumi Mogorosi, Tokelo Nhlapo, Tasneem Essop, Michael Hardt, Andy Clarno, Gillian Hart and the anonymous reviewers.

Disclosure statement

No potential conflict of interest was reported by the author(s).

References

Ally, N., and S. Ally. 2008. "Critical Intellectualism: The Role of Black Consciousness in Reconfiguring the Race-Class Problematic in South Africa." In *Biko Lives!*, edited by Andile Mngxitama, Amanda Alexander, and Nigel Gibson, 171–188. New York: Palgrave Macmillan.

Benjamin, W. 1968. "Theses on the Philosophy of History." In *Illuminations*, edited by Hannah Arendt, translated Harry Zohn, 253–264. New York: Schocken.

Biko, S. 2015. *I Write What I Like: Selected Writings.* Chicago: University of Chicago Press.

Biko, S. 2017. *The Testimony of Steve Biko.* Arnold, M. W. (Ed.). Johannesburg: Picador Africa.

Hall, S. 2019. "Race, Articulation and Societies Structured in Dominance." In *Stuart Hall: Essential Essays*, edited by David Morley, Vol. 1, 172–221. Durham: Duke University Press.

Laclau, E. 1977. *Politics and Ideology in Marxist Theory: Capitalism, Populism, Fascism.* London: New Left Books.

Motimele, M. 2019. "The Rupture of Neoliberal Time as the Foundation for Emancipatory Epistemologies." *South Atlantic Quarterly* 118 (1): 205–214. doi:10.1215/00382876-7281720

Naidoo, P., and A. Veriava. 2005. "Re-membering Movements: Trade Unions and New Social Movements in Neoliberal South Africa." In *from Local Processes to Global Forces, Centre for Civil Society Research Reports*, Vol 1, 27–62. Durban: University of KwaZulu-Natal.

Pontarelli, F. 2019. "Gramsci's Passive Revolution and Social Movements in South Africa, 2015-2018: The Student/Worker Rebellion and the National Union of Metalworkers." Unpublished PhD Thesis. University of Johannesburg (South Africa).

Veriava, A. 2019. "Leaving Solomon House: A(n Impressionistic) Portrait of the FMF Movement at Wits." *South Atlantic Quarterly* 118 (1): 195–204. doi:10.1215/00382876-7281708

Wolpe, H. 1972. "Capitalism and Cheap Labour-Power in South Africa: From Segregation to Apartheid1." *Economy and Society* 1 (4): 425–456. doi:10.1080/03085147200000023

Bernard Magubane on the political economy of race and class in South Africa

Bongani Nyoka [iD]

ABSTRACT
In his writings, Bernard Magubane theorizes racial capitalism but without necessarily invoking the term. Instead, he frequently refers to "the political economy of race and class" in the South African society. First, Magubane traces the roots of capitalism and racism in South Africa back to European expansionism. Second, he grapples with dispossession during the colonial period and calls it "the fact of conquest". This period was a significant prelude to apartheid capitalism and racism. Third, having analyzed these forms of domination, he argues that black people in South Africa would be liberated through the insurrection of the working people. Magubane's main contribution is his use of historical analysis to understand the next move by imperialism and its impact on the interaction of race and class and the struggle for liberation. Magubane seeks to develop a clear theoretical framework to understand the nature of the South African society. In this paper, I will attempt to illustrate Magubane's contribution to Marxist thought based on his study of South Africa's racially hierarchical political economy.

Introduction

There is currently a growing interest among social scientists in South Africa and elsewhere in the concept of racial capitalism (Ashman 2022; Phiri 2021). Less acknowledged in South African debates on race and class are radical black academics such as Bernard Magubane. Magubane's academic career spans over five decades and straddles the African and North American continents. Central to his writings are questions of national oppression, class exploitation, imperialism and racism in South Africa and other parts of the world. One of his main concerns has been the analysis of the experiences of black people in South Africa and the diaspora. Magubane's quest has been to understand the nature of oppression and exploitation of black people, and the struggles they wage to attain their freedom. Related to these concerns of his about race and class is the question of knowledge production. I argue that Magubane is a key figure to recover because some of the central questions debated today on the questions of race and class, the nature of the relationship between blacks in Africa and those in the diaspora, and the politics of knowledge production, are to be found in his early work. His broad sociohistorical approach to the growth of racial oppression and class exploitation in South Africa, and its link to the development of modern capitalism, makes Magubane a key figure to recover in current debates. In his study of any phenomenon, Magubane never loses sight of the character of the historical period that produced it. Before studying race and class, he defines that character of the said historical period. It is in understanding both the historical and contemporary elements – and not isolated incidents and episodes – that he is able to analyze the nature of race and class. For Magubane the race-class relation varies over time, and that race does different work for the capitalist economy in different historical moments. The question of race becomes more significant over time. For example, he argues that although colonialism has an ancient history, the colonialism of the last five centuries is closely associated with the birth of and consolidation of capitalism. Therefore, to study the development of capitalism is, for Magubane, the best way to study race inequality. This places socioeconomic relations at the heart of the problem, he maintains. This in turn shows how underdevelopment and racial inequality developed conterminously.

Magubane wrote on a wide variety of issues which included metacritical studies of the social sciences as social sciences as well as issues of race and class. Magubane is known for his series of essays: (i) the essays in which he Eurocentrism and coloniality in the discipline of anthropology; and (ii) those essays in which he criticizes the illegitimate regime of apartheid South Africa. Yet, he has several books which include *The Political Economy of Race and Class in South Africa, From Soweto to Uitenhage: The Political Economy of the South African Revolution, The Making of a Racist State: British Imperialism and the Union of South Africa, 1875–1910*, and *Race and the Construction of the Dispensable Other*. Magubane joined the University of Natal as a BA student in 1954. There, he met a number of African National Congress and Communist Party of South Africa underground activists. He argues that the University of Natal "was the environment in which my political consciousness and intellectual growth came into maturity" (Magubane 2010, 76). By 1961, Magubane had completed his BA(Hons) and MA degrees in sociology. He would spend the best part of his academic career as an exiled intellectual living in the United States, where he arrived in December 1961 to pursue his postgraduate studies at the University of California, Los Angeles (UCLA). He obtained his PhD in sociology in 1966 and left the US in March 1967 to teach sociology at the University of Zambia. Magubane left Zambia in

January 1970. He and his family returned to the University of California, Los Angeles on a visiting appointment. In August 1970, he took up a teaching post at the University of Connecticut in Storrs, where he taught until he retired in 1997. He returned to South Africa soon thereafter, and joined the Human Sciences Research Council (HSRC) in 1998. By the year 2000, he had left the HSRC to embark on a new project, South African Democracy Education Trust (SADET), whose goal it was to produce historical works dealing with South Africa's road to democracy.

Another of Magubane's books is *The Ties That Bind: African-American Consciousness of Africa*. This book began as a doctoral thesis, which he submitted to the Division of Social Sciences at UCLA in September 1966. Given the reputation of his doctoral dissertation committee, the sociologists Leo Kuper and John Horton, and the political scientist Charles R. Nixon, it was important for Magubane to produce a rigorous thesis. After a thorough and close reading of *The Times That Bind*, one concludes that Magubane accomplished just that. In addressing the question of African-American consciousness of Africa, Magubane set before himself a very difficult task, the outcome of which can only be said to be *sui generis* original.

In his autobiography, titled *My Life & Times*, Magubane criticizes South African neo-Marxists such as Belinda Bozzoli, Shula Marks, Stanley Trapido, Charles van Onselen and Harold Wolpe for advancing a class-centred analysis of colonialism and apartheid, at the expense of the race (Magubane 2010, 257). In this regard, he cites Jack and Ray Simons' book, *Class and Colour in South Africa, 1850-1950*, as having "impressed upon me once again the importance of understanding history and of conceptualising South African society as a totality" (Magubane 2010, 163; Simons and Simons 1969). He says he uses "'neo-' not in a disparaging or pejorative sense, but to describe an attempt to depoliticize Marxist categories. The neo-Marxist has effectively challenged the liberal orthodoxy dominant in South African history" (Magubane 1983). About the liberal historians he has this to say:

> The neo-Marxist has effectively challenged the liberal orthodoxy dominant in South African history. The weaknesses of the liberal school is four fold; it takes white settler colonialism and capitalist development as a natural order of the universe and concerns itself with studying how the poor, unfortunate peoples of the world, either adjusted or failed to adjust to the benevolent, if sometimes rough, expansion of western civilization. Second, liberal historiography is ideologically committed to the justification and preservation of the status quo. With this kind of commitment, liberal historiography has a built-in tendency to analyse South African history in terms of the virtues and vices of the English and Afrikaners. Africans intrude into their analysis as objects rather than as actors. A third aim of liberal historiography is to depoliticize history, i.e. to write it in such a way that the injustices committed against the indigenous peoples do not outrage. Liberal historians hence deprive the oppressed of lessons from the past useful for current and future struggles.

THE SOUTH AFRICAN TRADITION OF RACIAL CAPITALISM   83

Finally, race and racism are taken as the natural ideological baggage about which very little can be done. (Magubane 1983)

These are controversial remarks which warrant a close examination of Magubane's contribution to South African social and political thought. Although Magubane and fellow South African Marxists wrote on the question of race and class in South Africa, his work was hardly engaged either by his contemporaries or subsequent social scientists interested in these issues. In the book *Race, Class and Power: Harold Wolpe and the Radical Critique of Apartheid*, the South African political theorist Steven Friedman discusses in great detail the debates around race and class in South Africa (Friedman 2015). Tellingly, in the scholars whose works he discusses, Magubane's work is nowhere to be found. This has less to do with Friedman but more to do with the fact that Magubane's work was then, as it is now, largely ignored.

The making of race and class in South Africa

Cedric J. Robinson, whose usage of the term racial capitalism has come to represent the current standard, is not in fact the inventor of the term (Robinson 2000). South African intellectuals, Martin Legassick and David Hemson use the term as early as 1976 in a pamphlet entitled *Foreign Investment and the Reproduction of Racial Capitalism in South Africa* (Legassick and Hemson 1976). I should note that, in talking about racial capitalism, I understand the African American political theorist, Robinson, to mean that capitalism grew out of a Western society that was already immersed in racialism. Violence and slavery were central to European capitalism and imperialism primarily because racialism had already permeated feudal Europe. This position comes closer to the view that racism and capitalism co-constitute one another. For Legassick and Hemson, racism in South Africa developed historically from the changing nature of regimes of capital accumulation and how the South African state responded to these regimes of capital accumulation. In this regard, they argued that the discovery of gold in South Africa in the nineteenth-century, the early twentieth-century industrialization, and attempts at securing multinational investment capital during the apartheid period, meant that settler colonial racism was reorganized. Legassick and Hemson argue that,

> The creation of contemporary forms of racist ideology and the political forms of racial discrimination in South Africa ... was a consequence of capitalist development. From the beginnings of capitalist development, the masses of South Africa were involved in various forms of struggle against racism or capitalism. (Legassick and Hemson 1976, 1)

Elsewhere, Legassick notes, "The colonists became *dependent* on the role of the state in enforcing the race/class order: the state became 'the central institution upon which their colonial identity ultimately rested'" (Legassick 1993, emphasis in original). For Magubane, capitalism seems to require racism to sustain itself. Analytically, this seems like a functional explanation insofar as consequences are used to explain causes. In his critique of British imperialism, Magubane refers to Ireland and argues that it could legitimately be called the first colony of England. He says to understand British imperialism one must grapple with this "Irish Question".

Magubane notes in *The Making of a Racist State* that capitalism affected workers of all races. In this regard, there develops solidarity among the workers. But the ultimate goal for black workers would be live in a society where they are not judged by the colour of their skin. Magubane observes that:

> Africans in South Africa are an historically conquered and enslaved population kept in a subject state by the instrument of violence and by a system of vicious law and terror. The white ruling class imposes very severe constraints on Africans' aspirations for freedom. They try to determine what and how much Africans know. The powerless Africans are then exploited to enrich their conquerors. They perpetuate African enslavement, the ruling interests consistently wage psychological warfare against their heroes in order to disarm and destroy any independent national will among black people. The rulers first made Africans landless vagrants in their own country. They destroyed the best in their historical traditions and perverted the rest of their institutions to serve the purposes of alienation. By daily acts of dehumanization, an attempt is made to reduce them into a spiritually barren nation of slaves, thieves, murderers, dope addicts, and rapists. That is, a conscious effort is made to reduce them into literal monads. (Magubane 1989, 5–6)

In this regard, Magubane argues, there develops class and race consciousness on the part of the black workers. This class and race consciousness is a direct outcome of class exploitation and racial oppression. To add to this, Magubane argues that the formation of the Union of South Africa not only safeguarded white colonial interests, but also excluded blacks based on racial theories developed in the United Stated of America. Hard and low waged jobs in the mining sector were reserved for black work, while white workers were given better paying and less demanding jobs (Magubane 1996). The appalling working conditions in South Africa resembled the forced labour conditions in North America and the Caribbean. This was the lived experience of black workers both in South Africa and across the Atlantic.

What is important about Magubane's work is that he identifies similarities between Africans living in Africa and those who live in other parts of the world. The capitalist exploitation and racial oppression of black people everywhere had similar underpinnings. This led to a situation wherein whites considered themselves superior to blacks. White workers could choose the types of jobs they wanted but black workers could not. Magubane finds that the only time when white workers could not freely sell their labour was during the time of the indentured Irish. The inverse of white workers freely their labour was that they were sometimes amenable to the capitalist class. Magubane traces this racial affinity. Although the Irish had similar experiences to blacks, they were still white and could therefore enjoyed certain benefits. Unlike the Irish, not only were black people could not acquire property but were instead treated like property. But this is no more a paradox than a farmer who considers himself superior to his plough bull but depends, none-theless, on the bull for his "wealth." Essential to the logic of slavery is the idea that enslaved peoples are properties.

Magubane generally tends to adopt two lines of theoretical approach. The first is politico-historical: how did the unique political configuration emerge in South Africa? The second is sociological: how does the political economy of race and class in South Africa affect black people? Magubane needs theory as a guide, but at the same time he is not reductionist or mechanistic in his approach. His approach is that of sensitivity to context and historical specificity. This approach is not unique to Magubane. In *The Communist Manifesto*, Marx and Engels ([1848] 2008) rebuke German philosophers of the eighteenth century for their mechanist application and importation of French texts into the German society. Marx and Engels argue that while the French writings moved from France to Germany, the French social conditions did not move to Germany along with the said writings.

Although Magubane was a self-declared Marxist he nevertheless avoided being dogmatic about his Marxism. For Magubane class is not the primary contradiction in South African liberation struggles. He argues that South Africa cannot be understood without taking seriously the concept of race. He argues that racism is the primary contradiction in South African liberation struggles. Significantly, although he re-centred the concept of race, he does not discard the class category but points out that the two are mutually-rein-forcing. In spite of taking seriously the existence of race as a social construc-tion, Magubane is not a black nationalist. He seems to have had an uneasy relationship and contradictory relationship with black nationalism. He is sym-pathetic to Marcus Garvey and Garveyism, as can be seen in his book, *The Ties that Bind* (Magubane 1987a). For Magubane, change has to be driven by a mass movement. He sees Garveyism as having enjoyed a mass appeal in the African American society. Yet, in *The Political Economy of Race and Class in South Africa*, he portrays the Pan-Africanist Congress of South Africa as not only reactionary, but also opportunist. Epistemologically, Magubane refused to be tyrannized by concepts with universalistic pretensions. This is his attempt to show that taking seriously one's existential position yields deeper insights than merely superimposing theory to societal problems. Yet, in taking this approach Magubane is not an empiricist. According to him, studying facts cannot be limited to the level of description. The real meaning of facts lies in explaining them. The essence of facts has to be disclosed through theory. For Magubane, theory enables one "to see the overall picture of the process, and the interconnection of the facts engendered by this process" (Magubane 1973).

What is clear from the revolutionary writings of Bernard Magubane is that he believed that, given the political turmoil of the 1970s and 1980s, South Africa would be liberated through the insurrection of the working people. It is clear from his autobiography, *My Life & Times*, as well as his collection of essays, *From Soweto to Uitenhage*, that politically he had allied himself with the African National Congress (ANC). This is partly why he endorsed completely the idea that South Africa was a case of "colonialism of a special type" or a case of "internal colonialism". Magubane's proximity to the ANC came with its own theoretical limitations in the sense that he had no critique of both the colonialism of a special type thesis or the negotiated settlement, even though he had earlier argued that South Africa would be liberated through an armed struggle. It needs to be said, however, that the idea Magubane was not critical of ANC policies may fall into the narrative of the "betrayal of the revolution" that prevails within a younger generation of black intellectuals in South Africa, but one that understates that circumstances under which the transition took place. First, the texts of the second edition of the book were finalized before 11 February 1990, when Nelson Mandela was released from prison, much less the formal start of the negotiation. Second, embedded in the claims is the neglect of how inauspicious the circumstances were (international and local) for a socialist transformation in South Africa. This is apart from the tendency to treat the liberation movement as a monolith rather than a contested terrain of ideas and objectives. Finally, the point that Magubane makes is more about (a) the indeterminacy of the outcome of the negotiation that would follow the unbanning of the ANC and other liberation movements and (b) the acknowledgement of the ANC as the pre-eminent liberation movement, ideationally and organizationally, as a fait accompli.

Some of Magubane's contemporaries, such as Archie Mafeje were critical of the path chosen by the ANC and the South African Communist Party. For example, Mafeje asks, in the context of the alliance between the SACP and the ANC: "after the 'negotiated settlement' where will the communists and their celebrated program be? In jail or in the new bourgeois government"? (Magubane 1973, 83) In *From Soweto to Uitenhage*, Magubane defends colonialism of a special type against Marxists such as Alex Callinicos and Mafeje:

> Contrary to the shallow misrepresentation and disingenuous attempts by Callinicos and Mafeje to discredit the theory of internal colonialism at the time it was formulated, the SACP and the ANC had no coherent theory on the character of black oppression, and no comprehensive strategy for intervention and leadership in the struggle for national liberation and social emancipation. The great

THE SOUTH AFRICAN TRADITION OF RACIAL CAPITALISM   87

contribution of the Comintern Thesis on the national question, in 1928 and 1930, was that for the first time Communists and later nationalists confronted the specific nature of the South African state and broke with the liquidationist approach that had denied the fact that the African people in South Africa were subject to a form of oppression distinct from that of white class exploitation and oppression. Specifically, the theses recognised that black exploitation was a particular oppression and exploitation which required a comprehensive theoretical and historical analysis in its own right, and a special political strategy and programme to overthrow it. Specifically, the theses highlighted the fact that the struggle against white minority rule, was also a struggle against imperialism and a key to the struggle against for social emancipation in South Africa. (Magubane 1989, 203–204)

Yet, if South Africa was a case of colonialism of a special type, even Bantustan leaders would be justified in seeking independence from the apartheid state. Elimination of apartheid was not the only the solution. There needed to be an abolition of not only racial oppression, but also of imperialism and capitalism in South Africa and elsewhere. For Mafeje, apartheid South Africa was as a case of "*racial oppression* in an age of capitalism or imperialism" (Mafeje 1986, emphasis in original).

Magubane sees race as a biological category which under capitalist conditions is "articulated with class" (1987b). The idea that race is biological is one that Magubane later rejects. According to him, "any study of class and race must begin with the writings of W.E.B. Du Bois" (Magubane 1996, 5). He embraced Du Bois' position in *Dusk of Dawn* that "the black man is a person who must ride 'Jim Crow' in Georgia" ([1940] 2007, 77). By which he meant that race is not a matter of biology or even identity but often a matter of forced or forcible identification. In *Race and the Construction of the Dispensable Other*, Magubane points out that the race theory of the colonizing bourgeoisie became the ruling ideology by shedding the "overtly feudal trappings" and relied on the latest philosophical and scientific thinking. This pseudo-scientific view on race reflected the changing class character of the "regime of accumulation" as well as the fact that Europe had instituted a new civilization that was based on five hundred years of chattel African slavery. It is for this reason that Magubane argues that "one cannot talk about the vicious legacy of white supremacy without talking about the obscene economic inequalities on which it was built" (Magubane 2007, 30).

For Magubane, anti-black racism and white supremacy are not mere discourses, but practices that produce a prejudiced knowledge of blacks. This is what makes domination, exploitation and having an authority on blacks seem natural. Thus, Magubane examines racism and white supremacy historically in at least two ways:

(1) *genealogically*, in order that their provenance, their kinship and assent, their affiliation both with other ideas and with political institutions may be

demonstrated, (2) as practical *accumulation* (of power, land, ideological legitimacy) and negation of others, and their ideas of legitimacy. (Magubane 2001, 4, emphasis in original)

He goes on to argue that whilst racism cannot simply be correlated with material exploitation, it nonetheless produces forms of knowledge that justify the degradation of blacks. Racism, according to Magubane, serves to define the superior at the same time that it serves to regulate the inferior. Ultimately, racism, according to Magubane, is about inhumane social practices, exploitation and oppressive relations that brutalize, degrade and reduce blacks to less than human status.

Class, he argues, is about social relations which shaped by the way the means of production are distributed. In South Africa and the United States, the ruling class not only creates but also polarizes classes and races. This means that the ruling class creates conditions which enable inequality along racial lines. Thus, while black people in South Africa and the United States are largely members of the working class, they are also members of a particular race. They "cannot *disown* or *remove* their color" (Magubane 2007, 37, emphasis in original). "Racism *forces* them to remain as built-in scapegoats onto whom the burdens and contradictions of capitalism can be shifted" (Magubane 2007, 37, emphasis in original). In this sense, capitalism requires racism to survive, but racism does not birth capitalism. In *Race and the Construction of the Dispensable Other*, Magubane observes that:

> ... all human actions, beliefs and ideologies are purposeful and have some material basis. When the capitalist mode of production emerged from the womb of feudalism, it let loose the unprecedent, rapacious forces of greed that lie at the root of the enslavement of Africans and the slave trade. Those who went to Africa to capture Africans, transport them across the oceans and sell them into slavery, did not do so because Africans were 'black' or had facial features that were 'closer to those of apes', but because Africans, like all human beings, had the capacity to supply labor. The spirit of capitalism, as Weber called it, and the crisis of feudalism, drove Europeans to the four corners of the world. (Magubane 2007, 4)

For Magubane, it is difficult to accept class analysis as the only explanation of the South African society. As such, understanding the genealogy of racial inequality is not a mere academic exercise. This is so because without a sound understanding of the history of racism, one is unlikely to find solutions or strategies to combat it (Magubane 1979). For Magubane, apartheid South Africa must be understood as intrinsically linked to the history of white settlement in southern Africa. Moreover, apartheid was characteristic of a stage in the history of world capitalism. Thus, in order to analyze racial inequality and exploitation in South Africa, one must understand its historical roots. Important to note is the fact that inequality of income and wealth is not simply an economic issue but also "implies inequality of life chances" (Magubane 1979). As such, Magubane argued that, conceptually, racial inequality in South Africa must be understood as an aspect of imperialism and colonialism: the economic, political and cultural domination of black people by a white settler minority. He proposed to "use the term imperialism to refer to the specific relation between a subjugated society and its alien rulers, and colonialism to refer to the social structures created within the colonized society by imperialist relationships" (Magubane 1979, 3).

Magubane conceived of the South African problematic as that of intertwined struggle against racial and class domination. He argued that to study capitalism, and its development, was the best way to study "race inequality" because to do so was to place socio-economic relations at the centre of the problem and thus show how "underdevelopment" and "racial inequality" developed concurrently. For Magubane, the "ideology of racism" was fueled by expansionist and exploitative socioeconomic relations of capitalist imperialism. As a result, it became the primary motive for shaping and maintaining "unequal and exploitative relations of production along racial lines" (Magubane 1979). "The seemingly 'autonomous' existence of racism today does not lessen the fact that it was initiated by the needs of capitalist development or that these needs remain the dominant factor in racist societies" (Magubane 1979, 3). He was stressing the fact that, race and racism were not just epiphenomena or historical variables under apartheid but were central to its continuation. Magubane goes on to say:

> The political history of South Africa in the decade prior to the formation of the Union demonstrates quite clearly that 'race', while remaining a biological category, under exploitative conditions becomes a social category and an important element in the functioning of the socioeconomic formation. The structures of inequality in South Africa were the creation of people who systematically and deliberately fashioned conditions to separate blacks from whites in order to exploit the former. (Magubane 1979, 12)

Thus in the 1980s, while commenting on the nature or character of liberation, he had this to say:

> It is impossible to prophesy the duration of the coming struggle and revolution. But one thing seems quite obvious: victory will be achieved by the insurgent action of the working masses synchronized and complemented by the guerrilla army of the ANC and its allies. The African working class is being driven by the internal developments of the capitalist economy and white rule toward one realization: only the takeover of state power and a complete reorganization of society can alleviate their miserable lot. (Magubane 1989, 3)

The transition period and the road to liberation

For Magubane, imperialism is not only the colonialistic driving force, but also the engine of capitalism. Imperialism is the global system of national exploitation and oppression of the working peoples of the Global South by the ruling classes of the North. Hence anti-imperialism is as important as anti-capitalism and antiracism in South Africa. Anti-capitalism and anti-racism are meaningless if they are not based on anti-imperialism. The roots of racism are socio-economic and historical and therefore require an all-embracing anti-imperialist and anti-racist programme.

Indeed, the struggle in South Africa continued and the ANC took over through a popular vote which was preceded by negotiations, and not, as Magubane envisaged, an insurgent action. Further, we are yet to witness a "complete reorganization" of society which was said to alleviate the misery of the black majority. In the light of Magubane's unrealized projection, empirical questions about why the touted "insurgent action" never occurred immediately come to mind. Why did the revolutionary situation of the 1980s not lead to a revolution proper? The archive abounds with answers to this question. One reason, however, is easily seen: the ANC, which was arguably the biggest organization within the liberation movement, opted for a negotiated settlement with the apartheid government. The question then is why did the ANC opt to negotiate? The prevailing circumstances, among which include the fact that the apartheid regime was not militarily defeated on the battlefield; the changes in the international environment for emancipatory projects globally; and that the liberation movements and ANC, in particular, had arraigned against it not only the apartheid regime but several of the homeland regimes. The bloodiest encounters were in the killing fields of KwaZulu in the late 1980s and the 1990s, with the Inkatha Freedom Party as a driving force for the murderous violence in KwaZulu and Transvaal areas.

In an essay written in 1994, but published in 1995, "Reflections on the Confronting Facing Post-Apartheid South Africa", where Magubane writes about the transition period, he has this to say:

> [The] events that led to the collapse of apartheid in South Africa were disconcerting, even disappointing to some people. Apartheid, after bitter struggles, collapsed in a peculiarly quiet fashion. No grand, bold symbols of the old order marked its downfall. This makes it all the more easy for some people to underestimate what has happened ... Who could have imagined in February 1990, that the release of Mr. Mandela from life imprisonment, heralded at the same time the beginning of the end of white domination, that its architects had vowed would last forever? Or that de Klerk, instead of being reduced to irrelevancy like Ian Smith in Zimbabwe, would emerge as one of the vice presidents in a "new South Africa"? And that Buthelezi, whose movement has been embroiled in the savage carnage of the last ten years, would end up as a cabinet member of the Government of National Unity (GNU)? And, indeed,

THE SOUTH AFRICAN TRADITION OF RACIAL CAPITALISM 91

> that the white chief of the army and the minister of finance would retain their jobs? All this was part of the formula crafted under the power-sharing scheme as a five-year expedient to heal the bitter wounds of apartheid and reassure the whites that they have a future in a democratic South Africa. (Magubane 1995, 2)

From this, the question needs to be asked: has white domination in South Africa really ended? Indeed, the ANC itself would not now, some 28 years into democratic dispensation, continue to speak of a "second transition" to liberation without at least implicitly acknowledging its mistakes in the lead up to 1994. Magubane was impressed with the negotiated settlement and the subsequent GNU, in that he continues to say:

> It was a remarkable achievement when the ANC and the NP, bitter antagonists for decades, sought, and in the end found common ground whereby the white minority through power sharing found a face-saving way to negotiate its sur-render of power. It is still possible for many people to think of what happened in South Africa on May 10 as a temporal and reversible change. In the tedious negotiations that seemed to go on endlessly South Africans defied the logic of their past, and broke all the rules of political theory, to forge a powerful spirit of unity from a shattered nation. One cannot help but ponder history's ironies: of how we fight battles, and how, even if we win, things do not go the way we had hoped. That is, we do not get all that we fought for. We are, indeed, reminded once again of Marx's words who wrote in *The Brumaire of Louis Bonaparte* that: Men make their history, but they do not make it just as they please; they do not make it under circumstances chosen by themselves, but under circumstances directly encountered, given and transmitted from the past (Marx 1972, 120). The crucial question now is: Will the current paradox become a major contradic-tion in the months and years ahead? … Does it mean as some have already con-cluded that the ANC which heads the Government of National Unity (GNU) has made compromises that are tantamount to a "sell-out"? … The time separating the formal end of apartheid and the emergence of a democratic society in South Africa is simply too short for any judgment to be made. (Magubane 1995, 2)

The foregoing quote seems to me out of sync with Magubane's insurrec-tional writings of the 1970s and 1980s which were published at the height of the South African struggle for liberation. Indeed, certain of the questions he asks have been answered. Many have gone so far as to accuse the ANC of dis-playing arrogance in dealing with ordinary black South Africans. What we have seen, in the main, is an increase in inequality and the gap between the rich and the black majority. The promised "reorganization" of wealth for the benefit of the poor has not yet materialized. Instead, what we have witnessed is the realization of Fanon's warning that:

> The national middle class which takes over power at the end of the colonial regime is an under-developed middle class. It has practically no economic power, and in any case, it is in no way commensurate with the bourgeoisie of the mother country which it hopes to replace. In its willful narcissism, the national middle class is easily convinced that it can advantageously replace

the middle class of the mother country. But that same independence which literally drives it into a comer will give rise within its ranks to catastrophic reactions … . (Fanon [1961] 2001, 119–120)

I turn to Fanon because Magubane never really theorized post-1994 South Africa. And his analysis of the transition period seems to me sketchy. Indeed, the bulk of the work he wrote post-1994 is concerned primarily with rewriting South African historiography. Importantly, Magubane was heavily influenced by Fanon as I mention in the introduction. In *My Life & Times*, he states that *The Wretched of the Earth* "seemed to answer many questions that were swelling my mind" (Magubane 2010, 169). Having been influenced by Fanon's book, Magubane observes that after independence Africans in Zambia were in office but not in power. They were running the economy only in theory. Magubane's argument about Zambia could be extended to post-1994 South Africa under the leadership of the ANC. Although black people are not only in the majority in South Africa, but also lead the present-day government through the ANC, they continue to bear the full brunt of racism and capitalism. In the South African context, Mafeje argues that white people have no problem with not being in government, but they still enjoy the benefits of dominating blacks economically and ideationally (Mafeje 1998).

The current situation in South Africa resembles precisely what Fanon argues above. Although the ANC government has been able to provide low-cost housing, social grants and pension payouts, the educational system and the healthcare system are still abysmal. Fundamentally, issues such as land expropriation and reorganization of the economy for the benefit of the majority are still elusive. Again, Fanon's words are instructive in this regard:

In an under-developed country an authentic national middle class ought to consider as its bounden duty to betray the calling fate has marked out for it, and to put itself to school with the people: in other words to put at the people's disposal the intellectual and technical capital that it has snatched when going through the colonial universities. But unhappily we shall see that very often the national middle class does not follow this heroic, positive, fruitful and just path; rather, it disappears with its soul set at peace into the shocking ways – shocking because anti-national – of a traditional bourgeoisie, of a bourgeoisie which is stupidly, contemptibly, cynically bourgeois. The objective of nationalist parties as from a certain given period is, we have seen, strictly national. They mobilize the people with slogans of independence, and for the rest leave it to future events. (Mafeje 1998, 120–121)

Rather than "betraying" the "calling fate has marked out" for them, or "committing class suicide" as Cabral suggested, the ANC has opted to mimic their white predecessors. Further, against Fanon's warning above, they continue to mobilize people with slogans only during election time. In the intervening periods, everything continues as normal. Many a despondent and radical black youth have accused the ANC of selling out. It is necessary at this point to revisit Magubane's earlier writings to see what lessons we may learn and what opportunities we have missed.

Having said the above, to understand Magubane's analysis, one ought to take seriously what he called "the historical context/perspective". For him, present problems cannot be understood outside of the history and context which informs them. Apartheid, for example, could not be understood outside of the history of colonialism and slavery. As such, settler colonialism in North America and in South Africa differs slightly from other colonies in that, in these regions, it was not simply a question of class structure with a wealthy elite at the top and poverty-stricken natives at the bottom. Such socio-economic structures abound and the world is full of examples. In the main, settler colonialism in the two regions was further characterized by race or the question of colour (Magubane 1987b). Thus, for settler colonialism to be effective, colonists had to buttress their ill-gotten gains through racism. Here Magubane makes a preliminary distinction between racism and capitalism. He calls this twin evil project of settler colonialism "the fact of conquest" (Magubane 1987b, 9). This conquest, for Magubane, was a prelude to the totalitarian (apartheid) state. To drive his point home, Magubane argues:

> race and racism are not simply an expression of, nor a means for, guaranteeing the bourgeoisie's political dominance; in North America and South Africa discrimination has always had the full sanction of the monopolistic bourgeoisie. Jobs and investment opportunities could be denied to blacks, wages could be depressed below prevailing levels, and the white workers could enjoy substantial material rewards. The aim racism was to justify the very unequal incomes of classes *cum* races, to convince blacks that their wages reflected of their inferiority to whites and vice-versa. (Magubane 1987b, 21, emphasis in original)

For Magubane, in order to understand the genesis of apartheid, and black people's response to it, one ought to begin with the 1910 proclamation of independence. Magubane observes:

> The Union of South Africa was proclaimed an 'independent' White Dominion in the British Empire on 31 May 1910, the seventh anniversary of the signing of the 'Treaty of Vereeniging'. The African people paid a high political price when Britain decided to make South Africa an exclusive 'white dominion'. The Union of South Africa as it was constituted in 1910, was described by Lord Olivier as a slave state. The formation of the ANC in 1912 was an African response to one of the most unconscionable political betrayals of a people by a colonial power that prided itself as a paragon of virtue and mother of parliamentary democracy. (Magubane 1995, 4)

This crystallization of colonialism which had been at work in South Africa since the arrival of colonialists was the turning point in South African history.

Notwithstanding the implications of the 1910 declaration on black people in South Africa, few have sought to give it thorough historical and sociological treatment. Magubane argues:

> However, the revolutionary ideologies that have envisaged such a change are unable to take into their perspective the nature of his [colonized person] particular oppression and its implications for revolutionary strategy. This has been true even of white radicals who maintain that color oppression is no more than an aspect of class oppression, that color discrimination is only another aspect of working-class exploitation, and that the capitalist system is the common enemy of the white worker and black worker alike ... It is difficult to accept the class analysis *per se* in South Africa. An abstract class analysis not only liquidates the national question, but it ignores critical differences in the exploitation of black and of white workers which are due specifically to racism. What white Marxists often fail to grasp is that the African first suffered under slave trade and secondly under colonial exploitation. Under these forms of exploitation and oppression black peoples' suffering in Africa and the diaspora was total and devastating. With the emergence of so-called scientific racism, their exploitation became so systematic in its devastation as to make mockery of white working-class exploitation. Indeed, the exploitation and oppression based on race required constituting the African not only as the *Other* but as a species of *animal*. (Magubane 1996, 3–4, emphasis in original)

Not only must the struggle in South Africa be understood in its historical context, it must moreover be understood in the continental and global context. Oppression of the people of South Africa could not be understood outside of the context of oppression of black people in southern Africa, Africa and the African diaspora. There is no space to give this important issue its full treatment. The point, however, is that one has to be mindful of its relevance. Important as the 1910 catastrophe, are the events of the 1970s, particularly the 1976 student uprising. In this regard, Magubane argues: "June 16, 1976 was a turning point in the class struggle by the oppressed in South Africa. Developments that seemed only long-term possibilities became realities as a result of the events initiated by unarmed students of Soweto ... " (Magubane 1989, 41) Magubane continues:

> Thus with Soweto and its aftermath, the struggle of the black people for their liberation reached unprecedented heights. Never in the history of South Africa have so many millions engaged in open and 'armed' confrontation with the forces of ruling class oppression. The urban rebellion represents the most advanced aspect of class struggle in the history of South Africa. The students and workers have hit the South African ruling class and its international allies (where it matters most – in their pockets) as have no other events in recent history. (Magubane 1989, 42)

Magubane attributes this turn of events to the Black Consciousness Movement (BCM), comprising mainly the black youth in the townships, who had filled the political vacuum in South Africa following the banning of all

THE SOUTH AFRICAN TRADITION OF RACIAL CAPITALISM   95

liberation movements. Due to the BCM, the youth of all oppressed groups saw themselves, for the first time in South African history, as not only fighting the struggle for liberation but also as intrinsically belonging to the same race – black. Thus, Africans, Coloureds and Indians were self-referentially black. This racial solidarity among the oppressed groups put enormous amount of pressure on the apartheid government in that the ploy to divide and rule them proved unsustainable. Indeed, the apartheid regime grew increasingly isolated internationally. Internally, due to the formation of the United Democratic Front and the Congress of South African Trade Unions (COSATU), in the 1980s, South African townships were increasingly ungovernable, the youth became militant and the economy was plummeting. This constituted what Magubane called, following Lenin, a "revolutionary situation" – "a nation-wide crisis which affects both exploiters and the exploited" (Magubane 1989, 43). Not quite a revolution, but a revolutionary situation. Reading Lenin's (1920) text, *The Collapse of the Second International*, Magubane argues that a revolutionary situation is characterized by "three major symptoms": (i) it becomes impossible for the ruling class to maintain their rule without changes. So that not only does the working class refuse to live in the old way, it is also necessary that the ruling class be unable to live in the old way; (ii) the suffering and want of the oppressed grows more acute than usual; and (iii) as a result of the above, there is considerable increase in the political activity of the working people and thus taking matters in their own hands (Magubane 1989).

In concrete terms, or in the South African case, the revolutionary situation of the 1980s was marked by (i) an increasing attack on and bombing of strategic state entities; (ii) an increasing industrial action; (iii) an increasing unionization of the workforce which ultimately led to the formation of a trade union federation – COSATU; (iv) increasing waves of school boycotts (v) increasing arrests and police brutality and (vi) mounting pressure on the apartheid government internationally. While the said revolutionary situation is not in and of itself a revolution, for Magubane, the South African revolution was to be an armed revolution. That, of course, never took place.

In the late 1980s, Magubane had forcefully argued that: "the objective social situation in South Africa makes it impossible to struggle for democracy without also fighting against capitalism and advancing towards socialism" (Magubane 1987c). In the early 2000s, he notes that "until the labor market is democratized, South Africa's newly won freedoms will remain a chimera" (Magubane 2000). Moreover, "under capitalism, democracy is always restricted to the political domain, while economic management is held hostage to non-democratic, private ownership of the means of production. Such a democracy is incomplete … " (Magubane 2000, 77) I agree with Archie Mafeje when he says material conditions in South Africa may be ripe for a socialist revolution, but what is missing are "committed agents" to advance it (1997).

Concluding remarks

From an ontological as well as historical point of view, Magubane sought to demonstrate, for example, that the 1910 settlement of the Union of South Africa was not the starting point of South African history, but fundamentally a catastrophe for the indigenous populations. He made this point insistently and argued that to understand South Africa, we need to go beyond the colonial encounter because Africans are a people with histories, philosophies and knowledge systems which existed long before colonialism. Ultimately, Magubane's *oeuvre* draws inspiration from the ordinary people whose knowledge systems he seeks to explicate. In learning from the insights of the ordinary people, Magubane is able to interrogate universalistic tendencies of dominant theories of his time. In this way, it could be said that in his own way Magubane set out to shift dominant paradigms.

Magubane's work on race and class is concerned primarily with the ways in which blacks came to be enslaved, degraded and inferiorized. He does this by studying not only the nature of slavery, colonialism, imperialism and apartheid, but also by studying the ideologies and theories that undergird these forms of oppression and exploitation. Thus, whilst critiquing those who were at the forefront of these systems of oppression and exploitation, he also critiques theorists and ideologues who perpetuated these systems through their writings. Although Magubane draws inspiration from the Western canon and classical theorists such as Marx and Engels, he is not content with regurgitating their ideas in studying South African conditions. In this regard, Magubane's work is not only an interrogation of the ideologies of Western thought and social sciences, but also a study of the historical opposition between Africa and the West as well as blacks and whites. Magubane's work demystifies much of the obscurantism embedded in the social sciences and he demonstrates that colonialism, imperialism and apartheid were brutal systems which dehumanized blacks. For him, the end of white supremacy is the beginning of the process of black liberation. It is the dialectic between white supremacy and black liberation that Magubane's scholarship seeks to understand. In this paper, I sought to demonstrate that central to his writings are questions of national oppression, class exploitation, imperialism and racism in South Africa and other parts of the world. I sought to show that one of Magubane's main concerns has been the analysis of the experiences of black people in South Africa and the diaspora. Magubane's search to understand the nature of oppression and exploitation of black people, and the struggles they wage to attain their freedom, remains relevant to current debates. I sought to demonstrate that some of the central questions debated today on the questions of race and class, the nature of the relationship between blacks in Africa and those in the diaspora, and the politics of knowledge production and representation, have always been central to Magubane's writings. For me, the relevance of Magubane's work for ongoing debates consists in its call for a greater need for a clear theoretical framework in order to understand the complexity racism and capitalism. While mindful of imperialism and racism in other part of the world, Magubane understood that there is no one-size-fits-all approach to understanding racism and capitalism because this involves due regard to local variations.

Disclosure statement

No potential conflict of interest was reported by the author(s).

Funding

This work was supported by Andrew W. Mellon Foundation Turning the Tide: Early Career Scholars in the Humanities through Rhodes University.

ORCID

Bongani Nyoka (iD) http://orcid.org/0000-0002-8478-8725

References

Ashman, S. 2022. "Racial Capitalism and South Africa's Changing Race-Class Articulations." *New Agenda: South African Journal of Social and Economic Policy* 84: 29–35. https://journals.co.za/doi/epdf/10.10520/ejc-nagenda_v2022_n84_a8.

Du Bois, W. E. B. [1940] 2007. *Dusk of Dawn: An Essay Toward an Autobiography of a Race Concept*. Oxford: Oxford University Press.

Fanon, F. [1961] 2001. *The Wretched of the Earth*. London: Penguin Books.

Friedman, S. 2015. *Race, Class and Power: Harold Wolpe and the Radical Critique of Apartheid*. Pietermaritzburg: UKZN Press.

Legassick, M. 1993. "The State, Racism and the Rise of Capitalism in the Nineteenth-Century Cape Colony". *South African Historical Journal* 28 (1): 329–368. doi:10.1080/02582479308671985

Legassick, M., and D. Hemson. 1976. *Foreign Investment and the Reproduction of Racial Capitalism in South Africa*. London: Anti-Apartheid Movement.

Lenin, V. I. 1920. *The Collapse of the Second International*. Glasgow: The Socialist Labour Press.

Mafeje, A. 1986. "South Africa: The Dynamics of a Beleaguered State." *African Journal of Political Economy* 1 (1): 95–119.

Mafeje, A. 1997. *The National Question in Southern African Settler Societies*. Harare: SAPES Monograph Series No.6.

Mafeje, A. 1998. "White Liberals and Black Nationalists: Strange Bedfellows." *Southern Africa Political Economy Monthly* 11 (13): 45–48.

Magubane, B. 1973. "The 'Xhosa' in Town, Revisited Urban Social Anthropology: A Failure of Method and Theory." *American Anthropologist* 75 (5): 1701–1715. doi:10.1525/aa.1973.75.5.02a00310

Magubane, B. 1979. *The Political Economy of Race and Class in South Africa*. 1st ed. New York, NY: Monthly Review Press.

Magubane, B. 1983. "Nguni History Revisited." *Canadian Journal of African Studies* 17 (3): 539–543. doi:10.1080/00083968.1983.10804034.

Magubane, B. 1987a. *The Ties That Bind: African-American Consciousness of Africa*. Trenton, NJ: Africa World Press.

Magubane, B. 1987b. "Race and Class Revisited: The Case of the North America and South Africa." *Africa Development* 12 (1): 5–40. doi:10.57054/ad.v12i1.3054.

Magubane, B. 1987c. "The Current Situation in South Africa: A Sociological Perspective." *Journal of Law and Religion* 5 (2): 473–493. doi:10.2307/1051243

Magubane, B. 1989. *From Soweto to Uitenhage: The Political Economy of the South African Revolution*. Trenton, NJ: Africa World Press.

Magubane, B. 1995. *Reflections on the Challenges Confronting Post-Apartheid South Africa*. Paris: MOST Discussion Paper Series No. 7.

Magubane, B. 1996. *The Making of a Racist State: British Imperialism and the Union of South Africa, 1875-1910*. Trenton, NJ: Africa World Press.

Magubane, B. 2000. "Race and Democratization in South Africa." *Macalester International* 9 (1): 33–82. https://digitalcommons.macalester.edu/macintl/vol9/iss1/8/.

Magubane, B. 2001. *Social Construction of Race and Citizenship in South Africa*. Geneva: UNRISD Discussion Paper Series.

Magubane, B. 2007. *Race and the Construction of the Dispensable Other*. Pretoria: Unisa Press.

Magubane, B. 2010. *My Life & Times*. Pietermaritzburg: UKZN Press.

Marx, K., and F. Engels. [1848] 2008. *The Communist Manifesto*. Ware: Wordsworth Editions Ltd.

Phiri, M. 2021. "The South African Pandemic of Racial Capitalism." *Monthly Review* 73 (5): 36–50. doi:10.14452/MR-073-05-2021-09_4.

Robinson, C. J. 2000. *Black Marxism: The Making of the Black Radical Tradition*. Chapel Hill, NC: University of North Carolina Press.

Simons, J., and R. E. Simons. 1969. *Class and Colour in South Africa, 1850-1950*. Penguin African Library: Harmondsworth.

Whiteness and racial capitalism: to whom do the "wages of whiteness" accrue?

Zine Magubane

ABSTRACT
The writings of Neville Alexander and Bernard Magubane can be quite useful in resolving a debate that has grown ever more acrimonious between American Marxist scholars over the analytic purchase of the category "whiteness" and, by extension, the best way to conceptualize the relationship between "the logic of capital" and "racial identity". The essay describes the genesis, execution, and logics of the Report of the Carnegie Commission on the Poor White Problem in South Africa. It argues that middle class Afrikaner reformers framed charity as a means of securing racial dignity and solidarity for the Afrikaner poor while teaching the Afrikaner upper classes how to transform their feelings of distaste and loathing for the poor into feelings of respect and solidarity. The essay concludes that their main interest did not lie in extending "psychological wages" to the poor so much as in securing higher wages for itself.

Introduction

A 1994 review of David Roediger's *ouvere* that appeared in the *Journal of South African Studies* suggested that "scholars of Southern Africa would do well to attend to the writings of American historian David Roediger". The value of Roediger's work, the author argued, lay in his focus on "the social history of feeling oneself to be White" (Krikler 1994, 663–664). In a recent critique of how the construct "racial capitalism" has been deployed in the American academy, the editors of *Black Agenda Report* argued that the ubiquity of the term had led to "analytical emptiness" because "the [South African] origins of the phrase racial capitalism have become obscured, if not erased". Rather, the focus had shifted to American scholars like Cedric Robinson and David Roediger who did not "engage with African research on racial capitalism" (Black Agenda Report 2020, 1). The point made by the editors of *Black Agenda Report* is well taken. Roediger described his recent book, *Class, Race, and Marxism*, as a work of "racial capitalism, following Cedric Robinson" (Roediger 2017, 25). Although he gives a nod to the "somewhat older South African scholarship on racial capitalism" he does not cite the work of scholars like Martin Legassick (Legassick and Hemson 1976) or Bernard Magubane (1977). To his credit, Roediger mentions an interview that two scholars (Allison Drew and David Binns) conducted with Neville Alexander, but he does not engage substantially with Alexander's (1979) work.

The neglect of South African scholarship is unfortunate. A revived interest in the writings of Neville Alexander and Bernard Magubane, this essay argues, can be quite useful in resolving a debate that has grown ever more acrimonious between American Marxist scholars over the analytic purchase of the category "whiteness" (Arnesen 2001; Reed 2001; Fields 2001; Johnson 2019) and, by extension, the best way to conceptualize the relationship between "the logic of capital" and "racial identity" (Wood 2002). Whereas Roediger (2017, 19) argued that "the critical study of whiteness" was a means to "challenge the work of David Harvey and so many others that race is outside the logic of capital" his critics have argued that the critical study of whiteness reifies race because it is insufficiently nuanced in its approach to the logic of capital. Despite their stated aim of construing whiteness as "the product of evolving social relations", scholars who use whiteness as empirical datum and tool of analysis, Adolph Reed (2001, 76) observes, tend to underplay the importance of examining the class composition of the various movements and political programs that might broadly be seen as promoting whiteness and/or white supremacy.

The "wages of whiteness", one of the key analytical constructs deployed by a host of Whiteness scholars (Harris 1993; Ignatiev 1995; Roediger 1991) has come under particular scrutiny in this regard (Johnson 2019; Arnesen 2001; Fields 2001). Where Roediger (1991, 13) sees himself and other scholars working within the whiteness paradigm as engaged in a historical materialist project which places "the whiteness of the white worker in the broad context of class formation" their critics see them as having failed to deliver on these promises. A key source of this failure, they maintain, stems from the base assumptions that underlie how whiteness scholars frame the problem to be answered. The "central issue" to be investigated, Roediger (1991, 8) maintains, is "why so many workers define themselves as white" and, in so doing, eschew making common cause with Black workers and ultimately work against their material interests. To fully understand the psychological and cultural appeal of whiteness necessitates a turn to novel methods, such as psychanalysis. "The use of the ideas of Freud and other psychoanalytic writers in *The Wages of Whiteness* came out of Marxism and the Black Radical Tradition", Roediger (2017, 52) explains. Critics of whiteness studies argue that the turn to the psychoanalytic is precisely where the *elision* of the "broad context" of class formation takes place. When Barbara Fields (2001, 53) decries the "romanticism that besets whiteness scholarship" she is pointing to how the "strikingly romantic vision of solidarity as a state of nature for white people" lends itself too readily to analyses that underemphasize processes of capital accumulation and the class struggles through which they take place.

How can the South African scholarship on racial capitalism help us to be attentive to psychological and cultural issues while keeping our eyes firmly attuned to class struggle, class contradictions, and class forces? I have chosen to focus on the genesis, execution, and logics of the *Report of the Carnegie Commission on the Poor White Problem in South Africa* as a way of exploring how "charity" that is explicitly aimed at the alleviation of poverty amongst persons defined as white must, necessarily, engage issues of identity and consciousness. Middle class Afrikaner reformers framed charity as a means of securing racial dignity and solidarity for the Afrikaner poor while teaching the Afrikaner upper classes how to transform their feelings of distaste and loathing for the poor into feelings of respect and solidarity. I argue that their main interest did not lie in extending "psychological wages" to the poor so much as in securing higher wages *for itself*. Their actions were constrained, however, by the social relations of production within South Africa as well as South Africa's place in the imperial division of labour as a key supplier of gold for the world-wide exchange system. We can only understand why the bourgeoisie chose to see themselves as white, and tried to make other classes – who stood in quite a different relationship to the means of production – see themselves as white, too, if we examine how South Africa's dependence on foreign capital impacted the internal organization of the country – specifically as it relates to the forging of class alliances. Magubane (1979, 164) described the Afrikaner bourgeoisie, if they were to be compared to their counterparts in other capitalist countries in the inter-war years, as having used the state apparatus to achieve its aims in a way that is "without parallel". The policies they enacted, which sought to "curb the predominance of foreign capital" reflected the weakness of their position in both the domestic and global economies.

In the pages that follow I will demonstrate that the ideologies about whiteness (particularly "white solidarity") that the Afrikaner petty bourgeoisie promoted in the *Carnegie Report* were strategically chosen to achieve the following aims: to highlight their cultural authority as "lords of poverty"; promote the idea that they were the true and authentic representatives of generic "Afrikaner interests"; to demonstrate that the interests of mining capital and the Afrikaner bourgeoisie were in alignment; and (most importantly) to position themselves as the exclusive providers of their unique brand of "poverty management services" to the South African state.

Capital, labour, and the wage bill: the wages of whiteness reconsidered

In 1927 Frederick Keppel, Chairman of the Carnegie Corporation of New York, was approached by members of the Dutch Reformed Church, South African philanthropists and social workers, and academics based at the University of Cape Town and Stellenbosch University, to undertake a study of white poverty in South Africa. At first glance it would appear that the report is a straightforward example of the "wages of whiteness" in action. It argued, for example, that one of the functions of charity was to instill a sense of cross-class racial solidarity to act as a bulwark against the loss of "racial pride":

> Behind the poor white problem lies the native question. If the more privileged European grudges and refuses the poor his patronage and society, the latter will associate with non-Europeans, if he finds no members of his own race to consort with. (Albertyn 1932, 106)

Interpreting this statement within the "wages of whiteness" paradigm, which is focused primarily on the wages (psychological and otherwise) that *accrue* to workers, can only take us so far. Fortunately for us, South African scholarship on racial capitalism goes far beyond this. Alexander (1979) points out that the economic surplus, distributed to workers in the form of wages, is experienced by capital as a "wage bill". Capital's material interest lies in reducing this outlay as much as possible. The existence of a "reserve army" of poor, under-employed, and unemployed people is a crucial mechanism in this regard. Therein, however, lies a contradiction which places "charity" at the heart of the logic of capital.

> In industrialized capitalist economies a certain percentage of the working people is normally kept unemployed (Marx's reserve army of labor). This reserve army, through competition for jobs, (i.e. by raising the supply of labor above the level of normal demand), holds down the level of wages and at the same time helps to discipline the employed labor force which can, at least, theoretically in most cases, be replaced by the unemployed. *Since the unemployed must eat and live to be able to serve these functions, their existence involves the capitalist state in unproductive expenditure such as unemployment benefits, "doles", etc.* (Alexander 1979, 62, emphasis mine)

Charity – a type of expenditure that the capitalist class views as simultaneously necessary *and* unproductive – is a key part of the logic of capital. If we understand the contradictory role that charity plays in the logic of capital, we can better understand how the *Carnegie Report* discussed white identity, poverty, and culture. All of these issues were framed so as to highlight the "productivity" of "unproductive" expenditure. The utility of Alexander's analysis of the connection between charity and the labour market is aptly demonstrated by Wilcock's comments in *The Psychological Report*. The recipient of aid, he despaired, might conclude that "it is easier to get assistance from charity than it is to work" (1932, 92). Charity had the potential to disrupt the balance of class forces in other ways as well. Not only could it blunt the force of market compulsion, it could also have the unintended effect of making the distribution of the economic surplus a clear and tangible target of working-class struggle. "Another effect produced when charity is given frequently is that the recipients of it come to look upon it as their right. ... The assistance is no longer regarded as a favour" (Wilcocks 1932, 94). The notion, that state provided charity held the potential to change the outlook of the entire working class, raised alarm bells.

> The recipients of charity come all the more easily to believe that they have a right to such assistance, in that *the idea is linked up to a certain extent with notions that enter into the outlook of the people as a whole.* In the first place, it is connected with the view that the poor have a right to be assisted, that it is a duty of the "rich" towards the poor to give them this assistance, and hence also a duty of the "government" which, "of course is very rich." We also came across poor whites who believed that "charity is the right of the poor man". (Wilcocks 1932, 95, emphasis mine)

In addition to potentially making the state a target of class struggle, charity might also lead people to question the overall distribution of social goods and, in so doing, make redistribution of the means of production a target of struggle. Wilcocks (1932, 95) lamented that "now and again the claim to equal treatment is made by poor whites in a less naïve and more socialistic form. For example, the demand is put forward that no citizen of the State should be allowed to possess more than a certain amount of land, and that the State should buy up the rest and divide it amongst those who have none."

The *Report* demonstrates the Afrikaner bourgeoisie's wholesale commitment to shielding the state from any organized electoral pressure from the poor, acting in terms of their class interest. White men had universal suffrage and the poor were the majority of the electorate. The uneasy alliance between the Nationalist Party and the Pact government is made clear by the fact that an entire section of *The Poor White and Society* was devoted to the examining "The Influence of the Poor Man's Vote on State Policy". The report lamented that "the presence of a large number of settlers together very soon makes them aware of the power of their collective vote" and they would no doubt use that power to threaten political parties into compliance (Albertyn 1932, 77). This was a direct "jab" at the Labour Party. Supporters of the Nationalist Party often criticized the Labour Party for "buying votes" from the poor giving by them "greater privileges or assistance" which included cash grants, free land, and having their debt discharged (Albertyn 1932, 78). For all of these reasons, the middle-class reformers argued, their services were badly needed by the state to control what type, to whom, and how much charity was dispensed.

Knowledge of the above leads us to ask a different set of questions about both white identity and choice. Starting with the latter, how does the organization of the economy and its social relations of production set the terrain within which choices are made? A key objective of intra-bourgeois class struggle in 1920s and 1930s South Africa, it will be argued, was to win the contest to impose the parameters and define the horizons within which choices could be made. Before we ask why someone chooses to define themselves as white, we must ask how were the terms for making choices set in the first place? Secondly, people define themselves in any number of ways. The pertinent question, therefore, is how and why particular forms of self-identification become salient. For the petty-bourgeoisie, the preferred forms of self-identification for the poor were not only "white" and/or "Afrikaner" but also "supplicants of the bourgeoisie". Their preferred forms of self-identification for themselves were not only "white" and "middle-class" but also "protector and guardian of the poor" and "faithful defender of the interests of capital and the state".

Alexander, Legassick, and Magubane all refer to how the actions that the South African bourgeoisie took to alleviate White poverty are related to the class character of the South African capitalist state. Magubane (1979, 167) explains that from the 1890s onward, the "condition of the poor whites in the cities became a main preoccupation of the Afrikaner political class". These efforts escalated rapidly in the wake of the 1924 electoral victory of the Nationalist/Labor Party "Pact" government which embarked on an aggressive platform to ameliorate the conditions facing poor Whites. A number of scholars have pointed out that the Pact government rested on a shaky alliance between sections of industrial and agricultural capital. Class struggles over how, whether, and to what extent the surplus generated by mining capital would be put to unproductive expenditure on charity were a major source of instability within the Pact regime. As O'Meara (1983, 28) explains:

> The Pact's policies reflected the divisions within the capitalist class. The myriad forms of state assistance to agriculture (and industry) were possible only through various direct and indirect taxes, levies, etc. on the gold-mining industry. In effect, this involved the state transferring the surplus value generated in the mining industry to agricultural (and industrial) capital. The result was bitter political and ideological struggle at all levels between these capitals, together with their political and ideological representatives.

The *Carnegie Commission of Investigation on the Poor White Question in South Africa* was borne out of these struggles and reflected them in its methods of investigation, the questions it posed, and the answers it derived therefrom. The investigators were clearly concerned with structural issues. Volume I, *Rural Impoverishment and Rural Exodus*, stated that it intended to "discover the economic causes of rural indigency in its historical and social roots; to explain the rural exodus; to describe the entry into new occupations and the competition of the natives" (Grosskopf 1932, 20). At the same time, however, the *Report* stressed the importance of psychological and cultural factors, particularly as they related to ethnic or racial identity. Volume II, *The Psychological Report*, contained lengthy discussions of what we might term the "structures of feeling" amongst poor whites. One of the subsections of the *Psychological Report*, "The Consciousness of Being Impotent: The Feeling of Inferiority", described poor whites as having a "fatalistic attitude of mind" and lacking "national and personal self-esteem" (Wilcocks 1932, 71–72). Volume V, *The Sociological Report*, connected this fatalism and poor self-regard to the growing class divisions between Afrikaners. "With increasing riches and luxury, the gulf between the rich and the poor is becoming deeper and wider. On the one side, one finds impatience and even scorn of the indigent, and on the other a deepened sense of inferiority, or of bitterness and hatred" (Albertyn 1932, 103). The *Report* continued:

> The attitude of mind of prominent men all over the Union towards the problem was evident during their conversations on the causes of poor whiteism. Many spoke with real interest and sympathy, but others passed very severe strictures such as the following: "I have no patience with that class; I have no time for them; they are too lazy, indolent, untrustworthy, thankless, headstrong, deceitful – I would far rather employ natives than such wastrels." And even where the expressions used were not so sharp, very many people evinced an attitude of impatience and resentment which certainly did not argue an interest in the poor whites. (Albertyn 1932, 104)

Clearly, whiteness did not beget solidarity. In this excerpt, Albertyn does not identify exactly which "prominent men" expressed these attitudes of "impatience and resentment". The *Economic Report*, however, stated the matter plainly: "Important social legislation has been passed, a great variety of institutions founded, measures are taken to protect the health of the people, education has been furthered, charitable societies supported, child protection undertaken, relief works opened, and settlements established. *The expenditure as entailed is gradually becoming a fairly heavy burden on the country's taxpayers*" (Grosskopf 1932, xxx, emphasis mine).

The bourgeois ethic and the spirit of poverty

The fact that white poverty was primarily a matter of "spiritual" dimensions is mentioned numerous times throughout the *Reports* five volumes. E.G. Malherbe's (1932, 239) assertion that "one of the characteristics most readily developed through poverty and one frequently associated with the poor white is a certain spirit of dependence – sometimes described as a lack of some sense of responsibility or of duty or a lack of pride" was typical.

Alexander (1979, 17) makes the point that the "vacuity of bourgeois sociology" stems from the fact that it "approaches social phenomena with so-called operational definitions" that serve to obfuscate reality and thereby derail the types of analysis that might lead to a deep questioning of the sources of and solutions to inequality. "Dependency" is precisely that kind of concept. It subtly draws attention *away* from the systems of commodity production that expose workers to chronic uncertainty and *towards* the moral and spiritual deficiencies of the poor. It also reconceptualizes the relationship between labour and capital. The worker, who is in reality the source of the surplus value that is appropriated by the capitalist, is recast as a parasite.

> In the study of the relations of the poor to the government one is very strongly impressed by the excessive spirit of dependence on the Government, which exists on all sides. This pertains to matters like the provision of board and schooling ... relief work and provision of food and housing for the unemployed; the loan of stock on the easiest terms or gratis; free treatment of the sick; and free maintenance of the aged; and relief during times of distress. (Albertyn 1932, 12)

Who are the dependent? What social forces lay behind their emergence? Upon what (or whom) do they depend? The ways in which the *Report* defined the concept are intricately connected to the manufacturing of "racial identity" on the one hand, and the class struggles within the Afrikaner bourgeoisie on the other. These struggles, in turn, can only be fully appreciated if we situate the Afrikaner bourgeoisie within the matrix of a capitalist economy, paying particular attention to the "interaction between local and foreign capital in the political economy of South Africa" (Magubane 1979, 163). Embedded within the conflict between local and foreign capital lay a conflict between those segments of the Afrikaner bourgeoisie that sought to share power with British capital and those that sought to cut ties with the British and make national capital dominant in the whole of South Africa. The "poor white question" sat squarely within this conflict. The Afrikaner bourgeoisie, Alexander (1979, 37) explains, "set out to use all the ideological and cultural weapons in the arsenal of South African history in order to get a greater share of economic power for national capital". The clergymen, academics, and social workers (the petty-bourgeois professional class) carved out a special niche for itself as the self-appointed guardians of the poor. The ways in which they defined "dependency" not only reflected their desire to reframe charity as "productive expenditure" (as we saw above). It also ensured that the bulk of the state's expenditure would accrue *to them*, rather than to the poor.

It can never be forgotten, of course, that African workers were the major producers of value. The Native Reserves onto which they had been pushed

THE SOUTH AFRICAN TRADITION OF RACIAL CAPITALISM 107

after being dispossessed of much of their land provided the major subsidy to the capitalist class. The reserves operated as dumping grounds, where the owners of industrial and agricultural capital could extract labour as needed, pay an individual, rather than "family" wage, and then abandon their broken bodies once the last vestiges of productivity had been wrung out. The same held true for the migrant labour system. Therefore, the surplus that the bourgeoisie was so intent on guarding, and from which it would extract the means of its own survival, was produced largely by the African working class. It goes without saying that scant reference to this fact was made in the *Report*, save for a discussion of how whites suffered "unfair competition on the part of the non-European workers" (Grosskopf 1932, 165). The surplus accrued to mining and agricultural capital is, likewise, referenced in extremely oblique terms.

> A laborer who does not live by his wages alone, can easily offer his services more cheaply on the labor market. The majority of native laborers are not obliged permanently to support a family by their pay. ... For the rapid economic development of South Africa since about 1890, for the gold mines especially, the presence of a growing native population with low standards and simple wants was a decided advantage. (Grosskopf 1932, 166)

The silences around mining capital and its strategies for accumulation are hidden behind yet another "vacuous" concept – "adaptation" – which functioned alongside "dependency" to offer both a formulation of society and a solution to its problems that disguised the naked brutality of the capitalist system and the irreconcilability of the interests of exploiter and exploited. The poverty of white workers, the *Report* explains, is due to their failure to "adapt" to the imperatives of a modern economy. Their economic decline was "caused principally by inadequate adjustment to modern economic conditions" (Grosskopf 1932, viii). For the Afrikaner, adjustment meant disengaging from class struggle; being satisfied with wages that were commensurate with his "skill"; reinvesting their wages in Afrikaner owned banks, insurance companies, and pension schemes; spending their wages in Afrikaner run shops and businesses; and donating to organizations to further "Afrikaner culture" (Alexander 1979; Magubane 1979).

"Adaptation" for the African meant something else entirely. It meant accepting their place in the economy as the lowest paid members; abandoning all hope of fighting to regain the land from which they had been expelled; and aspiring to exist in South Africa as a consumer, rather than a citizen. *The Economic Report* advised that it was "far wiser to contemplate a future economic development of our country, in which native labor will play a valuable part in the productive system – and natives will be important consumers of the white man's products" (Grosskopf 1932, 244). In other words, the remedy for exploitation did not lie in the reorganization of the social relations of production and the ownership structure of the society. In this rosy future, the working class would be guided (some with carrots and others with sticks) along separate and profoundly unequal paths, all of which led away from class based anti-capitalist organizing and towards accommodation or "adjustment" with capital. In this they would be helped along by modern methods of social science and philanthropy – many of which were imported from overseas.

Local class reproduction and the political economy of global philanthropy

In the early 1920s, overseas ventures were still "unchartered territory" for American corporate sponsored foundations (Glotzer 2000, 97). The Carnegie study was a major milestone. The philanthropic foundations had long ago secured their place as the ideological directors of poverty management at home and, in so doing, harnessed philanthropy to the logic of business expansion by acting as intermediaries who provided the funding to individual academics and social science departments who would then produce studies that aimed at "solving Western capitalism's problems" (Fisher 1982, 239). Exerting their influence abroad opening up tantalizing possibilities for aiding American commercial interests in their quest to further penetrate South African markets. American capital began to penetrate South Africa during WWI. In 1917, Ernest Oppenheimer partnered with American financiers and formed the Anglo-American Corporation. American finance made it possible for the Far West Rand, the Klerksdorp Fields, and the Orange Free State Mines to commence operation. This was only the beginning. South Africa had a large industrial working class that were potential consumers of American exports. South Africa might also be a place to invest American surplus capital.

The South African clergymen and academics who collaborated with American researchers on the *Carnegie Report* also stood to gain by spearheading the effort to revise South Africa's entire system of welfare provision "in light of the best methods in vogue overseas" (Albertyn 1932, 114). Their interest was motivated less by academic curiosity than by naked financial interest. Americans had roundly rejected the idea that all (or even the bulk of) money the state and voluntary organizations collected under the guise of providing aid to the poor should actually go directly to the poor. Rather, Americans argued that as much (if not more) money should be devoted to the paying the salaries of the administrators who *oversaw* the poor. C.W. Coulter, an American sociologist who traveled with the Commission and gave lectures on the professionalization of sociology and social work in the United States, spoke enthusiastically about the fact that in a typical American charity, 70% of the funds went to the salaries of technical social workers, leaving only 30% for actual relief. *The Sociological Report* lamented that the majority of South African professionals did not as yet share this view.

> The opinion still is that the greatest possible amount of the available funds must be devoted to food and clothing for the necessitous. Only recently in a certain city when the question of coordination of the various charities and the opening of a central bureau for social welfare was being discussed, one of the most prominent social workers exclaimed "What! Do you propose taking the food out of the mouths of the poor and devoting the money to offices and salaries? No, my conviction is, as little money as possible for administration; if possible, nothing, so that everything may be available for food and clothing for the poor!" This view seems to obtain to a great extent in the Union. (Albertyn 1932, 118)

As members of the professional classes, the bourgeoisie had to make a case for getting a larger portion of the surplus in the form enlarged salaries and enhanced benefits. They decried the "dearth of well-trained social workers in the Union" and urged that the state must carve out an ever-growing portion of the surplus to provide money and scholarships for studying at home, endowing "well organized and well-equipped schools for social work", and funding overseas jaunts where students could to observe "best practices" in other countries (Albertyn 1932, 119).

They drew parallels between themselves and doctors, both of whom needed "years of study" because so much of their jobs involved making correct diagnoses (Albertyn 1932, 119).

When aspiring professional social workers stressed how dangerous it was to assume that "the social worker can diagnose social evils without the least training" (Albertyn 1932, 119) what kind of training and diagnostics were they talking about? The answer can be found in the final third of *The Sociological Report*, which discussed the "detrimental effects of wrong methods":

> The evil effects of injudicious relief are many and grave. In the first place it means that the recipient of relief is deprived of his self-reliance and self-respect. The chief distinction between the poor white and the respectable poor man is that the latter, though he may be as meagerly endowed with worldly goods as the former, still retains his self-respect. Like the unjust steward he says, "To beg I am ashamed." This sense of shame is the main bulwark between him and poor whiteism. (Albertyn 1932, 121)

Simply put, the bourgeois social worker set themselves up as the arbiter between the deserving and the undeserving poor, which they posed in racial terms as a difference between "poor whites" and the "white poor". The latter were redeemable and largely among the deserving. "Not every poor person is necessarily a "poor white". A man may be poor and have kept his independence and his ability to improve his position" (Grosskopf 1932, 18). The former ranged from the irredeemable – mendicants, beggars and criminals – to the more temporarily unemployed, and everything in-between. The value of the trained professional social worker to the capitalist state and, by definition, industry lay in their ability to protect both from unproductive expenditure. Armed with scientific diagnostics they would establish foolproof parameters to weed out the parasitic poor who, if they had their way, would suck the state dry with their demands.

> People often find fault with the charitable bodies which devote large sums to administration. This is usually the case with those who have no experience of charity. Many of the best and most efficiently organized societies in Europe devote fifty percent of their funds to administration. It is an axiom among people with technical knowledge that it often costs a pound to spend a pound wisely on charity. (Albertyn 1932, 117)

The lines they sought to draw between the deserving and undeserving poor underscore their commitment to making sure that the reserve army of labour remained fit and every ready to serve. Since it was the case that "unwillingness to work and lack of habits of industry are characteristic of many poor whites" social workers played the vital role of determining which whites were "prepared to work occasionally, but object to regular work, such as would be required from them if permanently employed". Diagnostics could also be used to determine which whites could easily be pressured to increase efficiency, whether they got paid more or not, and those who slowed down or ceased work entirely when they discovered that "increased exertion is not rewarded by an increase in pay" (Wilcocks 1932, 53). Diagnostics would also be used to ferret out which whites belonged to the permanent class of loafers, beggars, and mendicants who, because they would never cycle back through the labour market, would inevitably become a permanent drain on state finances. For these, too, they had a solution. Any persons who were discovered to be "thoroughly averse to any form of steady labor" would be assigned to forced labour colonies (Albertyn 1932, 108).

Solidarity and the wage of whiteness reconsidered

David Roediger credits the phrase (and the title) "wages of whiteness" to DuBois. He has often described how deeply impactful he found the following paragraph from *Black Reconstruction*:

> [T]he white group of laborers, while they received a low wage, were compensated in part by a sort of public and psychological wage. They were given public deference and titles of courtesy because they were white. They were admitted freely with all classes of white people to public functions, public parks, and the best schools. The police were drawn from their ranks, and the courts, dependent upon their votes, treated them with such leniency as to encourage lawlessness. Their vote selected public officials, and while this had small effect upon the economic situation, it had great effect upon their personal treatment and the deference shown to them. (DuBois 1992 [1935], 700)

In *The Wages of Whiteness* Roediger (1991, 13) trained his focus on the "public and psychological wage". As he put it:

> As important as the specifics are here, still more important is the idea that the pleasures of whiteness could function as a "wage" for white workers. That is, status and privileges conferred by race could be used to make up for the alienating and exploitative class relationships, North and South. White workers could and did, define and accept their class positions by fashioning identities as "not slaves' and as "not Blacks'.

Unlike *Black Reconstruction*, which is "firmly embedded in the Marxist tradition" and frames Jim Crow as a "class-based counterrevolution that destroyed the possibility of freedom for half the Southern working class" *The Wages of Whiteness* sees Jim Crow primarily as a system of racial oppression (Goodwin 2022, 54). Whereas DuBois approaches the issues of racial oppression and the racism of white workers from the perspective of political economy, and thus focuses on the ways in which Jim Crow enforced "a dictatorship of capital" (DuBois 1992 [1935], 630) *The Wages of Whiteness* focuses on the recipient of the "public and psychological wage". If, when reading the *Carnegie Report,* we adopt the perspectives provided by the South African tradition of racial capitalism, rather than the American one, we can shift our gaze from the class of recipients to the class who is extending the offer and, in so doing, query the extent to which ties of solidarity are actually formed.

On the face of it, theorists of racial capitalism approach the question of racial solidarity from a soundly "constructivist" perspective. In other words, they stress that neither racial categories nor the impulse to use "race" as a basis for group identification and social action are natural. Nevertheless, the idea that poor whites readily and easily accept the "psychological wage" as compensation for actual wages, often substandard at best and outright terrible at worst, has not only been readily accepted, it has become the basis for making theoretical claims. As is the idea that rich whites happily and enthusiastically extend psychological wages, and (if pressed) are not overly averse to extending additional material ones as well. Alexander (1979, 15) reminds us that solidarity "is a manifestation of consciousness, of what is assumed to be common to the entity concerned under particular historical circumstances. That which is common is seldom some simple and clearly defined element, nor does it remain constant and unchanging". It is worthwhile to explore the actual processes through poor whites are offered the "psychological wage" – what are the terms? What debates occur amongst those who are extending the offer? How are these offers received? And what is the impact on ties of solidarity?

The many critics of whiteness scholarship point to its reliance on "ventriloquism" and/or "psychohistory". As historian Eric Arnesen (2001, 22) observed in "Whiteness and the Historians Imagination", his "conceptual audit" of the field:

> If psychoanalysis requires the patient's extensive verbalization of his or her problems, whiteness psychohistory dispenses altogether with real people and their words and instead freely ascribes deep motivation and belief to its subjects on the basis of the historians' freewheeling interpretation of behavior and other people's words.

The *Carnegie Commission Report* was produced by the ruling class. By design, it records the opinions and ideologies of elites. To the extent that the voices of the poor and working-class Afrikaners who were the subjects and objects of study are heard, they are mediated through the petty – bourgeoisie. As the authors of Volume 2, *The Psychological Report*, explained:

> These interviews served as a means of getting into personal contact with poor whites and were held in an informal and elastic fashion, that is, as nearly as possible in the form of conversation. *They were, however, largely guided by certain points of view*. (Wilcocks 1932, 4, emphasis mine)

When the (heavily mediated) voices of the poor are heard, it is quite clear that the bourgeois reformers were aware that class antagonisms within the Afrikaner population not only existed, but were fierce and potentially dangerous. Reading the *Report*, one cannot help but be struck by how reluctant the wealthy were to extend the "public courtesy and acts of deference" that are said to be the "wages of whiteness". Albertyn ruefully observed: "The poor white realizes that he is unwelcome in his own fatherland" (1932, 106). One of the respondents, who succumbed to what the *Psychological Report* derided as the "easy lure" of a debauched life digging for diamonds, told the interviewer that he might be poor, but at least he was "not the rich man's dog" (Wilcocks 1932, 101). Whereas the Dutch Reformed Church saw itself as a mechanism for reducing inequality and fostering cross-class racial solidarity, the recipients of its "charity" saw the church as playing an active role in *producing* class inequality. This was not just a vague feeling. It was anchored in material realities. Churches are no different from any other institution in a capitalist society. Its practices, therefore, are not immune to the dynamics of profit and loss that prevail in other areas of the economy. The "structures of feeling" and solidarity between wealthy and poor parishioners were deeply and adversely impacted by the fact that churches rented the front pews at a higher-rates and the best pews went to richer parishioners; the church charged high baptismal and membership fees; and wealthy parishioners had a greater voice in church affairs because the church was dependent on donations and tithes. The commissioners had to tackle the uncomfortable question of whether or not the church was guilty of failing to "champion the rights of the poor when they come into conflict with the interests of the rich". The following responses were recorded: "The Church is a rich man's church; I have to pay to hear God's word and to have my child christened; The Church does nothing for me" (Albertyn 1932, 66). When asked about their lagging church attendance, informants replied: "We don't want to sit there and be ridiculed by others". The *Report* thus concluded: "Even if the poor man sometimes only imagines that others are looking down on him, the fact remains that he does actually feel it, and that it is to him a real drawback" (Albertyn 1932, 36).

One of the recommendations of the Carnegie commission was that the Church do more to emphasize the "essential brotherhood" of the rich and poor while taking care, however, "not to be so foolish as to antagonize the rich". This was no easy matter and the general consensus of the poor was that the church "hesitates to attack vested interests, even when they are wrong" (Albertyn 1932, 67). It was for this reason that feelings of "bitterness and hatred" towards the rich were growing amongst the poor (Albertyn 1932, 103). The wealthy, in turn, had no feelings of benevolence or brotherhood for the poor. Cross-class racial loyalty was by no means natural. Therefore, one of the services that the middle-class reformers pledged to carry out was that of a proselytizer who made sure that the "more prosperous citizens [would] be educated to a better sense of their duties and obligations to the less fortunate".

"Obligations" is a capacious term. It might mean nicer treatment. It could just as easily mean higher pay, which employers naturally balked at. "The farmer is apt to feel that, should he employ a European, he is also in duty bound to pay him a higher wage than he would a native. Being either unable or unwilling to meet the increased expenditure he prefers not to employ the European at all" (Wilcocks 1932, 60). Unsurprisingly, when poor whites pushed for "psychological" wages to be buttressed by higher material ones, they were rebuffed. "Farm owners who pay low wages to their European hands sometimes state that they are paying as much as the labor is worth, or that their own financial circumstances do not permit of their paying more. The laborer, on the other hand, feels that his wages are an inadequate reward for the work he does" (Wilcocks 1932, 69).

To trace the history of South Africa from the Act of Union in 1910, through the 1920s, when the Pact government came to power, ending with the ultimate triumph of the "Purified" Nationalist Party in 1948, is to trace the contours of several simultaneously occurring class struggles. On the one hand, there was class strife within the bourgeoisie. At the same time, fierce clashes occurred between the bourgeoisie and the poor and working classes. The compromise that underwrote the Union of South Africa in 1910 created a bifurcated society. There were "two separate spheres within the confines of a single state" (Magubane 1979, 164). On the one hand, there was a foreign "enclave economy" based on the mines and the contoured to meet the imperatives established by the Chamber of Mines. On the other hand, there was the domestic economy which was based on agriculture, over which the imperatives of the Union Government held sway. Thus commenced the struggle of the Afrikaner bourgeoisie to control the state to simultaneously "preserve and strengthen the interests of capital and imperialism and to fulfil their own economic aspirations". The entrenchment of imperial monopoly interests meant that these aspirations had to be pursued within fixed parameters. For the Afrikaner bourgeoisie and petty bourgeoisie to ensure their continued existence, they had to control the state and wield its influence to "mediate and tame the English dominance of the economy while advancing [their] interest in the same area". They couldn't achieve this by themselves. They needed the votes of the poor to gain control of the state apparatus. Thus, their willingness to address the problem of poverty and forge bonds of intra-class solidarity did not emanate from any sentimental sense of attachment to their fellow whites. Poor whites were their conduit to political power. There was nothing romantic about it. Although the commissioners toyed with the idea of having a law that would disenfranchise "any indigent person receiving a certain measure of state aid" and hoped thereby that the threat of losing the vote might deter some men from even seeking aid in the first place, this idea was never contemplated seriously because: "At present, however, even the person who is totally dependent on the State for his existence, has the vote, and so at least one of the means of breaking down this spirit of dependency remains inoperative" (Albertyn 1932, 78). Ultimately, political constraints, rather than bonds of racial solidarity, forestalled this possibility.

Final thoughts on the sociology of race and class

Bernard Magubane and Neville Alexander, both deceased, have given us sharp and insightful criticisms about bourgeois social science and the concepts it generates. Bourgeois sociology lacks the concept to study racism, Magubane (1977, 151) noted, "because its epistemological premises preclude its producing one". Alexander (1979, 223) made a similar point about ethnicity. When Sociologists "tried to reduce the diverse reasons for the emergence of group solidarities to a single quality called "ethnicity"", they wound up "obscuring precisely what has to be explained – the basis of such solidarity". Why does bourgeois social science exhibit such striking failures? Barbara Fields, echoing Magubane and Alexander, provides an answer. She made the prescient observation that "argument by definition and tautology [often] replaces argument by analysis in anything to do with people of African descent" (1990, 98). The tautological nature of "Whiteness studies" writ large stems from the derivation of the concept 'Whiteness' itself. Magubane (2000, 175) maintained that "concepts are meaningless apart from questions asked. The questions asked are determined by the problems we want to solve". We must ask ourselves whether "why do white workers choose to be white" is a useful question to ask. Does it bring us any closer to solving the problems of race and class oppression and exploitation? Or does it exhibit the same failures of bourgeois social science that Bernard Magubane (1977) pointed to in the article wherein he first used the phrase "racial capitalism"? Magubane argued that many of the concepts that guide mainstream sociological research served to do little more than obscure reality because "the bourgeois social scientist formulates concepts, categories, and uses methods which not only rationalize the existing social order but numb our minds to injustices" (164). My examination of the *Carnegie Report* leads me to conclude that it is not. While it would not be fair to accuse Roediger, a committed anti-racist and labour activist, to being numb to social injustice, nevertheless the "wages of whiteness" paradigm does not position scholars or activists to bring about the just world that he has spent the majority of his life fighting for. Were he alive today, Alexander (1979, 222) would likely view "Whiteness" with the same skepticism that he viewed the concept "ethnicity", which he described as having a "Humpty Dumpty" character. Just as "all the king's horses and men couldn't put Humpy together again", concepts like "ethnicity", "race" and "white identity", that were generated by apartheid and Jim Crow for purposes of social control, cannot be disarticulated from that context and then "put back together again" as analytical categories that guide antiracist and anti-capitalist sociological inquiry.

Whiteness is not a coherent analytical category. It is an ideology. And ideology, Fields reminds us, "is impossible for anyone to analyze who remains trapped on its terrain" (1990, 100). How can we step off of the ideological terrain? Fields provides an answer. Ideologies, she explains, "are not delusions but real, as real as the social relations for which they stand" (Fields 1990, 110). And what are those social relations? As was demonstrated above, the pertinent social relations had to do with the interactions between local and foreign capital and the intra bourgeois struggles they gave rise to as a result. These struggles, in turn, had an enormous impact on the poor and working classes, Afrikaner and African. The Afrikaner poor were offered a pathway out of poverty. They secured wages (psychological and otherwise) as well as job protection, political representation, and cultural dominance. The African working classes were subject to poverty, political disenfranchisement, starvation, violence, and sometimes death. In order to understand this historical outcome, our analyses must proceed at multiple levels. The level of analysis suggested by the "wages of whiteness" problematic is not entirely mistaken. It can provide interesting empirical insights. However, it does not provide the necessary analytical framework for understanding the historical movement of any given society. Fortunately for us, the South African scholarship that gave us the term "racial capitalism" does.

Disclosure statement

No potential conflict of interest was reported by the author(s).

References

Albertyn, J. R. 1932. *The Sociological Report (Volume V): The Poor White and Society*. Stellenbosch: Pro-Ecclesia-Drukkery.

Alexander, Neville. 1979. *One Azania, One Nation*. London: Zed Press.

Arnesen, E. 2001. "Whiteness and the Historians." *Imagination International Labor and Working-Class History* 60 (Fall): 3–32.

DuBois, W. E. B. 1992 [1935]. *Black Reconstruction in America, 1860–1880*. New York: Anthaneum.

Editors, Black Agenda Report. 2020. "Racial Capitalism, Black Liberation, and South Africa." *Black Agenda Report*. Accessed September 1, 2022. https://www.blackagendareport.com/racial-capitalism-black-liberation-and-South-Africa.

Fields, Barbara J. 1990. "Slavery, Race, and Ideology." *New Left Review* May/June: 95–118.

Fields, Barbara J. 2001. "Whiteness, Race, and Identity." *International Labor and Working Class History* 60 (Fall): 48–56.

Fisher, Donald. 1982. "American Philanthropy and the Social Sciences: The Reproduction of a Conservative Ideology." In *Philanthropy and Cultural Imperialism: The Foundations at Home and Abroad*, edited by Robert F. Arnove, 232–268. Bloomington: Indiana University Press.

Glotzer, Richard. 2000. "The Influence of Carnegie Corporation and Teachers College, Columbia University, in the Interwar Dominions: The Case for Decentralized Education." *Historical Studies in Education* 1 (2): 93–111.

Goodwin, Jeff. 2022. "Black Reconstruction as Class War." *Catalyst Journal* 6 (1): 53–95.

Grosskopf, J. F. W. 1932. *Economic Report (Volume I): Rural Impoverishment and Rural Exodus*. Stellenbosch: Pro-Ecclesia-Drukkery.

Harris, Cheryl I. 1993. "Whiteness as Property." *Harvard Law Review* 106 (3): 1710–1791.

Ignatiev, Noel. 1995. *How the Irish Became White*. New York: Routledge.

Johnson, C. 2019. "The Wages of Roediger: Why Three Decades of Whiteness Scholarship Has Not Produced the Left We Need." *Nonsite* 29 (September): 1–44.

Krikler, Jeremy. 1994. "Review Article — Lessons from America: The Writings of David Roediger." *Journal of Southern African Studies* 20 (4): 663–669.

Legassick, Martin, and David Hemson. 1976. *Foreign Investment and the Reproduction of Racial Capitalism in South Africa*. Cape Town: UCT Libraries Special Collections.

Magubane, Bernard. 1977. "The Poverty of Liberal Analysis: A Polemic on Southern Africa." *Review of the Fernand Braudel Center* 1 (2): 147–166.

Magubane, Bernard. 1979. *The Political Economy of Race and Class in South Africa*. New York: Monthly Review Press.

Magubane, Bernard. 2000. *African Sociology – Towards a Critical Perspective: The Collected Essays of Bernard Makhosezwe Magubane*. Trenton, NJ: Africa World Press.

Malherbe, E. G. 1932. *Educational Report (Volume III): Education and the Poor White*. Stellenbosch: Pro-Ecclesia-Drukkery.

O'Meara, D. 1983. *Volkskapitalisme: Class, Capital and Ideology in the Development of Afrikaner Nationalism, 1934–1948*. London: Cambridge University Press.

Reed, A. 2001. "Response to Eric Arnesen." *International Labor and Working-Class History* 60 (Fall): 69–80.

THE SOUTH AFRICAN TRADITION OF RACIAL CAPITALISM 117

Roediger, David. 1991. *The Wages of Whiteness: Race and the Making of the American Working Class*. London: Verso.

Roediger, David. 2017. *Class, Race and Marxism*. London: Verso.

Wilcocks, R. W. 1932. *Psychological Report (Volume II): The Poor White*. Stellenbosch: Pro-Ecclesia-Drukkery.

Wood, Ellen Meiksins. 2002. "Class, Race, and Capitalism." *Political Power and Social Theory* 15 275–284.

Reproducing "racial capitalism" through retailing in South Africa: gender, labour, and consumption, 1950s–1970s

Bridget Kenny

ABSTRACT

Using Stuart Hall's concept of articulation and the concrete with Bridget O'Laughlin's reminder of a focus on the struggles of living labour, this paper theorizes racial capitalism in South Africa from the concrete relations of retail labour in Johannesburg. The paper examines ways in which white working class women constituted retailing, struggling for their own claims in relation to gendered family and workplace orders, which in turn conditioned how black women organized when they entered front-line service jobs in the late 1960s, which then disrupted this order to explain a very different class politics and to constitute anew these meaningful spaces. These processes happened through multiple mediations. Retail capital not only contributed to economic expansion; labour relations in shops constituted specific affective spaces as meaningful terrains of collective belonging, projecting ideologies and explaining differentiated "subjects in struggle".

The recent flurry of writing on racial capitalism, especially in the United States, highlights the interlinked dimensions of racialized dispossession, exploitation and oppression as constitutive of the history of capitalism (Kelley forthcoming; Jenkins 2021; Jenkins and Leroy 2021; Johnson 2020; Taylor 2019; Bhattacharyya 2018; Hudson 2017; and see Gilmore 2007). Much of this literature takes inspiration from Robinson's (2000 [1983]) use of the term, and some have reminded readers that originally it came from South Africa debates (Kelley 2021; 2017; Makalani 2021; Hudson 2018; Go 2021). The phrase was first used by Legassick and Hemson (1976) in a piece arguing that new foreign investment in South Africa would not be a progressive force to eradicate racist rule, but was attracted to South Africa precisely because of the conditions of accumulation, which were constituted through a particularly low wage labour regime based on black migrant labour and state violent protection of these conditions. South African debate in the 1970s variously insisted that racism was not epiphenomenal to capital accumulation under successive regimes of white minority rule, but was necessary to the historical conditions and reproduction of accumulation (Alexander 1979; Mafeje 1978; Magubane 1979; Legassick 1974; Wolpe 1972).

This paper re-examines South African racial capitalism from a set of social relations that complicate our understanding of its reproduction. It explores the labour of commercial workers in the 1950s, 60s and 70s in greater Johannesburg, which centres a concrete analysis of white women workers and the shift to black women workers in the sector, and emphasizes the meaningful constitution of urban space and ideologies of nation in the intertwined dimensions of labour and consumption. White women disturb the category white worker defined in standard structuralist analyzes of South African racial capitalism in both their status as dependent workers and in how the meaningful expression of gender-race-class relations played out in the labour process and shaped urban space. Black women's entry in the late 1960s into these already-existing relations then disrupted this order to explain a very different class politics and to constitute anew these meaningful spaces.[1]

Through examining retail labour, the paper offers an explanation of racial capitalism that applies aspects of two important critiques of the functionalism of the earlier South African debate: Stuart Hall's (1980) concept of "articulation" together with his essay on Marx's method (Hall 2021 [1974]), and Bridget O'Laughlin's (2021) recent reminder of the imbricated struggles of "living labour". As a site, retailing in Johannesburg foregrounds how articulations (and rearticulations) of relations of race, class and gender produced particular struggles (as well as "subjects-in-struggle" (Hall 1985)), urban infrastructures and, indeed, signifiers of belonging and polity at a specific moment of change in South Africa. Examining retailing contributes to debates on racial capitalism in three ways, then: it centres white and black women's imbricated wage labour in South African capitalist development; it disassembles the reified category of "white working class", and thereby complicates apartheid hegemony; and, it shows how women's struggles mediated (and reshaped) racially territorialized hegemonies (see Gilmore 2002), explaining ongoing capital accumulation and shifting ideologies.

Making concrete racial capitalism in South Africa: articulations of living labour

In Harold Wolpe's (1972) well-known formulation, known as the "cheap labour thesis", black men entered wage labour in the mines and on the farms, but reproduced their labour elsewhere (in the rural "reserves") organized through non-capitalist social relations. This "articulation of modes of production" allowed capital to pay black workers far less than a social wage, as costs of reproduction were born by rural households (and women specifically) and communities involved in subsistence agriculture. Wolpe argued, though, that the quality of the (restricted) land on which migrant workers' families were expected to maintain themselves and their wage earners declined precipitously already from the segregation period. Yet capital now relied on the cheap labour of its black workers, and so the state had to ensure by force the reproduction of the conditions of this structure of accumulation. Apartheid was a system of despotic state intervention in the workplace and labour market (broadly mapped) to ensure the conditions for hyper-exploitation of the majority black workforce for the benefit of capital. Racism was thus functional to capitalist accumulation and not an ideological residue obstructing proper market efficiency, as argued by the liberals. This racial regime, then, was understood to structure other labour markets and sectors, like the secondary manufacturing industry developed around the mining sector (Legassick 1974).

Consequently, the division of labour between white and black workers defined racial capitalism in South Africa. White workers were incorporated into the industrial relations system as "civilised labour", that is, as "employees" with organizational and procedural labour rights and who were paid a wage befitting "civilised" ("European") living standards. In contrast, "pass-bearing natives", were excluded from the definition of employee, rights to join registered trade unions and the social wage. White workers benefitted directly from higher wages than black workers, as well as from job protections, and subsidies for welfare, housing and education (O'Meara 1975; Davies 1979; Wolpe 1976).

"White workers" as a category within South Africa's racial capitalism, then, were defined either as a labour aristocracy, or as middle class (working as supervisors and managers), or as non-productive (working in tertiary and distributive jobs) and therefore as not really members of the working class (Magubane 1979, 157; Davies 1973; O'Meara 1975; but see Wolpe 1976).[2] The key structural relationship which defined racial capitalism viz. white workers then was how white workers legitimated the white minority state as voters and supported capital's exploitation of black workers, either as a compromised fraction of the working class or as divided from the real working class. White workers and their unions functioned to provide (interested) support to the state, in turn reproducing capitalist accumulation.[3]

In multiple ways, the structuralist framings of racial capitalism in South Africa were functionalist, as many feminists critiqued. They implied discrete arenas of reproduction and production with the function of households to transfer surplus outward through biological and generational reproduction (see more broadly O'Laughlin 1977; Katz 1983; Mackintosh 1977); they did not explain women's subordination but took it as a premise (Bozzoli 1983;

O'Laughlin 1977); they obscured struggles within the patriarchal family, rural areas and between households and the wider economy (Cock 1980; Bozzoli 1983; 1991); they emphasized economistic relations between "race" and "class", without considering political and ideological meanings (Posel 1983); and, they focused on the technical requirements of capital to determine wage levels and not working class struggles (and their contradictory effects) (see O'Laughlin 1977; Bozzoli 1983). These debates, then, questioned structuralist arguments which assumed the needs of capital tautologically explained the reproduction of racial capitalism.

In his sympathetic review and critique of South African debate in his essay "Race, Articulation and Societies Structured in Dominance", Hall (1980) offers two critical interventions for understanding the social reproduction of capitalism and racism, which moves beyond the functionalism of Wolpe. First, how racism and racist hierarchies structure social relations is a matter of concrete analysis, and second, that in order to do such analysis a complex rendering of the co-constitution of "ideological" meanings and economic relations in place and time is necessary. South African debates offered him a specific instance of the stakes. In considering explanations for the development of capitalism, divisions of labour between white and black workers, and state legal and political action to uphold the migrant labour system, Hall discussed his concept of articulation. This was an intervention in debates about the trajectories of capitalism in colonial/post-colonial contexts and in debates about how ideology worked. He specifies in this essay that articulation refers to two senses of the term, the "joining up" and the "giving expression to" (Hall 1980, 328). He suggests that the latter sense is the least developed in theorizations, and that the two meanings combine to offer a "complex structure" in which the expression does not merely represent a simple correspondence of the relations; indeed, there is no "necessary correspondence" (Hall 1980, 329). He argues that attention to the concrete relations and conditions explaining the reproduction and transformation of "societies structured in dominance" offers a method for explaining the relationship of levels in any specific historical conjuncture. As a theory it mitigated against the functionalism and economic reductionism of Wolpe (Hall 1980, 322; but see later Wolpe 1988 and Hart 2007 discussion).

Using the South African debates, then, Hall outlined an imperative to examine concrete relations, forces and meanings to explain how domination worked through "race", co-constituting capitalist relations. Read together with his essay on "Marx's method" (Hall 2021 [1974]), he is explicit in his claim – to move from the abstract (that is, thought concepts) to the concrete, where the concrete is not the simple empirical but the specific conjunctions of components of a "complexly structured whole", a "differentiated unity" (Hall 2021 [1974], 28; 35). As Hall explains, "Both the specificities and the connections – the complex unities of structure – have to be demonstrated by the concrete analysis of concrete relations and conjunctions. If relations are mutually articulated, but remain specified by their difference, this articulation, and the determinate conditions on which it rests, has to be demonstrated" (Hall 2021 [1974], 36). For Hall this (non-teleological) dialectics countered functionalism, which presumed already (structurally, conceptually) to define categories and the relationship between parts (Hall 2021 [1974], 52–53; see Hart 2018).

For the purposes of analyzing the labour regime in retailing, as I will demonstrate below, this point is made explicit again by O'Laughlin (2021) in her recent critique of social reproduction theory in which she reminds us of the imbrications of "living labour" which explain the reproduction of capitalism. She argues that social reproduction theory bears resemblance to Wolpe's earlier "articulation approach" (following Meillassoux's articulation of modes of production) in maintaining a structural dualism between so-called "realms" of production and reproduction, without understanding their unity (O'Laughlin 2021, 9). O'Laughlin (2021, 4) instead calls for a focus on "class struggles over the reproduction of living labour", which cross-cut spaces of production and reproduction necessarily and force analysis of the co-constitution of race, class and gender within these processes. She asks: "given that capital is not accountable for the reproduction of the labour that it consumes, how does living labour survive and reproduce?" (O'Laughlin 2021, 17).

The generational shifts outlined in retailing in this paper can be viewed in such terms. Instead of beginning with a division of labour pre-constituted, the paper shows how and in what terms these divisions became created, how and in what ways "subjects-in-struggle" (Hall 1985, 112), emerged and acted as part of this process.[4] White women were not simply a privileged fraction. Instead their own (dependent) working class immizeration was mediated by white femininity, which was materialized in the labour process and constituted discourses of urban modernity in Johannesburg. Black women entered service jobs in conditions not of their own making and with very different pressures for reproduction. They contested these conditions through quite different politics, which in turn came to bear on later moments. These processes happened through multiple mediations, which I trace in the following sections. Retail capital not only contributed to economic expansion; labour in shops produced specific affective spaces as meaningful terrains of collective belonging, projecting ideologies of nation and explaining differentiated class struggles.

Commercial capital and city space

Commercial capital directed the colonial relationship in Southern Africa. Closely tied into finance from metropolitan banks, commerce extended trade relations throughout the region (see Legassick 1974). These networks facilitated retailing, and models of business were brought from the UK,

Eastern Europe or Russia with immigrants, who set up stores importing their stock (Kaplan 1986). By the early twentieth century across the Rand local merchants established profiles, and by the 1920s, many central Johannesburg shops were branches of chains, with "modern retailing" defining merchant practice.[5] This included transnational connections through industry journals and associations and global buying and supply networks (Kenny 2018, 31). The most contemporary retail practices, such as product display, standardized pricing, packaging and advertizing innovations, all contributed to ideas of settler colonial modernity (Kenny 2018, 31). In Johannesburg, the early concentration of capital in the sector partly resulted from the costly importation of goods, and larger wholesalers and retailers controlled channels, with exceptions being petty Afrikaner capital in smaller towns (O'Meara 1983). By the 1940s, the gross sales area of shops on the Rand had doubled and included multi-storey buildings, employing larger workforces (Kenny 2018, 32).

The shopping district in central Johannesburg was a heady space for white residents to shop and socialize (Kenny 2018, 30, 32–34). Tax laws that levied sites rather than improvements encouraged ongoing capital investment in regular extensions and refurbishments, and the architecture of many department stores contributed to the unique mixed style of Johannesburg as a "modern" city (Beavon 2004, 152–154; Chipkin 1993). Apartheid law restricted the growth of Chinese and Indian owned businesses to the far west of city centre, such that the property regime of downtown Johannesburg was white-owned (Beavon 2004, 153).[6] The spatial geography of the city's retailing mapped racial divisions.

In the 1950s and 1960s retailers expanded through new sites, opening new suburban branches and upgrading existing ones, facilitated through capital investment in property development (Beavon 2004, 179–180). This process of suburbanization marked another moment of changing spatial relations in the city, as white families moved to new neighbourhoods, buying their own homes often with state subsidy; car ownership increased and highway construction happened (Mabin 2005, 48). While retail capital investment in suburban infrastructure and shopping districts expanded in white areas, the Group Areas Act had ensured the forced removal of black families from locations closer to the city centre to segregated "townships" (Mabin 1992). Retail capital, then, helped to constitute apartheid's racialized spatial hierarchies.

Through these decades, retailers also enlarged economies of scale through developing supply chain systems and stock turnover efficiencies, focusing on bulk buying (Lambrecht, Meisel, and Rushburne 1967, 5). Supermarket formats were introduced in the 1950s and self-service in the 1960s. These scale and formatting changes required expanded investment and increased the concentration of commercial capital throughout the 1960s (Kenny 2018, 43). The state introduced competition regulation only in 1955, which resulted in prohibition of a range of monopolistic practices identified first in grocery retailers. This effort was meant to appease consumers complaining of rising prices, with the state continuing Resale Price Maintenance for key goods until 1967.[7] Nevertheless, retailing profited from the high growth of the economy in the 1960s of 6% per annum (Gelb 1991). Greater access to credit fuelled white consumption in this period (Grundlingh 2008). By the 1970s retail capital had further concentrated in national chains, and new mass discount stores and hypermarket formats, linked to international trends, had become the latest evidence of "progress" (Kenny 2018, 121–125). Raymond Ackerman, CEO of one of South Africa's largest chains, remarked of his decision to bring new "hyper" formats to South Africa in the 1970s that other businessmen thought he was "mad! ... You can't compare South Africa to Europe or America".[8] But, this comparison tracked chain retailer practices, abreast of a globalizing industry and keen to expand in similar directions. By the 1970s, the struggle between retailers and suppliers and producers had been resolved in favour of retailers as size and dominance determined their power ultimately (see Ackerman 2001).

The retail sector thus can be broadly defined through its history in greater Johannesburg as becoming increasingly concentrated over the decades. The state legislated white ownership for downtown and suburban shops. It stepped in when consumer prices became a public matter of concern, but as retailing developed along lines similar to, and indeed, articulated with global retailing, the size and control of market channels determined relationships with other capital in supply and production of stock. Retailers benefitted from South Africa's growth in the 1960s and were able to represent their efforts as opening markets to consumers and as offering access to cosmopolitan culture. Capital investment thereby instantiated city space through property development, aesthetics and formatting features, and selling global goods to middle class white consumers. In doing so, retailers constituted a meaningful city and, indeed, "nation" as modern competitor, contributing to and legitimating economic growth in its particular form. Retail capital accumulation thus buttressed apartheid hegemony through signifying chains linking the physical shopping spaces to ideas of advancement, consumerism and white belonging. Women's labour materialized such retail spaces through concrete relations with a predominantly white public in Johannesburg. These relations changed over time in ways that both generated the divided categories of black and white women workers and produced contradictions explaining subjects-in-struggle.

"Fixing meaning" through white women's living labour

The divisions of labour and forms of control within retailing relied on gendered and racialized difference to substantiate the affective meaning of shops in ways that legitimated the apartheid "nation". These articulations, as Hall suggests, then, specifically reinforced hegemony, doing so by territorializing racialized space (Gilmore 2002) and thereby reproducing racial capitalism.

White working class women worked in retail jobs from the turn of the nineteenth century, expanding in the 1920s through the 1970s with black women entering service jobs in the late 1960s (Kenny 2008; 2018). While white women worked as commercial workers alongside white men, there are important concrete differences obscured by the abstract category "white working class". White men worked as managers, supervisors and salespeople. When they worked as shop assistants, white men earned up to twice the wages of white women for the same job, as wage determinations legislated gendered pay differentials. Jobs in the sector accrued wage increments for years of experience up to four years, after which they were classified as qualified and paid a higher rate. Still, white women's qualified rates of pay for each occupational category could be as low as a half that of white men's. As the industrial relations system was being put into place, white women's labour was seen as "a character totally different from that of men. For women, employment is largely a stepping stone to marriage or better times" (Industrial Legislation Commission of 1935; quoted in Chanock 2004, 461; and see Berger 1992). The "civilised" wage that explained "white labour's" class-compromised position (Davies 1973; and see Wolpe 1976), then, described more accurately white men's wages, buttressed by discourses and state commitment to the white "male breadwinner" (see Kenny 2020).

While they were not seen to carry the household burden, white women indeed supported their families. In the 1940s, Ingrid du Toit, left school at fourteen to work in a department store. She said, "We were six in the family and I didn't have a dad, and my mom was dressmaking at the time … [I got a job] to get extra money".[9] In the 1950s Becca similarly got a job as a shop assistant to assist her mother, even as both her mother and her father worked.[10] These realities described the living labour of white women and influenced their struggles.

Regional occupational unions organized white men and women in the sector in the first decades of the twentieth century, with a national union, the National Union of Distributive Workers (NUDW), forming in 1937 from these associations. The NUDW actively organized white women in the sector and included many women shopstewards and officials in its ranks (Kenny 2018, 35–36). Shop assistants were higher educated young women than garment workers, as they had to be able to speak English and have basic numeracy skills (Kenny 2018, 36). Pay levels were portable between employers, which assisted with building standing through experience within the sector.

In this way, women shored up some status and seniority over time. Before the 1950s, women entering retailing were likely to be single, as with Ingrid and Becca, and they often (but not always) left when they got married. By the 1950s, however, married women frequently stayed in the job, often leaving when they had children and returning when their children were older in order to support their households. Mrs. Smith began working in a chain department store in Durban in the early 1950s. She left when she had her first child, and when she and her husband moved to Johannesburg, she went to work for the Post Office, left again to have her second child, and then in 1956, returned to find the Post Office offered her only the starting wage again. So, she walked across the street and got a job at the neighbouring store, instead. She worked at this chain until she retired.[11]

Forms of control within the labour process were decidedly gendered. The younger women "shop girls" were rigorously supervised by older women staff, often the main source of control on the shop floor, with white men in the distance above the shop floor in offices. Comportment and dress were a key measure of control (Kenny 2018, 36–40). White women took pleasure and pride in what they perceived to be their skill of sales and knowledge of the merchandize in these decades. Some Afrikaans speakers also felt they learned better English by practicing on the job, which conveyed class-inflected status to them.

White women earned some respectability from shop work through the 1950s, but by then, employers found it harder to keep white women in the job. In 1954 the state introduced a new category of parttime work in two job categories that white women held, designed to appeal to white women's concern to be home to care for children, even as black women served as domestic workers (Cock 1980). In the early decades of the twentieth century, legal bars operated to prevent married women from working in some sectors, with some continuing in the public service into the 1950s and 1960s (Berger 1992; Walker 2001). In the 1950s, a rise in concern over white juvenile delinquency pinned the social ill on working mothers (Mooney 2006). The benefits of apartheid subsidies to whites, and indeed the policing of boundaries of white society (Roos 2011; Freund 2020), had the effect that NUDW discourses shifted from a defence of white working class women's economic contribution to households to upholding their gendered purity despite ongoing employment (Kenny 2008). For instance, the union fought against the extension of store trading hours for decades; by the early 1960s, when some retailers pushed for "night trading", it defended against later hours by arguing that its members, "large numbers of married women … upon whom their husbands and children rely" needed to be home: "the provision of meals at normal hours and other reasonable amenities of life, domestic and family life would be subjected to considerable disruption [with extended trading hours]".[12]

In interviews with white women shopworkers who worked in the period, women spoke to me of their complicated household contexts, often having

THE SOUTH AFRICAN TRADITION OF RACIAL CAPITALISM 127

to deal with absentee or alcoholic husbands or remaining "spinsters" living alone.[13] Others, like Mrs. Smith, had the support of her husband, which she sought to continue to work. She enjoyed working, receiving the recognition of her manager: "He just liked me. I was promoted and promoted … .He said to me, 'Ek gaan jou maak' [I'm going to make you]".[14]

Against other more miserly authority, the union defended women workers' pay and working time as legislated. While the NUDW fought consistently for the removal of gendered pay differentials and other restrictions to white women's legal dependent status, it also deferred to husbands and fathers when they stepped in to opine around women's working time (Kenny 2018, 41). These battles occurred as individuated negotiations between men, the union officials and shop managers, or as national campaigns directed at a white public, such as those around trading hours (Kenny 2021). Negotiating these relations, some women proudly became supervisors and then trainee managers and eventually store managers with their own staff by the 1980s.[15]

In the 1960s, shop assistants, who may have accrued the status of working at an elite department store, nevertheless shopped at the lower end bazaar department store across the street (Kenny 2018, 32–33). The spaces of shopping were still de facto segregated by race. Thus, while working and middle class whites inhabited the same city streets moving between shops as workers and consumers, black consumers bought elsewhere, in Market Street in Indian-owned shops, in the townships or from a side window of a bazaar shop. Black men worked as distributive workers in city shops, stacking behind-the-scenes warehouses, moving equipment and doing deliveries (Hellmann 1953).

The built aesthetic and affective worlds of shops and consumption, evacuated as they were of the signifiers of black life, conditioned white belonging, ideas of nation and privilege during the middle twentieth century and legitimated South Africa. As one white woman shop assistant explained of 1950s Johannesburg, "All the shop assistants were white, the bus drivers were white, the lift operators were white. The menial jobs were black. Obviously the street sweepers, the toilet attendants, that sort of thing, remained black … .Very few black people were shopping … .[They did] the manual, heavy labour if there were things to be moved. Black people were around [in downtown Johannesburg] but they were very few".[16] These were "territorialized" hierarchies (Gilmore 2002), in which racial difference mapped affective belonging. White women domesticated retail spaces in these early years; their labour produced the connections between signifiers, maintaining the racist order through their comforting presence and through their very claims to knowing and doing their service jobs well (Kenny 2018, 36–38).

In Hall's terms, there was no "necessary correspondence" of these workers as "white women", but in retailing we can demonstrate how the gendered stakes of white femininity reproduced both possibilities for them to continue to work, to confront husbands, to contest managers, to bring up children, as well as limitations to their politics which reinforced divisions with black women, in ways which we will see in more detail in the next section. White working class women as "subjects-in-struggle", within concrete relations in labour processes and through the union, protected their basic conditions while affirming race and gender dispositions. As O'Laughlin emphasizes, struggles at the site of the wage, which appear separate, in fact, describe articulated real relations of living labour's sociality, cross-cutting production and reproduction.

The strict division of the labour market into white "employee" and black "pass-bearing native" that defined the racially bifurcated labour regime so definitive of analyses of racial capitalism in South Africa, thus obscures other relations. Retailing produced a complex differentiated set of relations in which shops were contested places of hegemony. White women as living labour struggled in these processes, becoming new subjectivities and also legitimating racist orders. City retailing not only accumulated surplus value through divisions of labour, but also constituted white settler modernity in Johannesburg through gendered service labour to a white public.

Disrupting signifying chains through black women's struggles

In the 1960s, service jobs in retail shops began to be deskilled. The expansion of retailing in terms of branch numbers and size increased corporate hierarchies, and new retailing "systems" developed with new merchandizing techniques. The bureaucratization of store relations by this time also broke down shop assistants' work. Self-service shopping removed the skill of knowing products and inducing a sale that white women had enjoyed in earlier decades. New job classifications in clerical and administrative work, gradations in counter-hands and supervisors, and the addition of end-of-line cashiers broke down the labour process, with each new occupation assigned its own pay rate. In the late 1960s, retailers intensified work with the union reporting that its members complained of having to cover more space: "one employee is expected to handle two or three counters which means considerably more work for them".[17]

The NUDW worked to maintain the integrity of occupational grades and the boundaries that separated service work from manual labour as a way to protect the respectability of white women's shop work as it was changing. The union wrote in 1970 to reassure a shop assistant's mother that she was not supposed to be conducting manual labour: "The Manager assured me that it is not normally necessary for white ladies to push heavy skips, and that the shop employs two Bantu for that purpose".[18] The "Bantu" were African men distributive workers, and the store was reorganizing work to reduce the number of general workers employed. In this instance, the young white woman shop assistant was made to do the additional work until the union complained to insist on the separation of the (racial and gender) job descriptions.

Indeed, until the 1960s, black workers in downtown shops consisted almost exclusively of men working in such distributive jobs. This generation of workers, slotted into the labour process as in many other sectors. They worked in what was understood as unskilled jobs. In the early 1940s they organized into the African Commercial and Distributive Workers Union (ACDWU), which won wage increases and even a temporary closed shop agreement for African workers in a strike in 1942, and they joined white workers in the sector's historic strike in 1943, but these possibilities closed after the 1946 black mineworkers strike and increased repression of black workers (Hirson 1990; Kenny 2018, 55). By the early 1950s, although employed through temporary work contracts through the labour bureaus like all African workers, distributive workers of one major chain retailer were reported to be longer urban residents with families living with them and with higher job stability than manufacturing workers. Still, they could not belong to a registered trade union, and their wage levels had remained the same over years. For the most part, they earned a labourer salary, set at a general worker's rate. Their labour process was dictated by black men supervisors ("baasboys"), who reported to white men in the warehouses or office, and who generally moved workers around to where they were needed (Hellmann 1953).

An expanding economy in the 1960s increased the demand for service and clerical work by the end of the decade and the early 1970s (Crankshaw 1997, 75). White women had more options for employment in the public sector (Kenny 2018, 47), and retailing faced white labour shortages. In this period, retailers began to hire black women into front-line service jobs, in Johannesburg, first Indian and coloured women (Kenny 2018, 47–50). The National Union of Commercial and Allied Workers (NUCAW), a separate union under NUDW leadership (to comply with labour legislation) represented coloured and Indian workers. Women entered service work sometimes employed as general workers, but in practice doing the work of shop assistants. When employed as shop assistants, they earned the lowest pay because of experience and gender pay differentials.

The changing labour market alarmed some National Party members, who called for job reservation in the sector,[19] complaining that black women worked alongside white women and served white customers. I discuss the failure of the effort to obtain job reservation elsewhere (Kenny 2018, 48–50), and neither the union nor employers supported it, nor were customers particularly bothered. In public discussions in 1969 around the job reservation inquiry for shop and clerical workers, the National Party and its

Minister of Labour argued that "separate development" was the aim with service workers serving their own "race" (Kenny 2018, 64). A newspaper interviewed customers in a "typical scene" at a major department store with "non-Whites serving White customers" and reported the "Coloured assistant(s)" as saying "I am accepted by customers as just another sales assistant, in spite of my race" and "Satisfied White customers ask to be served by me when they call again".[20] Black women service workers were praised publicly with similar language as white women, focused on their gendered politeness and their presentability.

Yet black women working in chain retailing faced various forms of discrimination, such as having to work longer hours than white women, being paid less, receiving no pension and being subjected to informal discrimination, such as having to do general workers' duties like cleaning while they were shop assistants. The NUDW and NUCAW defended coloured members arguing they should receive the correct wages and benefits for the job, and called out the racism by raising these differences to managers: "In at least one instance Coloured workers wore a different colour uniform or overall but were often also made to wear caps to distinguish them even more from the Whites".[21] Ultimately, the unions fought these grievances within a call for the "effective rate for the job", an argument for equal pay for the job, and which maintained existing occupational hierarchies to prevent the core membership from being undercut by a new workforce (Kenny 2018, 66). In other words, if black workers moving into the jobs were paid the same and treated the same, then its white membership's conditions would not be eroded.

In other ways, black women were subjected to bullying, distrust and abuse. In 1972, a group of coloured women workers stopped work in one store to complain to the union that their line manager, a Mrs. Edelman, checked their tills "three/four times daily". The union wrote to the branch manager, "Workers feel that they are under a constant cloud of suspicion and conditions were unpleasant".[22] These women workers contested such informal surveillance, which generated resonant affective meaning in these sites.

They argued against late night work assigned to them, because of the danger it put them into travelling home, and those that could, left for other jobs, such as one woman who requested not to stay late for stock take because she had been attacked coming home late to Lenasia, an Indian township. When her manager refused, she asked the union only to ensure that she received what was due to her in leaving. These women commented that they were often breadwinners of families but would find safer jobs in a context of a shifting economy (Kenny 2018, 69). The unions defended workers in a way to protect against individual discrimination and maintain the existing occupationally graded hierarchy in shops. When retailers pushed to extend trading hours into the evenings, the union argued that white women needed to be home for their families as we saw above, but to companies, acknowledged that later shifts could be staffed by casuals or black workers (Kenny 2021). Black women faced different reproductive constraints than white women as well as relations of control, which in turn influenced their responses (O'Laughlin 2021).

By the 1970s, retailers increasingly hired African women and men into service and clerical jobs. They organized into an independent union for black workers, the Commercial, Catering and Allied Workers Union of South Africa (CCAWUSA) in 1975 (Mashinini 1991; Kenny 2018, 71–89). Like white women before them, black women represented a better educated cohort than factory workers, and they were a second generation of urban township residents entering retailing after school to support families (where parents often worked in Johannesburg or East Rand factories). For instance, Mary Nkosi found work in a shop when she left school after Standard 7 (grade 9) in 1977. She needed to support her family as "the situation was not good".[23]

Unlike the prior generation of white women, they faced recessionary conditions and retailer cost-cutting, and changing capital investment as consolidation and new formats like discount retailing expanded linked, as noted above, to deskilling of the job as self-service became the norm. African workers entering in the 1970s and early 1980s confronted managers who paid them at the lowest rates of pay. Mary Nkosi explained that in 1981 she earned R154 per month starting salary,[24] and one study reported in 1982 that white women earned R80 per month more than coloured women and R120 more per month than African women (van der Walt as quoted in Kenny 2018, 72). Black workers endured racism and arbitrary dismissals. As one union official explained in 1982, "a manageress would phone the area manager to complain about one of the staff, and the area manager would readily say, 'Kick her out.'"[25] When women became pregnant they left, like white women before them, or more often, these women were fired from their jobs.

But, they were also politicized young people, and on the Rand, had been active in student politics in 1976, with many involved in the Black Consciousness Movement (Kenny 2018, 77). Unlike the prior generation of workers, this workforce organized through a militant race-class identity, generating new "subjects-in-struggle" out of articulations of legal exclusions, despotic control and reproductive urgencies.

CCAWUSA used the racialized differentials of pay between African, coloured and white workers to mobilize African workers to reject the explicit racial hierarchy in retail. The union organized by fighting for basic labour rights to be "employees" with the first recognition agreements won in the early 1980s following labour law reform (Mashinini 1991). The first maternity rights agreement in South Africa was won in OK Bazaars in 1983, which gave a year unpaid leave and, crucially, job protection upon return. Workers refused parttime work because they needed the hours to support families, collectively and forcefully struggled against racism and sexism, and organized against shop floor hierarchies between manual and service jobs, with the latter in particular affirming a clear race-class positioning (Kenny 2018, 71–89). By the 1980s, CCAWUSA (and its successor SACCAWU) became one of the most militant and largest unions, precisely for workers organizing against the articulations of gender, race and class relations.

Furthermore, by the 1970s, the social imaginary of shopping and consumption had shifted. Shopping became increasingly a cosmopolitan urban pastime, serviced by a new workforce. The obliging familiarity of white women was less required to generate consumer spaces. Indeed, the consumer public itself was changing as black residents began to shop more often in Johannesburg central stores. Retailers recognized changing consumer markets in larger black customer bases (Kenny 2018, 83). Shops offered lifestyle entertainment and consumption increasingly connected to worldly imaginaries extending meaning beyond national belonging (cf Posel 2010). Black consumers also provided communities of solidarity and by the 1980s, the union actively used consumer boycotts to shape labour struggles (Kenny 2018, 83–84).

This history tracks a complicated set of articulations describing changes to labour processes and divisions of labour that centre the articulated struggles of living labour to persist. These processes trace how categories were produced and reproduced in relation to each other and as retail capital expanded and built city space. Retailing has reproduced forms of racial capitalism in South Africa precisely through complex differentiations of labour markets, changing labour processes, and the semiotics of space, which emerged in and through these racialized hierarchies.

Conclusion

Retailing relied on proletarianized women's labour, both white and later black women's. In earlier functionalist analyses, women's labour appeared only as reproductive, to subsidize capital (Wolpe 1972; and see Bozzoli 1983; 1991). Yet with commerce, women's wage labour integrated the circuit of accumulation, and also produced and unravelled hegemonies. White women's union politics as well as informal everyday complicity constituted labour processes, reinforced normative white femininity, generated women's class politics and materialized a set of ideologies linking gendered care to social spaces of belonging for whites, which offered forms of consent legitimating apartheid's everyday worlds and ideas of a thriving nation.

Black women entered this constituted set of relations and came up against these limits: the contradiction of changing work, deskilled yet requiring gendered service; union protection in the midst of regular racist resentments; and, the very contradiction of liberation through employment. They rejected a politics of bureaucratic unionism and confronted not only their poor wages and job exclusions but also a range of conditions infantilizing them as women and subordinates. They organized into a militant union defined through a consciously race-class collective subjectivity in the 1970s and 1980s, rejecting the division of manual and service work so fundamental to white women's occupational integrity. In turn, they altered meaningful political subjectivity and action in the post-apartheid period, at the same time as reaffirming labour politics as a site of struggle (see Kenny 2018).

This paper contributes to theorizations of racial capitalism in that it returns to the centrality of labour in South African debates, as imbricated "living labour" to explain social reproduction through "a constant struggle by all working people to subsist, to nourish, to heal and to defend life against the depredations, drudgery and exertion of work under capital" (O'Laughlin 2021, 4). As Hall (1985, 98–99) explains, though, social reproduction is wider than the reproduction of labour power; it describes the "reproduction of social relations of possession and of exploitation and indeed of the mode of production itself". The South African debates in the 1970s were clear: racism was functional to the reproduction of capitalism, not epiphenomenal. Yet as Hall and others suggested, the logic of functionalism assumed the needs of capital explained these processes.

Rather, as we have seen, how living labour struggles concretely is relational, contradictory and meaningful. The constitution of "subjects-in-struggle" (Hall 1985, 93) emerges out of multiply determined processes, disrupts meaning, and co-constitutes the very orders of difference. White women's concrete relations both produced a specific politics contributing substantively to reproducing retailing and affirmed their sense of themselves as working class white women in the world. Black women rejected their insertion into these relations out of their own context of living, thereby altering the conditions of accumulation.

Hall (1980) explains articulation as a theory attending to the joining together of relations and forces as well as the forms of expression of these processes. If Robinson (2000 [1983]) showed the historical force of racist difference to capitalist development, Hall gives us a method for analyzing the relational and contradictory changes explaining the endurance of racialized capitalism. As Hall (1980, 338–339) argued, "Racism is not present, in the same form or degree, in all capitalist formations: it is not necessary to the concrete functioning of all capitalisms. It needs to be shown how and why racism has been specifically overdetermined by and articulated with certain capitalisms at different stages of their development".

The story of Johannesburg retailing explains how racialized and gendered class disunity was produced and reproduced, and it shows how retailing advanced through constituting apartheid hegemony. Through meanings of nation, modernity, consumer bounty and modern affective infrastructure, in Ruth Wilson Gilmore's (2002, 16) terms, a "territorialization" of racist difference *as* a "practice of abstraction .... organize[d] relations" in city streets and on shop floors in an unequal distribution of violence, reproducing rule and also prompting new subjects-in-struggle. If such processes produce "all kinds of fetishes: states, races, normative views of how people fit into and make places in the world" (Gilmore 2002, 16; 2007) then, retailing offers an important nexus.

Indeed, the stakes of this analysis of retailing in the 1950s to the 1970s register today. The gendered meanings of dependency returned later in the 1990s as casual labour expanded to serve extended trading hours in the evenings and weekends, and the union reinscribed new divisions between full-time and casual workers based on reincorporating gendered meanings, but now dividing black workers (see Kenny 2018, 185–208). Today, these arenas rely on the low wage labour of precarious black workers, still fighting to improve conditions but barely tied to liveable worlds. Retail capital redirects investment to distribution and logistics, reshaping affective geographies through mall expansion (see Luckett 2019) and buttressing South Africa's economy, itself serviced by debt, expanding new circuits of "racial finance capitalism" (Torkelson 2021). Johannesburg retailing in the mid-twentieth century demonstrates the conjunctural reproduction and transformation of gendered racial capitalism.

Notes

1. By "black", I refer to all oppressed by the apartheid regime in terms of their "race". When necessary to explain the history or as used historically, I specify African, Indian, and coloured. Official post-apartheid census classification maintains the categories of Black-African, Coloured, Indian, and White, and see Maré (2014).
2. White commercial workers were considered non-productive (not directly producing surplus value and only realizing it) or ideologically aligned to the petty bourgeoisie and therefore as not working class (see Davies 1979, 9–11, 21–25). In some renditions, white workers in fact benefitted "indirectly" from the surplus value produced by black workers, see Wolpe's (1976) critique of Davies' (1973) argument.
3. Recent work begins to challenge the homogenisation of white workers and the white working class in South and Southern Africa (Money and van Zyl-Hermann 2020; van Zyl-Hermann 2020; Money and van Zyl-Hermann 2021). Critique emphasises both the differences and messier histories of white workers in the region, and a growing body of scholarship shows the disciplinary efforts by the state on the white poor and white workers (Willoughby-Herard 2015; Freund 2020; Roos 2011).
4. Hall (1985, 112) describes "subjects-in-struggle" as new subjectivities which emerge out of existing relations and conditions, proffering new meanings for

categories, and hence disrupting chains of signifiers. His discussion of subjectivity in this essay (in relation to Althusser) suggests how he understands "social reproduction" to be a contradictory and contested process, one in which the concrete is "different levels and different kinds of determination" (Hall 1985, 94) and where ideology is the "work of fixing meaning through establishing by selection and combination, a chain of equivalences" (Hall 1985, 93).

5. The Rand (translated from the Afrikaans meaning the "ridge") is short for the Witwatersrand. It describes the geographic area following the gold seam extending from Johannesburg to its east and west.

6. Small Afrikaner traders secured the exclusion of Indian merchants from white areas through the Group Areas Act of 1950 (see O'Meara 1983, 213–218).

7. The Regulation of Monopolistic Conditions Act of 1955 was the first to prohibit certain forms of uncompetitive business practice seen to contribute to consumer price increases (Kenny 2018, 53).

8. "Boksburg: 10 Years of Hyper Magic," *Supermarket and Retailer* 32 (4), April 1985, p. 50; as quoted in Kenny 2018, 121.

9. Ingrid du Toit [pseudonym], interviewed by Bridget Kenny, Benoni, August 21, 2007; as quoted in Kenny 2018, 35. The research for this paper is covered by the University of the Witwatersrand, Human Research Ethics Committee (HREC) (Non-Medical) under ethics clearance protocol number H22/04/10.

10. Becca van der Walt [pseudonym], interviewed by Bridget Kenny, Johannesburg, March 19, 2007; as quoted in Kenny 2018, 36.

11. Mrs. Smith [pseudonym], interviewed by Bridget Kenny, Germiston, May 21, 2013.

12. Memorandum of Objection on the Proposed Extension of Trading Hours, J. R. Altman, National Secretary, NUDW, July 9, 1962, p. 5. University of the Witwatersrand Historical Papers, National Union of Distributive Workers (NUDW) archives, Head office AH 1494/Da 2.2; and see Kenny 2021.

13. Janice Tomlinson [pseudonym], interviewed by Bridget Kenny, Johannesburg, October 1, 2013.

14. Mrs. Smith [pseudonym], interviewed by Bridget Kenny, Germiston, May 21, 2013.

15. Mrs. Smith [pseudonym], interviewed by Bridget Kenny, Germiston, May 21, 2013.

16. Janice Tomlinson [pseudonym], interviewed by Bridget Kenny, Johannesburg, October 1, 2013; as quoted in Kenny 2018, 29–30.

17. Letter from D. Hartwell to Mr. J. Mitchell, October 9, 1968; University of the Witwatersrand Historical Papers Research Archive, National Union of Distributive Workers, Witwatersrand Branch, AH 1601 Ua 41.2.3; as quoted in Kenny 2018, 44.

18. Letter from M. Kagan to Mrs. Steyn, February 9, 1970; AH 1601 Ua 41.1.1; as quoted in Kenny 2018, 45.

19. "Job reservation" was a legislated provision in labour law (the Industrial Conciliation Act, 1956) whereby appeals could be made to the Minister of Labour to "reserve" any job, occupation or industry for whites, and prohibit black employment.

20. Paulette Dupree, "Inquiry into 'Mixed Serving in Shops,'" *Sunday Express*, October 5, 1969; as quoted in Kenny 2018, 64.

21. "Effective Rate for the Job Urged," *New Day*, July 1970, 6–7; University of the Witwatersrand Historical Papers Research Archive, National Union of Distributive Workers, Natal Branch AH 1202 Ua 41.2.5; as quoted in Kenny 2018, 65.

22. "OK Orange Grove, Temporary Work Stoppage," by Z. Farrah, May 15, 1972, AH 1601 Ua 41.1.3; as quoted in Kenny 2018, 67.
23. Mary Nkosi (pseudonym), interviewed by Bridget Kenny, Daveyton, August 26, 1999; as quoted in Kenny 2018, 75.
24. Mary Nkosi (pseudonym), interviewed by Bridget Kenny, Daveyton, August 26, 1999; as quoted in Kenny 2018, 73.
25. Isaac Padi, president of CCAWUSA, interviewed by Jeremy Baskin, April 17, 1982. Historical Papers Research Archives, University of the Witwatersrand, AH 2920; as quoted in Kenny 2018, 75.

Acknowledgement

I thank Zach Levenson and Marcel Paret for their encouragement and feedback.

Disclosure statement

No potential conflict of interest was reported by the author(s).

Funding

This work was supported by The Governing Intimacies Project, University of the Witwatersrand, under the project "The Materialites of Gender and Regulating Sex & Intimacies".

ORCID

Bridget Kenny ⓘ http://orcid.org/0000-0001-6255-4971

References

Ackerman, Raymond. 2001. *Hearing Grasshoppers Jump: The Story of Raymond Ackerman*. Cape Town: David Philip.

Alexander, Neville [No Sizwe]. 1979. *One Azania, One Nation: The National Question in South Africa*. London: Zed Books.

Beavon, Keith. 2004. *Johannesburg: The Making and Shaping of the City*. Pretoria: UNISA Press.

Berger, Iris. 1992. *Threads of Solidarity: Women in South African Industry, 1900–1980*. Bloomington: Indiana University Press.

Bhattacharyya, Gargi. 2018. *Rethinking Racial Capitalism: Questions of Reproduction and Survival*. New York: Rowman & Littlefield.

Bozzoli, Belinda. 1983. "Marxism, Feminism and South African Studies." *Journal of Southern African Studies* 9 (2): 139–171.

Bozzoli, Belinda (with M. Nkotsoe). 1991. *Women of Phokeng: Consciousness, Life Strategy, and Migrancy in South Africa, 1900-1983*. Johannesburg: Ravan Press.

Chanock, Martin. 2004. *The Making of South African Legal Culture 1902–1936: Fear, Favour and Prejudice*. Cambridge: Cambridge University Press.

Chipkin, Clive. 1993. *Johannesburg Style: Architecture and Society, 1880s–1960s*. Cape Town: David Philip.

Cock, Jacklyn. 1980. *Maids and Madams: A Study in the Politics of Exploitation.* Johannesburg: Ravan Press.

Crankshaw, Owen. 1997. *Race, Class and the Changing Division of Labour Under Apartheid.* London: Routledge.

Davies, Robert. 1973. "The White Working Class in South Africa." *New Left Review* 82: 40–59.

Davies, Robert. 1979. *Capital, State and White Labour in South Africa, 1900–1960.* Brighton: Harvester Press.

Freund, Bill. 2020. "White People fit for a new South Africa? State Planning, Policy and Social Response in the Parastatal Cities of the Vaal, 1940–1990." In *Rethinking White Societies in Southern Africa, 1930s to 1990s*, edited by Duncan Money, and Danelle van zyl Hermann, 79–96. London and New York: Routledge.

Gelb, Stephen. 1991. "South Africa's Economic Crisis: An Overview." In *South Africa's Economic Crisis*, edited by Stephen Gelb, 1–32. Cape Town: David Philip.

Gilmore, Ruth Wilson. 2002. "Fatal Couplings of Power and Difference: Notes on Racism and Geography." *The Professional Geographer* 54 (1): 15–24.

Gilmore, Ruth Wilson. 2007. *Golden Gulag: Prisons, Crisis, Surplus, and Opposition in Globalizing California.* Berkeley: University of California Press.

Go, Julian. 2021. "Three Tensions in the Theory of Racial Capitalism." *Sociological Theory* 39 (1): 38–47.

Grundlingh, Albert. 2008. "'Are We Afrikaners Getting Too Rich?' Cornucopia and Change in Afrikanerdom in the 1960s." *Journal of Historical Sociology* 21 (2&3): 143–165.

Hall, Stuart. 1980. "Race, Articulation and Societies Structured in Dominance." In *Sociological Theories: Race and Colonialism*, edited by Mary O'Callaghan, 305–345. Paris: UNESCO.

Hall, Stuart. 1985. "Signification, Representation, Ideology: Althusser and the Post-Structuralist Debates." *Critical Studies in Mass Communication* 2 (2): 91–114.

Hall, Stuart. 2021 [1974]. "Marx's Notes on Method: A 'Reading' of the '1857 Introduction'." In *Selected Writings on Marxism: Stuart Hall*, edited by Gregor McLennan, 19–61. Durham and London: Duke University Press.

Hart, Gillian. 2007. "Changing Concepts of Articulation: Political Stakes in South Africa Today." *Review of African Political Economy* 34 (111): 85–101.

Hart, Gillian. 2018. "Relational Comparison Revisited: Marxist Postcolonial Geographies in Practice." *Progress in Human Geography* 42 (3): 371–394.

Hellmann, Ellen. 1953. *Sellgoods: A Sociological Survey of an African Commercial Labour Force.* Johannesburg: South African Institute of Race Relations.

Hirson, Baruch. 1990. *Yours for the Union: Class and Community Struggles in South Africa.* Johannesburg: Witwatersrand University Press.

Hudson, Peter James. 2017. *Bankers and Empire: How Wall Street Colonized the Caribbean.* Chicago: University of Chicago Press.

Hudson, Peter James. 2018. "Racial Capitalism and the Dark Proletariat." *Boston Review*, February 20, 2018. https://bostonreview.net/forum/remake-world-slavery-racial-capitalism-and-justice/peter-james-hudson-racial-capitalism-and.

Jenkins, Destin. 2021. *The Bonds of Inequality: Debt and the Making of the American City.* Chicago: University of Chicago Press.

Jenkins, Destin, and Justin Leroy. 2021. *Histories of Racial Capitalism.* New York: Columbia University Press.

Johnson, Walter. 2020. *The Broken Heart of America: St. Louis and the Violent History of the United States.* New York: Basic Books.

Kaplan, Mendel. 1986. *Jewish Roots in the South African Economy*. Cape Town: C. Struik.

Katz, Cindi. 1983. "Book Review: Maidens, Meal and Money." *Antipode* 15 (1): 42–45.

Kelley, Robin D. G. 2017. "What did Cedric Robinson Mean by Racial Capitalism?." *Boston Review*, January 12, 2017. https://bostonreview.net/race/robin-d-g-kelley-what-did-cedric-robinson-mean-racial-capitalism.

Kelley, Robin D. G. 2021. "Why Black Marxism, Why Now?" *Boston Review*, February 1, 2021. https://bostonreview.net/race-philosophy-religion/robin-d-g-kelley-why-black-marxism-why-now.

Kelley, Robin D. G. forthcoming. *Black Bodies Swinging: A Historical Autopsy*. New York: Metropolitan Books.

Kenny, Bridget. 2008. "Servicing Modernity: White Women Shop Workers on the Rand and Changing Gendered Respectabilities, 1940s–1970s." *African Studies* 67 (3): 365–396.

Kenny, Bridget. 2018. *Retail Worker Politics, Race and Consumption in South Africa: Shelved in the Service Economy*. Basingstoke: Palgrave Macmillan.

Kenny, Bridget. 2020. "To Protect White men: Job Reservation in Elevators in South Africa, 1950s–1960s." *Social History* 45 (4): 500–521.

Kenny, Bridget. 2021. "Trading Time: Retail Working Time and Precarious Labour in South Africa, 1960s–1980s." *Journal of Labor and Society* 24: 163–186.

Lambrecht, B., E. Meisel, and J. Rushburne. 1967. *A Survey of the Retail Trade in South Africa*. Cape Town: Stasinfrom.

Legassick, Martin. 1974. "South Africa: Capital Accumulation and Violence." *Economy and Society* 3 (3): 253–291.

Legassick, Martin, and David Hemson. 1976. *"Foreign Investment and the Reproduction of Racial Capitalism in South Africa." Foreign Investment in South Africa Discussion Series No. 2*. London: Anti-Apartheid Movement.

Luckett, Thembi. 2019. "Hope in the Debris of Capitalist dys/Utopia? Historical Progress and the Intricacies of Everyday Life in Lephalale." *Anthropology Southern Africa* 42 (1): 74–85.

Mabin, Alan. 1992. "Comprehensive Segregation: The Origins of the Group Areas Act and it Planning Apparatuses." *Journal of Southern African Studies* 18 (2): 405–429.

Mabin, Alan. 2005. "Suburbanisation, Segregation, and Government of Territorial Transformations." *Transformation: Critical Perspectives on Southern Africa* 57: 41–63.

Mackintosh, Maureen. 1977. "Reproduction and Patriarchy: A Critique of Claude Meillassoux, 'Femmes, Greniers et Capitaux'." *Capital and Class* 2: 119–127.

Mafeje, Archie. 1978. "Soweto and Its Aftermath." *Review of African Political Economy* 5 (11): 17–30.

Magubane, Bernard Makhosezwe. 1979. *The Political Economy of Race and Class in South Africa*. New York and London: Monthly Review Press.

Makalani, Minkah. 2021. "Cedric Robinson and the Origins of Race." *Boston Review*, February 2, 2021. https://bostonreview.net/race/minkah-makalani-cedric-robinson-and-origins-race.

Maré, Gerard. 2014. *Declassified*. Johannesburg: Jacana Press.

Mashinini, Emma. 1991. *Strikes Have Followed Me All My Life: A South African Autobiography*. New York: Routledge.

Money, Duncan, and Danelle van Zyl-Hermann. 2020. *Rethinking White Societies in Southern Africa, 1930s to 1990s*. London and New York: Routledge.

Money, Duncan, and Danelle van Zyl-Hermann. 2021. "Revisiting White Labourism: New Debates on Working-Class Whiteness in Twentieth-Century Southern Africa." *International Review of Social History* 66 (3): 469–491.

Mooney, Katie. 2006. "'Die Eendstert Euwel' and Societal Responses to White Youth Subcultural Identities on the Witwatersrand, 1930–1964." PhD diss., University of the Witwatersrand.

O'Laughlin, Bridget. 1977. "Production and Reproduction: Meillassoux's Femmes, Greniers et Capitaux." *Critique of Anthropology* 2 (8): 3–32.

O'Laughlin, Bridget. 2021. "No Separate Spheres: The Contingent Reproduction of Living Labor in Southern Africa." *Review of International Political Economy* 1–20. doi:10.1080/09692290.2021.1950025.

O'Meara, Dan. 1975. "White Trade Unions, Political Power and Afrikaner Nationalism." *South African Labour Bulletin* 1 (10): 31–51.

O'Meara, Dan. 1983. *Volkskapitalisme: Class, Capital and Ideology in the Development of Afrikaner Nationalism, 1934–1948*. Johannesburg: Ravan Press.

Posel, Deborah. 1983. "Rethinking the 'Race-Class Debate' in South African Historiography." *Social Dynamics* 9 (10): 50–66.

Posel, Deborah. 2010. "Races to Consume: Revisiting South Africa's History of Race, Consumption and the Struggle for Freedom." *Ethnic and Racial Studies* 33 (2): 157–175.

Robinson, Cedric J. 2000 [1983]. *Black Marxism: The Making of the Black Radical Tradition*. Durham, NC: University of North Carolina Press.

Roos, Neil. 2011. "Work Colonies and South African Historiography." *Social History* 36 (1): 54–76.

Taylor, Keeanga-Yamahtta. 2019. *Race for Profit: How Banks and the Real Estate Industry Undermined Black Homeownership*. Durham, NC: University of North Carolina Press.

Torkelson, Erin. 2021. "Sophia's Choice: Debt, Social Welfare, and Racial Finance Capitalism." *Environment and Planning D: Society and Space* 39 (1): 67–84.

van Zyl-Hermann, Danelle. 2020. *Privileged Precariat: White Workers and South Africa's Long Transition to Majority Rule*. Cambridge: Cambridge University Press.

Walker, Liz. 2001. "'Conservative Pioneers': The Formation of the South African Society of Medical Women." *Social History of Medicine* 14 (3): 483–505.

Willoughby-Herard, Tiffany. 2015. *Waste of a White Skin: The Carnegie Corporation and the Racial Logic of White Vulnerability*. Berkeley: University of California Press.

Wolpe, Harold. 1972. "Capitalism and Cheap Labour Power in South Africa: From Segregation to Apartheid." *Economy and Society* 1 (4): 425–454.

Wolpe, Harold. 1976. "The 'White Working Class' in South Africa." *Economy and Society* 5 (2): 197–240.

Wolpe, Harold. 1988. *Race, Class and the Apartheid State*. London: James Currey.

Geographies of racial capitalism: the July 2021 riots in South Africa

Ashwin Desai

ABSTRACT
In July 2021, riots involving large-scale looting of businesses enveloped parts of South Africa. The "spark" for the violence was the incarceration of the country's former President, Jacob Zuma. While referring to the broader dynamics of the riots, this article focusses on one township of Durban, Phoenix. Here, the violence was headlined as taking a racial turn, setting African against Indian. By situating the analysis against the African National Congress (ANC) led government's failure to confront inherited apartheid geographies and racialised forms of capital accumulation, the article foregrounds the explanatory power of racial capitalism, with the understanding that, while "dynamic and changing", its "temporality … is one of ongoingness … a process not a moment … ". (12) (Jenkins, D., and J. Leroy. 2021. "Introduction: The Old History of Capitalism." In *Histories of Racial Capitalism*, edited by D. Jenkins, and J. Leroy, 1–26. New York: Columbia University Press.).

Introduction

In July 2021, widescale rioting and looting erupted in two of South Africa's largest provinces by population, KwaZulu-Natal (KZN) and Gauteng. The immediate context was the imprisonment of former President Jacob Zuma for contempt of court, on the direct instruction of South Africa's highest judicial body, the Constitutional Court. The riots had a decided ethnic character. The epicentre lay in areas where mainly Zulu-speaking South Africans lived; Zuma being Zulu himself. However, the socio-economic tinder was dangerously dry with unemployment levels running beyond 40 per cent. Delivery on government promises of development for poor black communities through conservative economic policies has all but ground to a halt. This was exacerbated by endemic theft of public monies by cadres of Nelson Mandela's once proud liberation movement, the African National Congress (ANC)

(Basson and du Toit 2017; Bhorat et al. 2017). Inequality in South Africa is, almost literally, a powder-keg. Having said that, as destructive as the riots were, the near insurrection observed one very specific rule of engagement. South Africans of different races and classes did not set upon each other. Looters did not invade personal property and suburbanites did not venture beyond their neighbourhoods to attempt to quell the lawlessness in factories, shopping centres and on highways. One of the exceptions was the township of Phoenix; townships being dormitory-style districts servicing white cities and towns, set aside under apartheid for Black workers to live in. In line with apartheid's strict and perverse social-engineering, Black people were themselves divided into groups; Africans, being the majority, coloureds (or people of mixed race) and Indians (mainly the descendants of British indenture in the second half of the nineteenth century). When Phoenix was created in the 1960s, it was to receive Indians forcibly removed from their footholds in the port city of Durban under South Africa's infamous Group Areas Act.

Marxists writing on South Africa argued that racial domination and capital accumulation were inextricably linked and that the fight to defeat apartheid was also a struggle to end capitalism. Racial capitalism was the term used to show this interconnection.

(Alexander 1985, 1986; Legassick and Hemson 1976). History was to show that this script was not followed and capitalism was given a new lease of life with the coming of the ANC to power. As Clarno puts it:

> The South African transition has reproduced racial capitalism while transforming the dynamics of exploitation and exclusion. Deindustrialization and casualization have weakened the labour movement, intensified the exploitation and precariousness of the Black working class, and produced a growing racialised surplus population ... .Coupled with their increasingly precarious economic situation, the Black poor confront a severe shortage of decent housing. The crises of unemployment and homelessness are compounded by landlessness. Accepting constitutional protections for private property, the new government rejected the use of state-centred mechanisms to redistribute colonised land. Instead, South Africa adopted a market-based program through which the state helps subsidize the purchase of white-owned land by Black clients. This "willing-seller, willing-buyer" program depends not only on the ability of Black clients to access capital but also on the willingness of white landowners to negotiate a price and sell their land. The program has facilitated the emergence of a small class of wealthy Black landowners but has only led to the redistribution of 7.5 per cent of South African land. (Clarno 2017, 34)

What is argued in this article is that, given the continuing power of racial geographies and inherited forms of capital accumulation, racial capitalism still has great explanatory value in contemporary South Africa, and it provides ways of understanding the events that unfolded in Phoenix. In this context, Bhattacharyya's recent work on racial capitalism has resonance, urging that attention be given to "new and unpredictable modes of dispossession to be understood alongside the centuries-old carnage that moistens the earth beneath our feet" (Bhattacharyya 2018, 9). Bhattacharyya acknowledges "the sedimented histories of racialised dispossession that shape economic life in our time" and upon which much scholarship still rests a languid eye. After all, history lies heavy on the neck of Black people, of all places in South Africa, the country which spawned the starkest exemplar of racial capitalism; apartheid. However, Bhattacharyya opens the way to understanding "the place of racialisation in particular instances of capitalist formation, most of all when those instances are now" (2018, 9). This "permission" to seek explanatory force in contemporary events for phenomena in which race and capital appear to intertwine is theoretically useful and liberating. Yes, the historical framework is important but new questions may be entertained. How does the logic of capital, seeking ever higher profit, tending towards monopoly when it can, and often dispossessing the already poor, resolve around racial lines in the here and now?

In the story of Phoenix township and the fatal violence that took place there in July 2021, this article proposes that newer social forces played a significant role. In particular, it suggests that a particular strata of post-apartheid Black capitalists have found it useful to operate within an ethnically charged market and society. This is the market for tenders that the local and provincial state awards for goods and services to private companies; a lucrative market with high rates of profit. Although in a limited sector of the economy, some Black entrepreneurs have in recent years discovered the value of *capitalizing on race* in their dealings with an African nationalist state. This is no moral accusation. They would probably not be good businesspeople if they did not. Yet, this racialization can have consequences in the way social conflict is handled. Racial categories to be ticked in boxes on supply chain management forms do not always stay on those forms. They assume political substance.

Where I take issue with Bhattacharyya is the dismissal of intentionality, when she argues that "racial capitalism does not emerge as a plan" (2018, 9). While taking the point that one must be wary of the idea of a puppeteer pulling the strings according to some preordained script, one has to take cognisance that in South Africa, capital accumulation and racist exploitation have been handy bedfellows. These histories and methodologies of profiting from racial division continue to impact on contemporary social relations. As Jenkins and Leroy put it, "violent dispossessions inherent to capital accumulation operate by leveraging, intensifying, and creating social distinctions" (2021, 3).

Notwithstanding this, Bhattacharyya's intervention is relevant to my own enquiries: this is to better understand events in South Africa that took place a quarter of a century after apartheid ended. As Bhattacharyya tells us:

Racial capitalism helps us to understand how people become divided from each other in the name of economic survival or in the name of economic well-being. One aspect of its techniques encompass the processes that appear to grant differential privileges ... and the social relations that flow from these differentiations. (2018, 10–11)

Bhattacharyya's willingness to consider whether "new and unpredictable modes of dispossession" have proximate causes and are not simply a distant *sine qua non*, is worth emulating. Also stimulating is Bhattacharyya's concession that racial capitalism

operates both through the exercise of coercive power and through the mobilisation of desire. People are not only 'forced' to participate in economic arrangements that cast them to the social margins; they also rush to be included in this way and to become edge-subjects of capitalism. (2018, 9–10)

Except for casting local elites as sell-outs, dupes or pawns of imperialism, a fair portion of left analyses gives little attention to the desires of victims, the sometime "edge subjects of capitalism". This is a regrettable oversight. Both racialization and commodification can be processes that people or groups come to actively desire. Ignoring this underestimates the true scope of the problem. As Bhattacharyya put it, we need to understand "the seductive character of capitalist living, even for those who are most damaged by the workings of capitalism" (2018, 18). When we ascribe to racial-capitalism yet another outrage or dehumanizing loss, we might have to ask, how did its victims go along with it for so long and why do they apply its sharp edges to their own veins?

Phoenix

In July 2021, our television, telephone and computer screens ignited with scenes of looting in KZN and parts of Gauteng. The violence and destruction were so widespread that it resembled a war. For ten days, shops, warehouses, factories, a harbour, highways, and entire neighbourhoods had acrid palls of smoke hanging above them, as if these structures had been hit by airstrikes. Instead of a sneak attack by a foreign adversary, however, hundreds of civilians poured onto the streets to do damage with their bare hands and rudimentary tools; crowbars, jerry-cans and matchsticks. They grabbed what they could, set fire to what they could not, and then receded back into the suburbs, shacks and townships.

It is hard to imagine that any single participant's lot improved, no matter how many TVs or groceries they managed to snag. Indeed, for most, it demonstrably worsened. Local shops never reopened, thousands of jobs were lost, the local state, already bankrupted by corruption and skewed development priorities, had little patronage to dispense.

The riots were destructive in both human and financial cost. Over 500 people died. Tragically, many were trampled or burned alive inside shops and factories when rioters further back-torched buildings. Billions of rands worth of damage was done to infrastructure, not to mention markets, supply chains, tax receipts, investment, and morale. No pro-poor gains were made on the economic policy front. No-one owned the uprising, which remains mired in negative and derogatory ethnic (it was a Zulu thing) and criminal (it was a Zuma thing) loops of association.

Among those in the crowd, we are told by a subsequent Expert Panel, a few hardened and organized instigators directed the violence (Africa, Sokape, and Gumbi 2021). *They* pulled the strings on Twitter, on secretive WhatsApp groups and even in connivance with seditious elements in the state. Their presumed purpose was an old tactic employed *against* the apartheid state by liberation movements: to make South Africa ungovernable. Judging by the hashtags on social media, the spectre of violence in 2021 was to some extent leveraged (not caused) to pressure the government into releasing from jail former President of the country and Kwa-Zulu-Natal native, Jacob Zuma. This most brazen politician is widely and notoriously implicated in corruption during his term of office, involving eye-watering amounts. He currently stands accused on several fronts of bartering access to state power for kick-backs that foreigners could give his substantial familial and political cohort.

My focus is not on the general cause of the July 2021 violence, however. I hone in on the course the violence took in Phoenix, twenty-five kilometres north of Durban. Designated during apartheid as an Indian township, Phoenix houses around 300,000 people, many poor or of working-class social origin. Phoenix stands out as the reputed site of a massacre by Indian South Africans against African compatriots. Labelled as looters, some Africans moving around in Phoenix were set upon by vigilante groups and assaulted or killed. Reports of these events sowed immense social discord and, for a time, threatened to ignite a race-war in South Africa.

It is worth pausing for a moment and going back a few decades before the 1990s to understand how Phoenix came to contain Indian people during apartheid. In the second half of the 1960s, with the apartheid state at the zenith of its' powers, tens of thousands of Indians were forced out of their homes. This dispossession was part of the weaponry of "Grand Apartheid" where the government enacted even more zealous laws to separate black from white; in the labour market, sexually, and where they lived. Phoenix was designed to receive many of these families put on the move, evicted mainly from areas closer to the CBD of Durban. The barren township far outside of Durban was laid out in a swirling grid, encompassing some stand-alone houses, but also many two or three storey tenements, row after row of them. After the fall of apartheid, a large proportion of middle-class residents moved to formerly white suburbs. Many industries, such as the huge textile factories that employed Indian workers during the 1970s and 1980s collapsed, as tariffs were hastily decreased and imports flowed. Positions in the civil service also became harder to access. Under apartheid, Indians benefitted from a certain level of job-reservation. Since 1999, affirmative action targets in effect reserved 85 per cent of jobs and promotions for African work-seekers and only around 2 per cent for Indians. While this quota accurately represents South Africa's overall population demographics, it is out of kilter with Durban's population statistics.[1]

In response to receding economic prospects in the state, many Indian breadwinners adopted trades, such as plumbing, tiling, and so on. Others opened stores or spaza shops, rented out backyard rooms or ran taxis. Others clung onto their existing jobs as teachers, clerks, salespeople, waiters, attorneys, accountants, hairdressers, caterers, and technicians. Phoenix's economy also came to encompass (and bleed from) organized criminality, mainly through a drug-trade conducted by rival gangs, but also the popular illegalities of knocking off name-brand goods and evading tax and import duties.

The end of apartheid thankfully saw the end of Group Areas. For reasons irreducible simply to being better resourced, schools in Phoenix were widely regarded as having higher standards of education than those in African townships. Poorer parents in search of better opportunities for their children, who lived outside the area, thus eagerly sought placement in Phoenix schools. With the state, through legislation, gradually clawing back school admission authority from parent-run governing bodies, by the mid 2000s, the racial profile of learners in Phoenix schools changed dramatically. This created its own tensions and conflicts. The same applied to hospitals and other social services. Anyone moving around Phoenix before (and after) the riots will see a mixture of African and Indian consumers, workers, public servants, small business-owners and pedestrians going about their business, the racial admixture of which one does not see in many former "group areas".

Geographically wedged between the affluent Umhlanga, Gateway Mall, Mt. Edgecombe, Inanda and Kwa-Mashu, the latter two being African townships, Phoenix has absorbed far greater cultural and demographic change than either (white) Umhlanga or (African) Kwa-Mashu could dream of. Crucially, for Indians living in working class areas like Phoenix, this "opening up" of community resources, coupled with their own modest financial standing has provided them with no credit as to their legal identity. Legally, Indian and African South Africans are distinct groups and the state, through legislation, differentiates between them in assigning opportunities, giving preferential treatment to Africans.

This would perhaps not be a recipe for conflict in a growing economy or one where the government spends its tax revenues properly. However, since 1999, the ANC government's economic policy has predominantly rested on redistributing existing resources, whilst neglecting infrastructure investment that would serve people's basic needs. This has led to a decade of punishing electricity black-outs and water shortages. An ageing infrastructure, catering mainly for whites, has not been extended or even maintained. Houses built in Durban have been of laughable quality and shack settlements have sprung up everywhere. Arguments by the ANC government that this stems from the legacy of apartheid are specious twenty eight years after the first democratic elections. Similarly specious are arguments that a neo-liberal economic policy imposed upon South Africa by the West is to blame. Even with the development inequalities of apartheid factored in, and even within the social spending brackets imposed by international lenders and investors, the ANC government had trillions of rands at its disposal over the years to build and equip new schools, hospitals, power-plants, pipes and to build proper houses. Not only has this money been available, but it has been stolen by ANC cadres.

For rich whites and Indians, the following fact is something they can absorb. While Group Areas have ended, group classification has not. What this means is that the state can still pick winners and losers in the game of life based on the colour of their skin. In its very constitution, the new South Africa entrenches apartheid's racial categories of African, coloured, Indian and white. The rationale is that differential treatment based on these categories is necessary to redress the stark social imbalances of the past. Thus, preferential treatment may be given to Africans in the workplace in hiring and promotion. Similarly, universities may adjust their admission requirements to permit a greater number of African students. Even in sport, it is not sufficient that provincial or national teams have a certain split between white players and players of colour. Cricket teams, for example, must have a certain proportion of Africans in them.

And so, where does a place like Phoenix stand? Unlike either the suburbs or townships, it has transformed, on the North Coast of KZN, into arguably the most racially diverse location. Social divisions are the least stark in schools, hospitals and queues for social services. Because government policy is sensitive to brute race and not class, the formal inequality which an Indian learner from Phoenix faces when she does not make the cut for medical school with 93 per cent aggregate is appreciably higher when an African learner from a rich background in Umhlanga gets the place. These policies form part of the broad, everyday brooding lament of working-class Indians in places like Phoenix. While similar complaints of "losing out" may be muttered by wealthier Indians, this is said with a hint of irony. There is always a way around that money or connections can buy. But for poor Indians, this sense of racial grievance ironically has not bubbled up. For many, it has helplessly seethed.

In keeping the focus local and contemporary, we are bound to ask what kind of racial capitalism defines social relations in Phoenix? At a very abstract level, one could seek to implicate the Washington consensus. One could point a finger at red-lining banks scared to advance credit to the poor. One might even blame the continuing stranglehold of white monopoly capital on industries like mining or farming. It is a matter of record that, as the transition unfolded, "infrastructural rights" initially won "(such as access to water, sanitation and energy)" were rolled back "by linking the scope of services provided to buyer affordability, rather than providing an acceptable level of services and charging an acceptable amount" (Bond 2000, 110). However, what is argued here, is that if one looks more closely at the manner in which capitalist interests racialised the episode of looting in 2021, other players, not properly described before, may be discerned. It comes down to this: by the time the riots erupted, many working-class Indians in Phoenix arguably faced the brunt of a "fraction of capital" seeking hegemony in significant sections of the KZN economy. These were African chauvinists feeding off contracts with the local and provincial state, whose business model was to steal state resources and displace the resultant disaffection of the poor onto racial minorities.

Between borders and business forums

As the looting spread, many looters in the north of Durban walked along the highway between Kwa-Mashu and the warehouses, malls and businesses at Cornubia, where they wanted to be. Their journey took them past or through Phoenix. Although these lamentable events took place during a widespread episode of social unrest, this geo-spatial fact is crucial for what happened later. Oddly, Phoenix was also singled out quite early for attention in the "Twitter streets". Social media was awash, first with a threatened invasion of Phoenix by Africans, followed by news of vigilante violence by Indians, which triggered further threats. Similar fears of attack and isolation may have permeated other neighbourhoods. But in Phoenix, they had an obvious substantive, geographic and psychological resonance that did not apply in other locales, as I argue below. My approach takes locale seriously, with the understanding that broader economic and political factors "are refracted through the prism of locality into the conditions in which the individual functions. However mobile our society, the local spatial dimension is a necessary and major part of our experience" (Parry, Moyser, and Wagstaff 1987, 213).

While figures vary, it is estimated that some thirty six people were killed in Phoenix; thirty three were African. A total of fifty six people have been arrested in connection with the murders. Most of those killed came from the African settlements adjoining Phoenix; Zwelisha, Bhambhayi and Umaoti. Here, RDP housing rests alongside shack settlements. For the first

20–30 h, when the looting spread and threats of attack made the digital rounds, there was little if no police presence.

When a group of nearby African residents made their way into Phoenix, stones rained down on some houses. Twitter and Facebook lit up with stories of attacks on Phoenix. On 11 July 2021, a WhatsApp message went viral: "Tomorrow we are coming in all your Indian people town to close everything. You will wake up and see flames". A siege mentality took over, as visuals of widespread looting were captured live on television, and stories abounded of Phoenix being invaded and shopping malls going up in smoke. One must also remember the historical backdrop of antagonism that turned to violence in 1949 and 1985.

In Cato Manor in 1949, violent clashes took place between Indian and African. Probably more importantly, in 1985, Indians were driven out of Inanda. This conflict was caught up in the escalating resistance to apartheid that also saw the ANC aligned United Democratic Front (UDF) pitted against the Zulu nationalist Inkatha Freedom Party (IFP). The IFP were pushing for Inanda to be incorporated into the KwaZulu-Natal Bantustan, while the ANC/UDF opposed this. Indian presence was seen as holding this process up. Most of the Indians driven out found a home in Phoenix. These events remain fresh in the memory and one can discern how this fed into a siege mentality (Hughes 1985).

Much is made of white mainstream antipathy to Indians which, under white minority rule, portrayed Indians as an unwanted community and a scourge on the economic prospects of white businesspeople. After 1994, some of these attitudes have been adopted, quite casually, in mainstream black majority rule. Famous anti-apartheid playwright, Mbongeni Ngema, released a popular song titled "AmaNdiya" in 2002, excoriating Indians as a group and, worryingly, calling on the "strong men" of the Zulu "nation" to resist. In Kwa-Zulu-Natal, an African grassroots movement, the Mazibuye African Forum sprang up purportedly to oppose against Indians' "racism". It portrayed Indians as foreigners. The Black nationalist political party, the Economic Freedom Fighters (EFF), also articulates anti-Indian sentiment, most noticeably ahead of elections. Much of this delicate historical balance of Afro-Indian relations would have been known and experienced by Phoenix residents (Desai and Vahed 2019).

In a bail application for nine people from Phoenix, accused of a variety of crimes including murder during the riots, a voice note was played in court by the lawyer of three of the accused. "In the voice note, an African man speaks of meetings allegedly held in KwaMashu, Umlazi and the Inanda Hostel where attacks on Phoenix residents were discussed. The speaker claims a special traditional medicine would be used to kill people in Phoenix" (*Post,* October 27–31 2021). It remains unclear why the focus was on Phoenix, but it created something of a siege mentality. The near total absence of police or army

THE SOUTH AFRICAN TRADITION OF RACIAL CAPITALISM

responses to widescale, serious and obvious illegality only added to the impulse of self-security among Indians.

Around Phoenix, the Kwa-Mashu highway was barricaded by mobs who stoned passing cars, and on the R102 near Ottawa, on its eastern border, municipal refuse trucks commandeered by Zuma supporters dumped tons of refuse on the road. Within a day, columns of black smoke rose from the townships that girdle the area, as malls, shops and spazas were pillaged. Anxiety – the fear of what would come next, with the police patently over-whelmed – began to tighten its grip. The disquiet was inflamed by an array of WhatsApp messages and voice notes that spelled out plans to attack Indians in their own homes. Phoenix resident Aldino Padayachee recorded:

> Voice notes were all over saying the Zulus were coming, but it made people scared. We were hearing that and at the same time we could see hundreds of people coming toward us. (Hunter, Wicks, and Singh 2021, 192)

Were these voice notes designed to create racial tension and as much mayhem as possible? Were they to ensure that those who attacked shops in Cornubia and later Nandi Drive would have "safe passage" through Phoenix? It is doubtful there was any strategic command centre. The threats were at best ad-hoc, in-group mobilization efforts, the enunciation of a desire to constitute blocs of identity for their own sake, such as soccer teams from adjoining towns devising bloodcurdling chants. The effect however was very different. The chants were taken seriously.

In Phoenix, roadblocks were set up by residents of the flats. These were first defensive barricades, intending to slow traffic. As the looters made their way through Phoenix though, this took on a more offensive turn, with cars and bakkies stopped and searched, especially vehicles laden with goods, some still in boxes. And then the drug lords, gangsters and their runners moved in. They began looting the looters in the name of "defending the community". When some of these "community defenders" were arrested, their own homes contained washing machines, fridges and other looted items. This re-looting was accompanied by gratuitous violence. Vehicles belonging to suspected looters were pummelled with cricket bats. African people walking in Phoenix were assaulted. Some were shot. None of this is to say that the victims were selected for mob "justice" based on any under-lying facts. Afterwards, African people reported being targeted simply for trying to fill up at petrol stations in Phoenix, or walking home from work, being as innocently present on public thoroughfares as any South African has the right to be anywhere in the country.

In understanding the violence, the enduring power of two phenomena seems dominant. The spatial logic of apartheid saw Phoenix placed between white suburbs and high-end shopping centres and African town-ships. To get from the latter to the desired former meant physically traversing

Phoenix roads. The constitutional logic of democracy saw Africans and Indians in Phoenix still separated as economic and political subjects. Phoenix, housing the lower middle-class and poor, was thus a site where the sharing of state resources with African neighbourhoods was most visible, but for which residents were given no credit. Both of these factors made the settlement potentially explosive in times of trouble. Economic decisions, either to violently acquire or violently guard property, became cloaked in racial identities, African versus Indian. The looting, screened on television, the clear incapacity or lack of police will in protecting people, the heightened social media posts, led to apocalyptic thinking in a narrow strip of Phoenix, a sense of an ending, of betrayal.

Debates surrounding the looting have taken two opposed forms: orchestration or spontaneity (Africa, Sokape, and Gumbi 2021; Hunter, Wicks, and Singh 2021). In what has emerged so far, there is some evidence of local mobilization to protest Zuma's imprisonment. However, the jailing of Zuma stands for something more profound: It was widely seen as the courts drawing a line in the sand against the impunity of a professional caste of looters embedded in and around the ANC, who in concert with foreigners and local businesspeople, had bankrupted state coffers while Zuma was president. Zuma, still on trial for corruption, and with more charges pending, had been jailed for a relatively minor infraction: contempt of court. The jailing of the figurehead of state capture sent shockwaves through the tender mafias of KZN. These shockwaves filtered through to the livelihoods of community leaders at a very local level. How so?

To benefit from corruption around the procurement of state contracts in KZN, one had to be in favour with the politicians. For they held sway over the bureaucrats who evaluated bids and awarded contracts. Under Zuma, a vast network of rent-seekers had been installed in senior positions within the executive. Since the favour of senior ANC leaders was crucial to businesspeople seeking to win tenders in certain sectors of the KZN economy, this also meant the opposite. As an ANC member, unless one acquired a leadership position, you were not worth bribing. To acquire a leadership position in turn meant contesting, every two and half years, for ANC leadership positions in branch or provincial executive committees. This was – and still is – an expensive business. Rival factions of ANC members must pay branch members and delegates to vote them in, with the price of a mark on an ANC ballot reportedly running into tens of thousands of rands. Insidiously then, ANC leadership is monetized all the way down the ranks. Along with this monetization comes loyalty, or at the very least, mutual self-interest. The arrest of Zuma and the threatened dismantling of corrupt networks of patronage which he headed up, understandably agitated local Kwa-Mashu and Inanda leaders, as much financially as ideologically.

So, while my own view inclines towards the looting being a spontaneous response to the opportunities that such a moment afforded, especially as law enforcement agencies were either over-run or seemed unwilling to intervene, one cannot completely ignore the political interests that would be served in encouraging racial discord. This is a key feature, as described above, of the business model of the fraction of capital operating in KZN alongside ANC elites. Steal, and then deflect blame for the resulting non-delivery of basic services. Indeed, the alleged racism of Indians increasingly garnered more public headlines than the actions of looters, the incitement by Zuma supporters, and the woeful inaction of the state. In some quarters, Indian racism became the *sine qua non* of the rioting and looting itself, as if attacks on Black people from Phoenix preceded the widescale looting. While the riots were still simmering down, some African politicians saw fit to march on Phoenix to decry racism. Simultaneously, calls by Black nationalist politicians for Indians to be shot attracted an insipid push-back from black political parties, whose key mobilising promise is to win for their constituents, through control of state purchasing, the biggest slice of the economy (Hunter, Wicks, and Singh 2021).

It is one thing to criticize local business mafias. At a central level, the ANC's economic model was, in practice, also bereft of coherence, realism and honesty. With no real plan to make good on the vision of past leaders in the first half of the twentieth century, who were committed to self-help schemes and opportunities for the small trader to grow, they concentrated instead on the idea of creating a Black patriotic bourgeoise, through a legislative opening up of the upper echelons of the economy through Black Economic Empowerment (BEE) rules and preferential procurement policies weighted in favour of Black business. BEE was supposed to, in the words of Mbeki, be the catapult for creating and strengthening a black capitalist class (Saul and Bond 2014, 223). Much was expected of this black bourgeoisie which the ANC held would be committed to redressing the inherited inequalities of apartheid (MacDonald 2004, 649). This expectation did not age well. Access to the commanding heights bred aloofness and entitlement (as well as airs and graces). By the time of Zuma's presidency, it was clear that BEE had become the preserve of a few, that there were few genuine businesses created, and many of the deals were mired in debt. By 2014, the ANC's once Premier of Limpopo Ngoako Ramatlhodi, held that the ANC was the foot-soldier of an economy that was still commanded by whites (Saul and Bond 2014, 223).

In the face of this, we have those grouped around former president Zuma and his infamous cronies in the Gupta family, who used proximity to the president to allegedly steal billions of rands during Zuma's nine years in office. They argued that they were seeking to tip the balance away from monopoly capital and Mbeki's BEE beneficiaries in favour of tender-based black capitalists (Pauw 2017). This would deal the final death-knell to white monopoly capital, old-money concentrated in sectors of the economy that white people were able to monopolize under apartheid such as agriculture, banking, insurance, engineering and mining. Tender-based capitalists in practise, however, simply looked to use the state as a way to accumulate capital. They were not in the business of using this capital to invest in ways that would create jobs, develop national industry and expand internal markets. Jeremy Cronin, former deputy general secretary of the South African Communist Party (SACP) and ANC Member of Parliament referred to "a process of primitive accumulation" in contemporary South Africa, in which would be capitalists "without capital … could only really emerge in any substantive way through taking on indebted shareholding from existing monopoly capital (with all the dangers of fronting and compradorism), or through the diversion of public resources into private pockets (parasitism)" (*Daily Maverick*, 14 August 2020).

In Durban, ANC ward councillors are at the centre of not only primitive accumulation but also a network of patronage and backhanders. This was given free rein in the Zuma years, but once he was forced prematurely from office, has been stymied, with some of his closest allies in KZN being charged for alleged roles in patronage networks surrounding tenders. A form of primitive accumulation was further "legitimised" by so-called Business Forums which targeted large projects of private companies and, at the barrel of a gun and in the name of transformation, forced companies to pay over a percentage of contracts and employ workers on the books of the Business Forums. Ahead of Zuma's arrest, these forums, while still operating in KZN, were substantially pushed back by special law enforcement attention.

While arguably still nascent and with their slice of the economy not measured, no social history of Durban in 2021 can ignore the existence of these tender barons. They exist, they cohere as a class or faction of a class and, given that the effect of their business practices is to deepen poverty, they need a scapegoat for non-delivery in the next financial year. This scapegoat may just as well be an Indian family terrified by threats of violence, as it may be an African breadwinner assaulted by Indian thugs on a Phoenix sidewalk. As long as there is someone else to blame for the mess of corruption, it does not really matter whose blood is spilt.

Present futures

Where are we now? The streets have returned to the kind of normalized violence which has characterized the area for the last decade. This is true both in Phoenix and Kwa-Mashu. Drug-lords, some with registered security companies and fire-power, rule the streets. Many of the young are anchored

THE SOUTH AFRICAN TRADITION OF RACIAL CAPITALISM 153

within the limits of a few square kilometres. Sugars[2] addicts wander the streets. Drug lords enforce their will with brutality.

The areas contiguous to Inanda, Kwa-Mashu and Phoenix, Umhlanga and Mount Edgecombe saw incredible development post-1994 into what urban economists call an "edge city". Writing in 2007, Bill Freund described the development:

> On the ridge overlooking the sea and the oceanside suburb of Umhlanga Rocks, one now finds hundreds of houses of the newly rich (no longer racially defined, of course), the largest shopping complex in South Africa modelled on activity-based U.S. shopping malls and a growing array of corporate service offices and headquarters. ... Just inland, Mount Edgecombe sugar estate has been largely turned into a golf course and network of affluent gated suburbia. (Freund 2007, 190)

A few kilometres away, we have another world. The shacks of Inanda sit alongside rudimentary government-built houses. Many places have no electricity and running water. In the government-built flats in Phoenix, things are better, but here too, the Indian working class has taken a battering. Wealth and poverty bare their teeth at each other.

In this area of the KZN North Coast, we witness an unfolding of what Neil Smith has referred to as "satanic geographies of uneven development" which "represent a striking spatialization of the class and race, gender and national relations that make global production a social process" (Smith 1997, 188).

On an overcast September weekend in 2021, with the violence subsided, I was in Phoenix. The Ubuntu (Friendship) Committees and Social Cohesion workshops were in full swing, but the youth of Phoenix stayed away. At the bottom of a stairwell in the Phoenix flatlands, in Lenham, I met an Indian man in his mid-20s. Let me call him Gupta. He used to work in the local taxi rank, but for two years has been unemployed. When asked about jobs, his persistent refrain is "they do not want Indians". He was at the barricades during the unrest; "protecting his grandmother". His life is spent "hanging", as he put it.

A mere road away lives a young man in the shack settlement of Umoati. Let me call him Zuma. During the looting spree, he had garnered a few goods from the Phoenix Mall. But the takkies and clothes had been sold. He worked for a while in the Umhlanga strip as a cleaner. It is a 15-minute ride away from his home but a world away. He too is "hanging". He is fiercely anti-Phoenix Indians, but could laugh and crack a joke with me.

As we speak, I gaze over the view from his shack. Distant car-dealerships, malls, the high-end apartments of Umhlanga in the distant haze, even a descending aeroplane. Wealth drips around him but just out of reach. Except during the riots. According to Zuma, it was so very easy. He walked across a bridge that covers a stream and the Mall was immediately in sight. He grabbed a few things and made his way back. More would have been possible if the Indians hadn't got in the way.

One thinks of Achille Mbembe telling us of a society in which something is within eyesight but beyond reach: "an economy of desired goods that are known, that may sometimes be seen, that one wants to enjoy, but to which one will never have material access" except through "pillage and seizure" (2002, 271). Life is "assimilated to a game of chance, a lottery, in which the existential temporal horizon is colonized by the immediate present and by prosaic short-term calculations" (2002, 271).

So close, yet so far apart. Both Zuma and Gupta feel powerful within their areas but powerless outside it. Gupta circulates in the flats, picks up a few "lucks", as he terms it. His manning of the barricades has reinforced his reputation as a tough guy. Zuma also links into the power structures of the ward councillor. He will mobilize for him in the ANC branch and elections. He'll get an odd-job here, a handout there.

They eye each other with resentment from within spitting distance. As Bourdieu tells us: "Social identity lies in difference, and difference is asserted against what is closest, which represents the greatest threat" (Bourdieu 1984, 479).

But there is something deeper as one probes, a kind of ressentiment from both sides, a willing adoption of racialised identities that are assumed to best advance the economic interests of individuals, under a local capitalist formation, who live but a road apart from each other. The flats are slightly better but are in free-fall, as Gupta senses that all the resources go across the road; "the government gives us nothing". Both have histories of evictions and dispossessions, but as Bhattacharyya states, these experiences are "complicated by other differentiating processes and the battle to retain access to increasingly scarce resources is mobilising differences, and commonalities, between groups" (2018, 21).

Endings and beginnings

Pockets of looting also popped up during the July 2021 riots in Gauteng. In Soweto, African residents mobilized to protect their property, using violence to ward looters off. These actions were framed as righteous, law-abiding civilians standing up to the incipient barbarism of the lumpen proletariat. In complete contrast, in Phoenix, the story is of the working classes of Inanda (African) and Phoenix (Indians) turning on each other. This says much about the enduring ability of apartheid lexography to shape political perceptions of events decades after its fall. Rendered invisible in these narratives are the luxurious estates lying beyond the battlefields. Near Phoenix, this is Mount Edgecombe, acres of green-roofed luxury homes set around golf courses and water-ways. After the riots, these and other gaudy private

THE SOUTH AFRICAN TRADITION OF RACIAL CAPITALISM 155

developments in Umlanga will continue, increasing populated by Indian and African families wishing to escape the township and suburbs by visibly cutting themselves off from it. As Freund put it:

> The logic of capital is one that the ANC government is very unwilling to counter; there is complete acceptance of the need to accommodate and attract business through "competitiveness" as the key dictate in urban policy. Countering unplanned development (or better put, development planned purely in the interests of the affluent) is no longer considered a sensible way to conduct urban politics. And thus the continuing edge city development of north Durban can be considered a certainty for the future. (Freund 2007, 191)

The challenge of organizing Zuma and Gupta into a radical subjectivity from below is that they are not part of the employed, working alongside each other. They are part of "the disposable poor" who "must constantly invent creative life strategies to survive. Yet, these spaces of abandonment are never external to the dynamics of racial capitalism". They are there as a potential "desperate workforce", recruiting ground for drug lords and foot soldiers of local politicians and tender mafias (Clarno 2017, 2002).

Their exploitation, their immiseration in poverty is in their demarcated "group areas". The recent violence illustrates how the lines have been drawn; recruitment grounds for the entrepreneurs of Indian racism and African chauvinism.

Do we all end up with the promise of nuance and complexity, but end in the same place of a re-racialization of society, a society of blood? Or is there something else? Can a politics emerge that can close the distance? How do we build the future in the present? At the moment, the social cohesion and *ubuntu* workshops are, uninspiringly, all we have. Even the churches mainly keep to their "own" flock. The efforts of out-reach are laudable, but at the same time simply a holding pattern.

Standing in Phoenix, one can say that the dream of a non-racial inclusive democracy is rendered into ashes. Can it ever rise? Can we build an anti-racist movement of young people in the area? School assemblies are crucial. In most schools in Phoenix, between 30 per cent and 60 per cent of the students are African. It is the one shared social space where identities may be contested and reformed. The flats and council houses of Phoenix have progressively deracialised and social relations are really good. Witness Lloyd Cele who found fame as a runner up in SA Idols, the main singing contest in the country. Born in Kwa-Mashu, he grew up in Phoenix. In the aftermath of the riots, he spoke about the impact on his family:

> From what they have expressed, it was nothing but fear. Fear in their own homes that had them in tears. I could only pray for their safety and hope that it would be over as soon as possible and that unity would be restored again.

Talking about growing up in Phoenix, he remembers it as a special time: "the only people who had problems with us was the Aunty who didn't want to give our tennis ball back" (*IOL News*, 21 August 2021).

At the top echelons of society, Gupta and Zuma merged into the Zuptas. But at the bottom, they eye each other with fear and anger. Can we bring working-class youth together? What kind of language will appeal? How can we break this re-racialization of society?

One of the first challenges is to understand local dynamics. To situate oneself on the ground. To not shy away from the challenges that come with it. To take a step back.

The violence in Phoenix has monopolized our political energies. Given us choices to make in either Black or brown. Some see the moment as fostering "One Indian, One Bullet" sentiments (Hunter, Wicks, and Singh 2021, 180). Others instead urge an attitude of "let's all just get along". Both duck the harder insight. It needs us to look near and far as well as the ground beneath our feet. Getting along depends on the categories of Indian and African dissolving into a practical neighbourliness between Phoenix and Inanda, as much as it is also a struggle to develop an orientation that prioritizes the poor and marginalized, rather than simply ploughing resources into mega-projects and infrastructure for the speedier import and export of goods.

Patently also obvious is that government restitutionary measures that only take race into account, and not class, hinder practical solidarity. Race is no longer a reliable placeholder concept for disadvantage. Social policies using this measure alone thus facilitate the sharp social divisions that flow from a sense of injustice. Indeed, inequality within South Africa is now most deepened within the African income spread. Making legal distinctions between people of colour in South Africa (African, coloured and Indian) may have made sense a quarter of a century ago, but no longer.

Meanwhile, the everyday violence of the area marches on. Drug lords hold sway and mete out instant retribution to those who cross them. Police are either invisible or in on it. Political murders are commonplace.

In African communities, in language reminiscent of the Phoenix uprisings, a determination to defend the community against "foreigners" (mainly African migrants) has gained traction. Operation Dudula, a loose movement of vigilantes popular in many African areas, object most stridently to African migrants walking their streets, seen to be criminals up to no good. It is useful to keep in mind Jenkins and Leroy's argument that

> Racial capitalism is a highly malleable structure. It has at times relied on open methods of exploitation and expropriation that wrench racialized populations into capitalist modes of production and accumulation, such as slavery, colonialism, and enclosure. But racial capitalism also relies on exclusion from those same modes of production and accumulation in the form of containment,

> incarceration, abandonment, and underdevelopment for a racial surplus popu-
> lation. The maintenance of racial capitalism can even rely on the limited
> inclusion and participation of racially marked populations; by extending
> credit and political rights to these populations, the pervasive "racial" of racial
> capitalism recedes, entrenching itself through obfuscation. (Jenkins and Leroy
> 2021, 3–4)

Returning to the racialization of tender-based capitalism, it seems safe to say that the motive to limit competition to ensure higher profits has found expression in legal and political discourses, which propose that African and Indian citizens *should* be treated differently. This division of people based on race however rests on a fundamental obfuscation. Only a small percentage of people deploying this ideology truly benefit from it. The rest scrabble around to make ends meet under an economic system that excludes them all. Unfortunately, this is not clear when racial identities are mobilized, in the midst of a riot or vigilante action. To the extent that many of the foot sol-diers would, if you surveyed them, likely swear by the racial identity that they have been assigned, they too are the edge subjects of capitalism.

There is possibly also a material basis to this assumption of identity. South Africa, like almost every society in the world, is undergoing profound socio-economic stresses. These are brought about by forces as profound as pan-demics, tanking economies, movement of people, inflation, unemployment, loss of trust in traditional institutions, and the shocks of war. In this situation, groups of people contending for dwindling resources may find it useful to form identities that place them first in line to *receive* state largesse. These identities would also serve to excuse any illegal *taking* they may do. Phoenix/Inanda has heralded what "new and unpredictable modes of dispos-session" may be essayed under conditions of socio-economic stress, especially where people of visibly different races live cheek by jowl in places as "edge-subjects of capitalism" (Bhattacharyya 2018, 10).

Edge subjects like Gupta and Zuma come with histories of racialised differ-ential incorporation. Zuma sees historic privilege across the road, Gupta sees the new political arrangements as discriminating against him. Bhattachar-yya's argument that "Racial capitalism is a way of understanding why we seem so divided and yet so intimately intertwined with each other" is haunt-ingly apposite (2018, 11).

So it will go. On. What will break the cycle in a context where the spatiality and "temporality of racial capitalism is one of ongoingness, even if its precise nature is dynamic and changing … a process not a moment … "? (Jenkins and Leroy 2021, 12). It would be easy to shake one's head and bemoan our broken dreams. Returning to the streets of Phoenix one year after the riots, there are tensions and recrimination, but also a determination to build something beautiful, as once more a key shibboleth of anti-apartheid struggle, non-

Notes

1. Indians make up 2 per cent of South Africa's overall population but could easily be 15–20 per cent of Durban's.
2. Cheap, addictive drug swhich has burgeoned in these areas.

Disclosure statement

No potential conflict of interest was reported by the author(s).

References

Africa, S., S. Sokape, and M. Gumbi. 2021. "Report of the Expert Panel into the July 2021 Civil Unrest, 29 November 2021." Pretoria: The Presidency.

Alexander, N. 1985. *Sow the Wind*. Johannesburg: Skotaville.

Alexander, N. 1986. "Approaches to the National Question in South Africa." *Transformation* 1: 63–95.

Basson, A., and P. du Toit. 2017. *Enemy of the People: How Jacob Zuma Stole South Africa and How the People Fought Back*. Jeppestown/Johannesburg: Jonathan Ball Publishers.

Bhattacharyya, G. 2018. *Rethinking Racial Capitalism: Questions of Reproduction and Survival*. London: Rowman and Littlefield.

Bhorat, H., M. Buthelezi, I. Chipkin, S. Duma, L. Mondi, C. Peter, M. Qobo, M. Swilling, and H. Friedenstein. 2017. *Betrayal of the Promise: How South Africa is Being Stolen*. Stellenbosch: State Capacity Research Project.

Bond, P. 2000. *Elite Transition: From Apartheid to Neoliberalism in South Africa*. Pietermaritzburg: University of Natal Press.

Bourdieu, P. 1984. *Distinction*. London: Routledge & Kegan Paul.

Clarno, A. 2017. *Neoliberal Apartheid: Palestine/Israel And South Africa After 1994*. Chicago: University of Chicago.

Desai, A., and G. Vahed. 2019. *A History of the Present: A Biography of Indian South Africans, 1990-2019*. New Delhi: Oxford University Press.

Freund, B. 2007. *The African City: A History*. Cambridge: Cambridge University Press.

Hughes, H. 1985. "Violence in Inanda, August 1985." *Journal of Southern African Studies* 13 (3): 331–354.

Hunter, Q., J. Wicks, and K. Singh. 2021. *Eight Days in July: Inside the Zuma Unrest That set South Africa Alight*. Cape Town: Tafelberg.

Jenkins, D., and J. Leroy. 2021. "Introduction: The Old History of Capitalism." In *Histories of Racial Capitalism*, edited by D. Jenkins, and J. Leroy, 1–26. New York: Columbia University Press.

Legassick, M., and D. Hemson. 1976. *Foreign Investment and the Reproduction of Racial Capitalism in South Africa*. London: Anti-Apartheid Movement.

MacDonald, M. 2004. "The Political Economy of Identity Politics." *The South Atlantic Quarterly* 103 (4): 629–656.

Mbembe, A. 2002. "African Modes of Self-Writing." *Public Culture* 14 (1): 239–273.

Pauw, J. 2017. *The President's Keepers: Those Keeping Zuma in Power and out of Prison*. Cape Town: Tafelberg.

Parry, G., G. Moyser, and M. Wagstaff. 1987. "The Crowd and Community. Context, Content and Aftermath." In *The Crowd in Contemporary Britain*, edited by G. Gaskell and R. Benewick, 212–254. London: Sage Publications.

Saul, J., and P. Bond. 2014. *South Africa – The Present as History: From Mrs Ples to Mandela and Marikana*. Johannesburg: Jacana.

Smith, N. 1997. "The Satanic Geographies of Globalisation: Uneven Development in the 1990s." *Public Culture* 10 (1): 169–189.

Racial capitalism: an unfinished history

Robin D. G. Kelley

ABSTRACT
This afterword considers Cedric J. Robinson's theory of racial capitalism in relation to the South African tradition as advanced in this special issue. Both formulations of racial capitalism developed in the same global conjuncture. And much like the South African tradition, Robinson's theory of racial capitalism was always fundamentally a *strategic* one. As in the South African context, this meant transcending the stale impasse between Black nationalists and Marxists and developing novel theories to inform revolutionary strategy. Ultimately then, racial capitalism is "a concept forged and developed in struggle", as the editors put it – and it cannot be considered otherwise.

[T]he character of capitalism can only be understood in the social and historical context of its appearance.

Cedric J. Robinson ([1983] 2021), 24, *Black Marxism*.

These essays incisively advance our understanding of racial capitalism. They move us beyond what has been an unproductive and manufactured debate over who "owns" racial capitalism, who coined it first and who deserves credit, resulting in an obsession over the term's lineage rather than deepening our discussion of its application. This volume resists such traps. The key takeaway here, as Zachary Levenson and Marcel Paret write, is that we "focus on reading racial capitalism as a strategic, rather than a purely analytic, concept – a concept forged and developed in struggle". I also agree that South Africa's engagement with racial capitalism can be understood as "conjunctural", whereas Robinson's is "a global, mode of generalization". And yet, we should still reckon with the fact that *Black Marxism* appeared as debates over racial capitalism in South Africa were raging. In other words, even if they were not in conversation, both formulations of racial capitalism developed in the same conjuncture – the period marked by neoliberal restructuring in response to capital's global crisis, the precipitous increase of Third World debt due to rising interest rates, the defeat of the New International Economic Order, the weakening of Soviet communism *and* the apartheid regime in the face of heightened popular resistance, and a wave of Marxist-oriented revolutions, from Nicaragua to Grenada to Burkina Faso.

My own thinking was profoundly shaped by this conjuncture. In 1983, I entered a doctoral programme in African history at UCLA, where I had planned to study the colonial "underdevelopment" of Mozambique's economy in order to better understand the challenges facing the then ruling Frente de Libertação de Moçambique (FRELIMO). Reading Walter Rodney's *How Europe Underdeveloped Africa* is what brought me to graduate school. As a "student" of Rodney's, as it were, I took for granted that colonial extraction, the processes of proletarianization, the violence of dispossession and discipline were structured by racism. Rodney ([1972] 2018, 103) insisted that colonial racism "became indistinguishable from oppression for economic reasons". He reinforced the point with C. L. R. James's oft-quoted line from *The Black Jacobins* ([1938] 1963, 283):

> The race question is subsidiary to the class question in politics, and to think of imperialism in terms of race is disastrous. But to neglect the racial factor as merely incidental is an error only less grave than to make it fundamental.

The question of which is subsidiary or primary spawned a perpetual "chicken-and-egg" debate over race and class, but for me James, Rodney, the history of colonialism, the African liberation movement, and growing up Black and poor in Harlem proved that "race and class constituted a single site of struggle". This fact was never in dispute.

When I decided to change my dissertation topic to the South African Communist Party at the end of my first quarter, "racial capitalism" became a staple of my vocabulary. I joined the editorial board of *Ufahamu*, a graduate-student run journal of African Studies, where we published essays about South Africa by Magubane (1986), Campbell (1986) and Byrne (1982) that referenced "racial capitalism" or "racially structured capitalism".[1] My colleague Drew (1991), a brilliant fellow graduate student at UCLA in Political Science and contributor to *Ufahamu*, was working on a dissertation about the South African Left and racial capitalism. She generously shared her notes, contacts and ideas, and I did my best to reciprocate. And, of course, anyone working on or from the Left in South Africa was familiar with Neville Alexander. We all read, debated and re-read *One Azania, One Nation* (Alexander 1979). Meanwhile, sometime in late 1983 or early 1984, Zed Press sent a review copy of Robinson's (1983) *Black Marxism* to *Ufahamu's* editorial office. As the book review editor, I received it with the aim of reviewing it, but forty pages in, I realized I was ill-equipped. Instead, I asked Cedric to join my dissertation committee, and he became my primary mentor.

It never occurred to me or anyone in my graduate cohort in African history to link Robinson's brief analysis of the origins of racial capitalism to the current debates in South Africa. And in the proliferation of articles and discussions on the character of racial capitalism in South Africa and what it portends for the coming struggle, Cedric Robinson's name is *never* mentioned.[2] Nor should we expect otherwise. In the 1980s and early '90s, Robinson was at the margins and *South Africa was at the center*. Arguably, the most important international movement of the period was the struggle to end apartheid, what some might cheekily call "the highest stage of racial capitalism". On the other hand, *Black Marxism* attracted very few readers, and most reviewers either misunderstood or disparaged it. And the few critics sympathetic to Robinson had little or nothing to say about racial capitalism. We shouldn't be surprised since his analysis of racial capitalism – a phrase he uses only four times in the book – was never at the heart of his argument. However, Robinson's death in 2016 was followed by a rather dramatic pivot towards his use of "racial capitalism" since it coincided with new directions in Black Studies and, even more importantly, a sudden interest in the study of capitalism, or "new capitalism studies". That opening led to an explosion of scholarship, conferences, symposia and debates which elevated "racial capitalism" as an idea to be reckoned with, and a critique of the "whiteness" of new capitalism studies. Meanwhile, the sudden interest in Robinson coincided with a renewed appreciation of Neville Alexander in South Africa.[3] Unfortunately, the latest U. S. academic fascination with racial capitalism has not only paid scant attention to Alexander and other key thinkers but contributed to South Africa's shift "from centre to margin".

For South Africans, the question behind the theory of racial capitalism in the conjuncture of the late '70s and early '80s was whether to support a one- or two-stage struggle against apartheid. The authors here remind us that Neville Alexander's critique of the two-stage theory was not merely strategic, and certainly not specific to South Africa. It descends from a much older debate over whether a bourgeois democratic revolution must precede socialism. It's a debate that goes back at least to the Russian Revolutions of 1905 and 1917, during which Marxists argued over whether a "backward" country could "leap" over the stages of development straight to socialism. Of course, once the Bolsheviks seized power it was no longer a theoretical question. A similar debate was on full display during the Second Congress of the Communist International in 1920, when Lenin and Indian Communist M. N. Roy differed over whether anti-colonial movements should be bourgeois democratic or revolutionary socialist. Roy distrusted the bourgeois and petit-bourgeois elements leading anti-colonial nationalist movements. Conceding that proletarian revolution was out of the question, Roy believed that workers and peasants under the guidance of a disciplined Communist party were capable of building a mass revolutionary socialist movement. Whereas Lenin was willing to support nearly all anti-colonial movements, Roy feared that the petit-bourgeois leadership of the respective nationalist movements "would compromise with Imperialism in return for some economic and political concessions to their class" (Haithcox 1971, 14–15).[4] Like Roy, Alexander did not believe liberation came piecemeal or that the fight was for a "nonracial" capitalist order, hence his vehement opposition to the two-stage theory.

How was *Black Marxism* a response to the conjuncture? In some respects, it, too, was shaped by much older questions – questions that had been gestating in Robinson's consciousness since he spent two months in Zimbabwe in 1962, just as the white settler state forced the liberation movements (ZAPU and ZANU) underground. Early glimmers of his arguments also appear in his graduate papers at Stanford in the late 1960s. Nevertheless, *Black Marxism* was inspired by struggles in Southern Africa and the wave of revolutionary rebellions in the Caribbean during the 1970s. But he wanted to understand why Black resistance on a global scale had taken on certain shared characteristics. He did not think the answer could be found in contemporary struggles between Black nationalists and Marxists, so he set out to trace "the revolutionary consciousness that proceeded from the whole historical experience of Black people" and not merely formed by capitalist slavery and colonialism (Robinson [1983] 2021, 169). This he called the Black Radical Tradition. It questions the capacity of racial capitalism to re-make African social life and succeed in generating new categories of human experience stripped bare of the historical consciousness embedded in culture. For this reason, Robinson focused on the *long* origins of capitalism, its antecedents and the consequences of its particular form.

Unfortunately, his interpretation of the origins of racial capitalism is still misunderstood, subjected to misguided criticism. For example, Robinson does not privilege "race" over "class", subordinate economics to racial ideology, or claim that there is no economic basis for what he calls "racialism" – the ways in which early European economies used difference as a means of structuring the social order, not to be confused with the rise of modern "racism" in the Enlightenment era. He is most concerned with the geographical and historical limits of Marx and Engels' understanding of capitalism's emergence. Slavery, Robinson argues, was not an aberration or a relic of the past. Slave labour within the Mediterranean and emerging Atlantic economy existed at least three centuries *before* the beginnings of modern capitalism, along with other forms of labour exploitation and coercion (peonage, serfdom, indenture). These were class struggles that not only shaped capitalism's embryonic development, but they directly fly in the face of the "presumptions that Europe itself had produced, that the motive and material forces that generated the capitalist system were to be wholly located in what was a fictive historical entity. From its very foundations capitalism had never been – any more than Europe – a 'closed system'" (Robinson [1983] 2021, 4).

He does not say that Europeans were inherently racist but that the idea of superior and inferior "stocks" or categories of people had already permeated much of Europe in the feudal era. We can, therefore, expect that it would affect the class consciousness of European (namely English) working classes. In fact, Robinson's analysis here is consistent with Levenson and Paret's first thesis: "class struggle from above" produces racism in the quest for profits and resources. But class struggle is as old as classes, and as Robinson reminds us, the bourgeoisie did not suddenly appear with capitalism. There is a much longer history in which different middle strata and bourgeoisies often vied with each other for power, resources and access to trade and commerce.

The same holds true for the "lower orders" in that they did not represent some unified class or undifferentiated "masses". Such differences, often determined and reproduced by the state, were used to assign value, occupation and citizenship status. The excluded or marginalized were usually assigned to certain occupations, such as military service (mercenaries), household labour, handicrafts, manufacturing, the ship and dock workers, and agricultural labour. Most scholars, Robinson ([1983] 2021, 23) asserts, miss the significance of the migrant or immigrant in European economies – even prior to the rise of capitalism – because of their "mistaken use of the nation as a social, historical, and economic category". He is criticizing the assumption that there is a stable "English working class" bounded together in a national identity. Robinson's insights certainly apply to contemporary South Africa, where xenophobic violence against alleged foreigners, migrant workers from Zimbabwe, South Asians with century-old roots in South Africa, and so forth, suggest the limits and instability of the category of the nation. It is also a stark reminder that class struggles from below do not *automatically* lead to undoing racism, even when they may disrupt profits.

Ultimately, racial capitalism is, indeed, "a concept forged and developed in struggle". As such, it is theory made and remade on the fly. Or to put it differently, the most consequential "revisionists" are not renegade intellectuals but people in motion. As a concept, it has already been remade – and renamed – in the current conjuncture. We now speak of gendered racial capitalism. As post-apartheid South Africa faces deepening inequality, extreme levels of poverty and houselessness, a ruling regime that is fundamentally anti-labour and completely enmeshed in the neoliberal order, the two-stage theory debate is moot. A new generation is reckoning with the violence of gendered racial capitalism and looking back to history to understand it in order to kill it.

Notes

1. It's not as if these early debates on racial capitalism were limited to South African publications or specialized African Studies journals. See for example contributions from Milkman (1977) and Posel (1983).
2. See for example pieces by Bernard Magubane (1984, 1986), Adam (1984), Saul (1986), Campbell (1986), and Byrne (1982). Incidentally, Robinson and Magubane were friends and interlocutors. It apparently did not occur to either of them that they were engaged in the same conversation.
3. See especially Clarno and Vally's (2022) contribution to this volume, as well as pieces by Cloete (2014) and Motala (2013).
4. A copy of Roy's theses is available in Karnik (1978, 107–110). For Lenin's views on Roy's supplementary theses, see Lenin (1967 [1920], 30–37).

Disclosure statement

No potential conflict of interest was reported by the author(s).

References

Adam, Heribert. 1984. "Racist Capitalism Versus Capitalist Non-Racialism in South Africa." *Ethnic and Racial Studies* 7 (2): 269–282. doi:10.1080/01419870.1984. 9993444.

Alexander, Neville [No Sizwe]. 1979. *One Azania, One Nation: The National Question in South Africa*. London: Zed Press.

Byrne, Hugh. 1982. "Review: The Crisis in South Africa." *Ufahamu* 11 (3): 268–273.

Campbell, Horace. 1986. "Popular Alliance in South Africa." *Ufahamu* 15 (1–2): 58–83.

Clarno, Andy, and Salim Vally. 2022. "The Context of Struggle: Racial Capitalism and Political Praxis in South Africa." *Ethnic and Racial Studies*. Advance online publication. doi:10.1080/01419870.2022.2143239.

Cloete, Michael. 2014. "Neville Alexander: Towards Overcoming the Legacy of Racial Capitalism in Post-Apartheid South Africa." *Transformation: Critical Perspectives on Southern Africa* 86: 30–47. doi:10.1353/trn.2014.0032.

Drew, Allison. 1991. *Social Mobilization and Racial Capitalism in South Africa, 1928-1960." PhD Dissertation*. University of California Los Angeles.

Haithcox, John. 1971. *Communism and Nationalism in India: M.N. Roy and Comintern Policy, 1920–1939*. Princeton: Princeton University Press.

James, C. L. R. (1938) 1963. *The Black Jacobins: Toussaint L'Ouverture and the San Domingo Revolution*. New York: Vintage.

Karnik, V. B. 1978. *M. N. Roy: A Political Biography*. Bombay: Nav Jagriti Samaj.

Lenin, V. I. (1920) 1967. "The Report of the Commission on the National and Colonial Questions, July 26, 1920." In *Lenin on the National and Colonial Questions*, 30–37. Peking: Foreign Languages Press.

Magubane, Bernard. 1984. "The Mounting Class and National Struggles in South Africa." *Review* 8 (2): 197–231.

Magubane, Bernard. 1986. "South Africa: On the Verge of Revolution?" *Ufahamu* 15 (1–2): 22–57.

Milkman, Ruth. 1977. "Apartheid, Economic Growth, and U.S. Foreign Policy in South Africa." *Berkeley Journal of Sociology* 22: 45–100.

Motala, Enver. 2013. "Enough Is as Good as a Feast." *Mail & Guardian*, July 19. Available online: https://mg.co.za/article/2013-07-19-00-enough-is-as-good-as-a-feast/.

Posel, Deborah. 1983. "Rethinking the 'Race-Class Debate' in South African Historiography." *Social Dynamics* 9 (1): 50–66. doi:10.1080/02533958308458333.

Robinson, Cedric J. 1983. *Black Marxism: The Making of the Black Radical Tradition*. London: Zed.

Robinson, Cedric J. (1983) 2021. *Black Marxism: The Making of the Black Radical Tradition*. Chapel Hill: University of North Carolina Press.

Rodney, Walter. (1972) 2018. *How Europe Underdeveloped Africa*. New York: Verso.

Saul, John. 1986. "South Africa: The Question of Strategy." *New Left Review* 160: 3–22.

Index

Note: Endnotes are indicated by the page number followed by 'n' and the endnote number e.g., 20n1 refers to endnote 1 on page 20.

African Commercial and Distributive Workers Union (ACDWU) 129
African National Congress (ANC) 2, 3, 5, 7, 12, 13, 15, 26, 32, 37–9, 47, 61, 81, 86, 89–93, 140–1, 145–6, 148, 150–2, 154, 155
Alexander, Neville 7, 9–13, 25–9, 34, 36, 38, 39, 100, 106, 111, 114–15, 162
Alter-Globalisation Movement (AGM) 78n1
Althusser, Louis 34
AmaNdiya 148
American civilization 53
anti-apartheid movement 2–4, 16–17, 26, 72, 148, 157–8
anti-capitalism 14, 90
anti-imperialism 90
anti-racism 12, 14, 90
anti-racist and anti-capitalist struggle 12–14
apartheid 1–6, 8–10, 24, 27, 32, 33, 35–9, 64–7, 71, 75, 76, 82, 83, 87–91, 93, 120, 123–6, 132–4, 141–9, 162
Arnesen, Eric 111–12
articulation 14–16, 25, 34, 35, 48, 49, 51, 54, 57, 60, 63, 65–8, 77, 119, 121–2, 125, 131–3
Azanian People's Organisation (AZAPO) 5, 9, 13

Balibar, Etienne 34
Bannerji, Himani 29
betraying 92
Bhattacharyya, Gargi 141–3
Biko, Steve 6, 15, 63, 69–72
Black Agenda Report 99, 100
Black Consciousness Movement (BCM) 2, 24, 41n11, 61, 94–5, 131

Black Economic Empowerment (BEE) 151
The Black Jacobins 161
Black Marxism 3–5, 25, 28, 160–3
blackness 11
Black Panther Party 35
Black people 5, 6, 11, 33, 35, 37, 47–58, 69, 71, 73, 75, 80–1, 84, 85, 89, 92–4, 96, 127, 141, 142, 151, 163
Black People's Convention (BPC) 5
Black radical tradition 16, 36, 100, 163
Black Reconstruction 15, 46–7, 49, 53, 57, 110–11
Black Victorian 47
black women service workers 129–30
Bozzoli, Belinda 82
Breckenridge, Keith 50
Burawoy, Michael 8, 32
bureaucratization 128
Buthelezi, Sipho 11
Byrne, Hugh 161

Cabral, Amilcar 11, 24–5, 35
Campbell, Horace 161
Cape Action League (CAL) 3, 26
Cape Youth Congress (CAYCO) 2–3
capital accumulation 15, 28, 29, 40, 83, 101, 119, 124, 141, 142
capitalism 28, 47, 58, 97
Carnegie Commission 15, 101, 108, 111, 112, 115
casualization 37
Chandler, N. D. 47, 48, 50, 57
cheap labor thesis 8
city space 122–4
civilised labour 120
Clarno, Andy 4, 15
Class and Colour in South Africa, 1850–1950 (Jack and Ray Simons) 82

Class, Race, and Marxism (Roediger) 100
Cohen, Cathy 40
The Collapse of the Second International
  (Lenin) 95
colonialism 2, 4, 9, 32, 36, 48, 64, 81, 82,
  86, 87, 89, 93, 96, 156–7, 161, 163
colonialism of a special type (CST) 2
commercial capital 122–4
Commercial, Catering and Allied
  Workers Union of South Africa
  (CCAWUSA) 131–2
The Communist Manifesto (Marx and
  Engels) 85
Communist Party of South Africa (CPSA)
  11, 16, 17n2
Congress of South African Trade Unions
  (COSATU) 95
conjuncture 4, 9, 24, 25, 31, 33, 34, 66,
  121, 160–4
consumption 67, 119, 124, 127, 132
Coulter, C. W. 108
Cradock 26

Darkwater: Voices Within the Veil (Du
  Bois) 53
deindustrialization 37
delicately disinter 5
dependency 106
deracialization 33, 37
Desai, Ashwin 16
de-subjectification 72
dialectical frame 76
Drew, Allison 161
drug lords 152–3, 156
Du Bois, W. E. B. 24–5, 31, 40, 46–54, 57, 87
Durban 144, 152
Dusk of Dawn (Du Bois) 87

economic foundation 47
Economic Freedom Fighters (EFF) 148
economic monstrosity 47, 51
The Economic Report (Grosskopf) 107
edge-subjects of capitalism 157
emancipation 11, 27, 51, 86, 87
enclave economy 113
ethnicity 114, 115
Executive Committee of the Communist
  International (ECCI) 17n4

Fanon, Frantz 24–5, 35
#Fees Must Fall /#End Outsourcing
  (FMF/EO) movement 61–3, 77
Ferguson, Roderick A. 40
feudal agrarianism 47
Fields, Barbara 101

*Foreign Investment and the Reproduction
  of Racial Capitalism in South Africa*
  (Legassick and Hemson) 83
Frente de Libertação de Moçambique
  (FRELIMO) 161
Friere, Paolo 35

Gauteng 140, 143, 154
Gelb, Stephen 8, 33
gender 118–32
Gilmore, Ruth Wilson 134
global horizon and modernity 48
global philanthropy 108–10
Goodwin, J. 49
Gramsci, Antonio 28, 31

Hall, Stuart 4, 5, 28, 34, 35, 40, 63, 119,
  121, 133
Hemson, David 25, 83
Hudson, Peter James 24, 34
Human Sciences Research Council
  (HSRC) 82

internal colonialism 86
intersectionality 46, 61

James, C. L. R. 24–5, 31, 35, 40, 161

Kelley, Robin D. G. 3, 16, 24, 25
Kenny, Bridget 16
Koshy, Susan 4
Kundnani, Arun 29
Kwa-Mashu 148, 152–1534
Kwa-Zulu-Natal (KZN) 16, 90, 140, 143,
  144, 146–8, 150–3

Legassick, Martin 6, 7, 9, 14, 25, 28, 83,
  100, 118
Lenin, V. I. 31
Levenson, Zachary 160
Limb, P. 47
living labour 119–22, 132

Mabasa, Lybon 13
Machel, Samora 35
Magubane, Bernard 10, 15, 25, 80–1, 84,
  86, 93–4, 100, 114, 115, 161
*The Making of a Racist State: British
  Imperialism and the Union of South
  Africa, 1875–1910* (Magubane) 81, 84
Malherbe, E. G. 105
Marks, Shula 82
Marxist Workers Tendency (MWT) 3, 5, 14
Marx's method 119, 121
Meillassoux's articulation 122

INDEX

169

Mkhize, K. 50
modern retailing 123
Molteno, Frank 9
Motala, Enver 29
Mullen, B. V. 49
multi-racialism 12
My Life & Times (Magubane) 82, 86, 92

Naidoo, Prishani 15
National Democratic Revolution
   (NDR) 2, 32, 38
National Forum Committee 26
National Liberation Front (NLF) 26
National Union of Commercial and Allied
   Workers (NUCAW) 129, 130
National Union of Distributive Workers
   (NUDW) 125–30
National Union of South African Students
   (NUSAS) 72
Native Life in South Africa (Mkhize)
   47, 54, 57
Neville Alexander Commemorative
   Conference, 2021 25
Nixon, Charles R. 82
Non-European Unity Movement
   (NEUM) 6, 10, 11, 26
nonracialism 12
Nyoka, Bongani 15

Odendaal, A. 50
O'Laughlin, Bridget 119, 122
One Azania, One Nation (Alexander) 25,
   32, 36, 161

Pan Africanist Congress (PAC) 61
Paret, Marcel 160
Phadi, Mosa M. 15
Phoenix 16, 141–57
Plaatje, S. T. 48, 49–51, 54–7
*The Political Economy of Race and Class in
   South Africa, From Soweto to Uitenhage:
   The Political Economy of the South
   African Revolution* 81, 85
privatization 37, 38
psychohistory 111–12

race and class 2, 3, 25, 47, 53, 58,
   65, 80, 81, 83, 85, 96, 114–15,
   132, 161; concept of articulation 65–9;
   debates 63–5
*Race and the Construction of the
   Dispensable Other* (Magubane)
   81, 87, 88
Race, Articulation and Societies
   Structured in Dominance 63

*Race, Class and Power: Harold Wolpe
   and the Radical Critique of Apartheid*
   (Magubane) 83
racial capitalism 4, 48, 49, 57, 100, 111,
   115, 120, 141, 160, 162, 164; after
   apartheid 36–9; concept of 80; South
   African tradition 2–5
racialization, primary agent
   of 8–10
racialized class fractions 31
racialized dispossession 30, 37
racialized exploitation 30
racialized job reservations 30
racial oppression 87
Racial Oppression in America
   (Blauner) 17n3
racism 8, 9–10, 12, 17, 28, 31, 39, 41n9,
   54, 58, 77, 80, 83, 88, 92, 97, 120, 148
Reed, Adolph 49, 100
regime of accumulation 87
retailing 119, 122–34
riots 16, 140–58
The Road to Freedom 38
Robinson, Cedric J. 3–5, 34, 47–8, 83, 99,
   100, 118, 133, 161–2, 164
Rodney, Walter 24–5, 161
Roediger, David 99, 100, 110, 111
Roy, M. N. 162

Saul, John S. 8, 33
Saunders, C. 50
Singh, Nikhil Pal 4
The Sociological Report (Albertyn) 109
solidarity 110–14
The Souls of Black Folk (Du Bois) 51
South African Communist Party (SACP) 2,
   7, 8–9, 11, 12, 32, 38, 152
South African Democracy Education Trust
   (SADET) 82
South African Students' Congress
   (SASCO) 72–3, 75, 76, 78n4
South African Students' Organisation
   (SASO) 5
South African tradition of racial
   capitalism (SAT) 3–5, 9
Sow the Wind (Alexander) 27–8
split labor market 7
Stalin, Joseph 12
struggle: anti-racist and anti-capitalist 3;
   context of 31–4
The Study of the Negro (Du Bois) 48, 51
subjects-in-struggle 119, 122, 131,
   133–4, 134n4
subversive movements 78n5
superstructural phenomena 77

Tabata, I. B. 6, 13
Talented Tenth 47, 49–50
Taylor, Keeanga-Yamahtta 4
tender-based black capitalists 151–2
territorialization 134
The Ties That Bind: African-American Consciousness of Africa (Magubane) 82, 85
township, Phoenix 141–7
Trapido, Stanley 82
Tri-Cameral Parliament 27

Ubuntu (Friendship) Committees 153
Ufahamu 161
Umlazi 148
unchartered territory 108
United Democratic Front (UDF) 2, 148
United Stated of America 84
United States 30, 36, 47, 51, 88, 108
University of California, Los Angeles (UCLA) 81, 82, 161
University of Cape Town (UCT) 26

Vally, Salim 4, 15, 29
van Onselen, Charles 82
ventriloquism 111
Veriava, Ahmed 15

The Wages of Whiteness (Roediger) 100, 102–5, 110–15
whiteness 15, 71, 74, 99–115, 162
white workers 120, 134n3
white working class 13, 30, 33, 49, 53, 54, 57, 58, 119, 125, 126, 128, 134n3
white working class women 125, 128
Witwatersrand (Wits) 60, 62, 77
Wolpe, Harold 8, 9, 28, 34, 35, 82, 119–21
women's labour 124–8
Workers' Organisation for Socialist Action (WOSA) 5, 13, 27
The Wretched of the Earth (Fanon) 92

xenophobic violence 164

Milton Keynes UK
Ingram Content Group UK Ltd.
UKHW051657141024
449570UK00005B/34